COOKING COMICS!

SIMPLE SKILLS, FANTASTIC FOOD

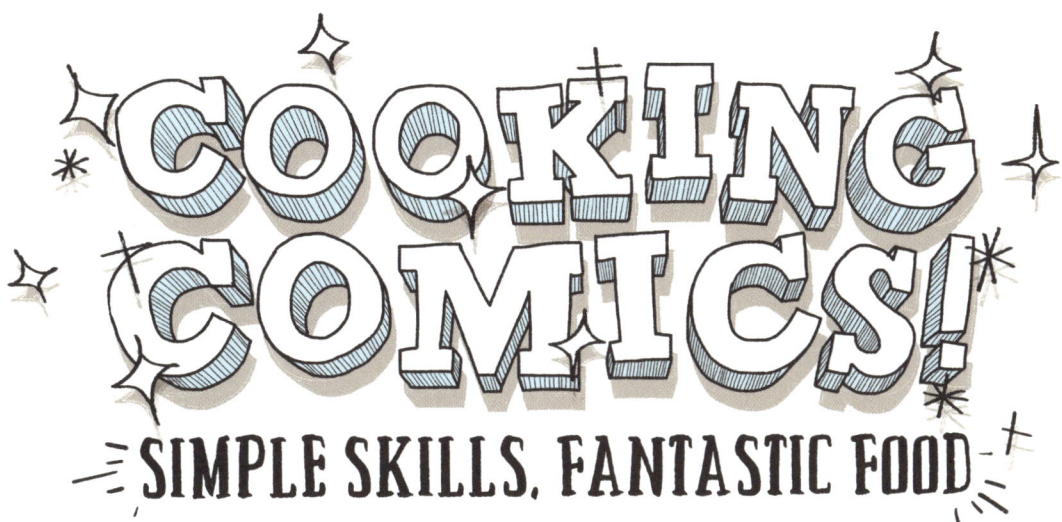

Cooking Comics! Simple Skills, Fantastic Food
Copyright © 2016 One Peace Books, Inc.

ISBN 13: 978-1944937041

No part of this work may be reproduced or transmitted in any form or by any means, electronic or mechanical, including photocopying, recording, or by storage and retrieval system without the written permission of the publisher. For information contact One Peace Books.

This is a work of fiction. Names, characters, places, and incidents either are the product of the author's imagination or are used fictitiously. Any resemblance to actual persons, living or dead, events, or locales is entirely coincidental.

Corrections to this work should be forwarded to the publisher for consideration upon the next printing.

Written by: Lauren Thompson
Illustrated by: Tsukuru Anderson

One Peace Books
43-32 22nd Street #204 Long Island City, NY 11101 USA
http://www.onepeacebooks.com

Printed in Korea
1234546789

COOKING COMICS!

SIMPLE SKILLS, FANTASTIC FOOD

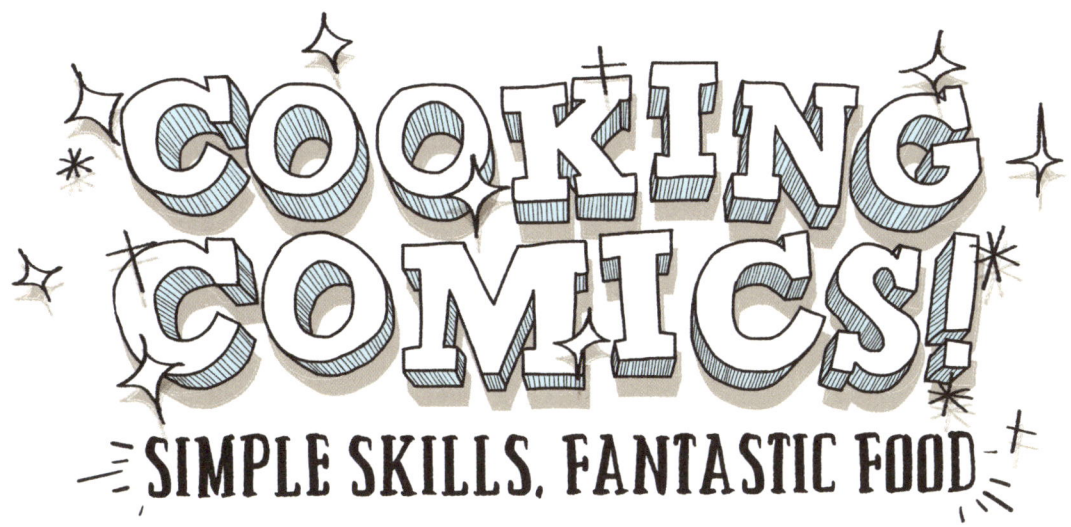

Table of Contents

Introduction..6

Equipment..8

Pantry / Groceries.......................................10

Basic Skills..12

Soups..20
    Technique
    Potato Leek Soup
    Sausage and Bean Soup

Salads...28
    Technique
    Bitter Greens Salad
    Shaved Root Vegetable Salad

Eggs..36
    Tecnhiques
    Baked Eggs

Pasta...44
    Technique
    Carbonara with Pancetta
    Tortellini with Sage

Rice..52
    Technique
    Chicken and Kimchee Fried Rice
    Tomato Risotto

Sautéing..60
    Technique
    Chicken with Summer Vegetables
    Skirt Steak Yakisoba Stir Fry

Grilling..68
    Technique
    Jerk Chicken with Cucumber Salad
    Sausage with Grilled Peach salad

Roasting..76
    Technique
    Roasted Pork Belly
    Roasted Chicken and Gravy

Frying..84
    Technique
    Vegetable Tempura
    Fried Clam Po' Boy

Braising..92
    Technique
    Lamb Shanks with Cheesy Polenta
    Braised Chicken with Balsamic Vinegar

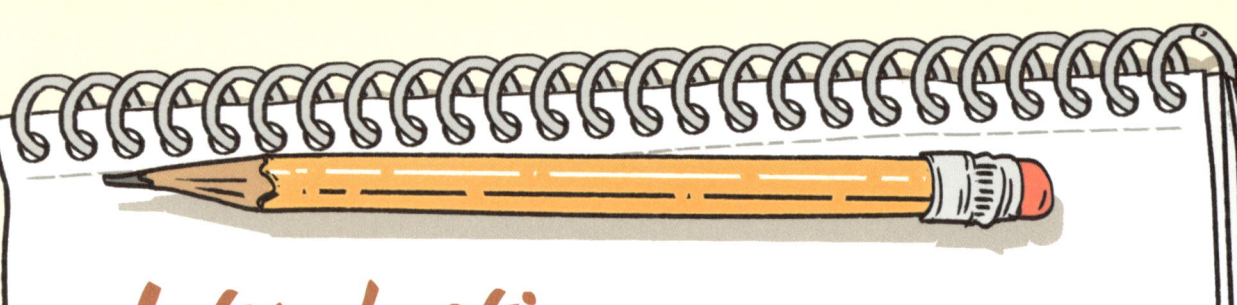

Introduction

Before I was a professional cook I followed recipes like they were the bible. If the recipe said to cook something for 10 minutes, I set my timer. I **loved** cooking, and I was willing to go to great lengths to meticulously follow the instructions exactly as they were written, line by line, minute by minute. I wanted to make sure I was "getting it right," but what I didn't know was that such a thing is **impossible**.

I should have been asking myself, is this delicious? Do I know **why** this is delicious? Could I make this same dish again without the needing a recipe? Could I take the technique of the recipe and translate it to other dishes, with different ingredients?

Before I started to study on my own, I had a friend who was a chef, and his ability to make something out of nothing was awe-inspiring. I still thought that cooking meant clutching a recipe and meticulously measuring ingredients. But then this guy could just look in the fridge and whip something up that was unbelievably delicious. At the time, I thought that kind of spontaneity could only be earned through arduous study and years of training in a professional kitchen.

I was **completely** wrong. Knowing how to cook does **not** mean that you have a library of recipes in your head, that you have a collection of reference cookbooks, or that you frequent online recipe libraries. Actually knowing how to cook means that you can make something delicious out of whatever you have on hand. That ability comes through learning basic techniques and understanding how and why they work.

Giving you that **understanding** is the goal of this book. Each section covers a specific cooking technique. They are basic techniques that most culinary students learn in their first classes. Some are broad and some are quite specific, but each was chosen so that when you make your way through the whole book and learn each one, you will have an arsenal of techniques to choose from when you open the fridge to see what you've got to work with. In addition to illustrating the technique, each section also has a couple of recipes that show that technique in action.

When using this book, trying focus on the **techniques** themselves. Follow the recipes, but then try to get creative and make your **own** dish. You will learn the most by implementing these techniques with your own ideas. When I tought culinary school, nothing made me happier than seeing my student's faces light up when it all finally clicked and they realized they knew what they were doing, and they gained the confidence to get creative and have fun. Although I won't be there to see any of you readers, I hope that you find that same excitement my students did.

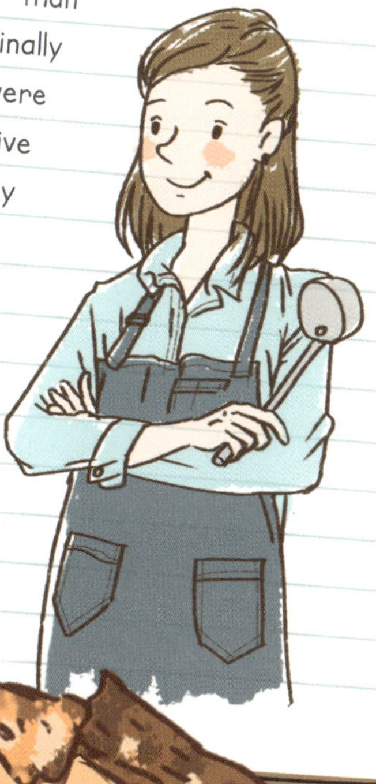

I hope it keeps you cooking!

Lauren Thompson

EQUIPMENT

This collection of equipment is enough to cook pretty much anything you can think of, and the majority of these things can be bought for very little money. Some things, like knives and enameled cast iron, are worth spending more money on. If treated right, they will last a lifetime.

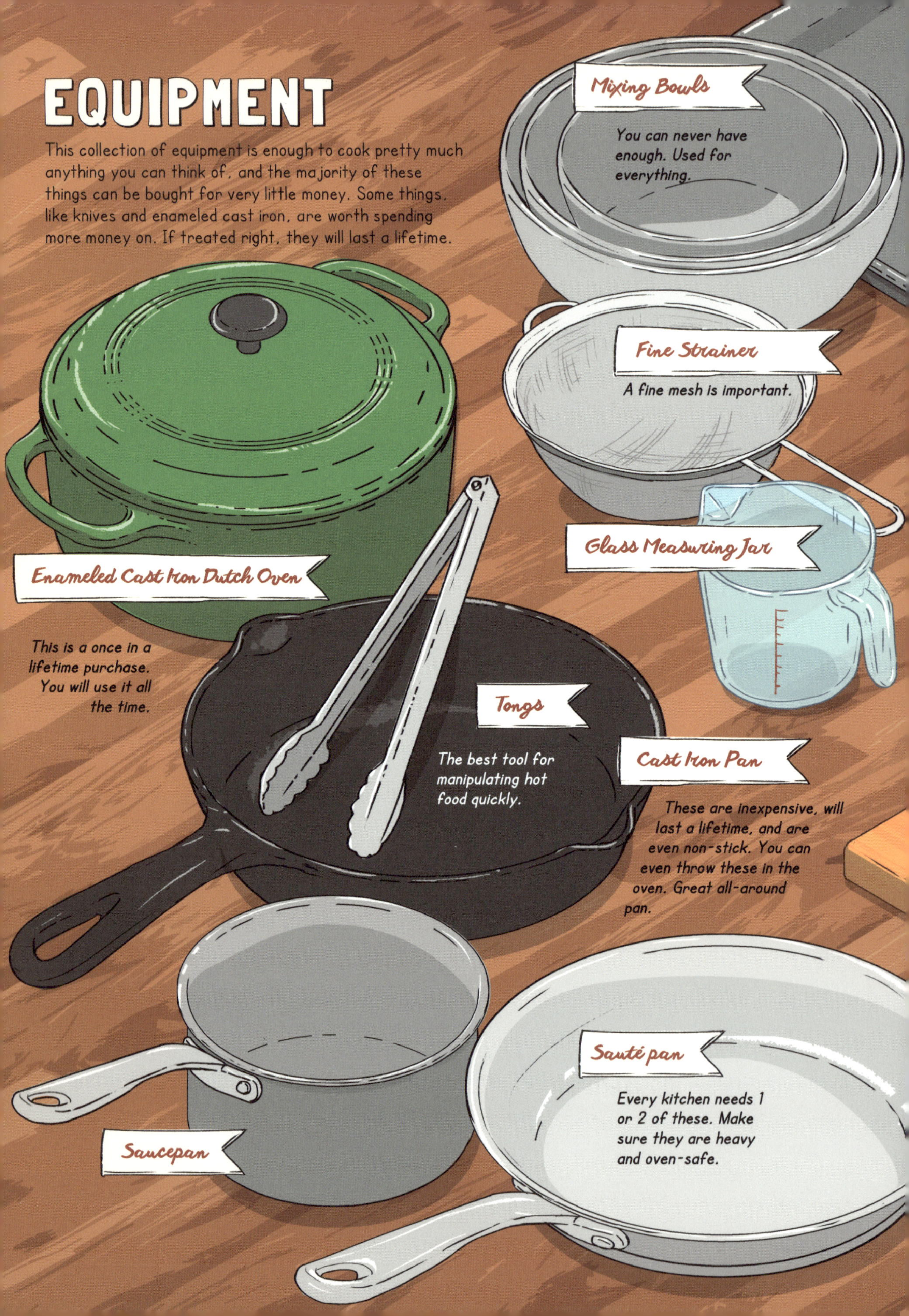
Mixing Bowls
You can never have enough. Used for everything.
Fine Strainer
A fine mesh is important.
Glass Measuring Jar
Enameled Cast Iron Dutch Oven
This is a once in a lifetime purchase. You will use it all the time.
Tongs
The best tool for manipulating hot food quickly.
Cast Iron Pan
These are inexpensive, will last a lifetime, and are even non-stick. You can even throw these in the oven. Great all-around pan.
Sauté pan
Every kitchen needs 1 or 2 of these. Make sure they are heavy and oven-safe.
Saucepan

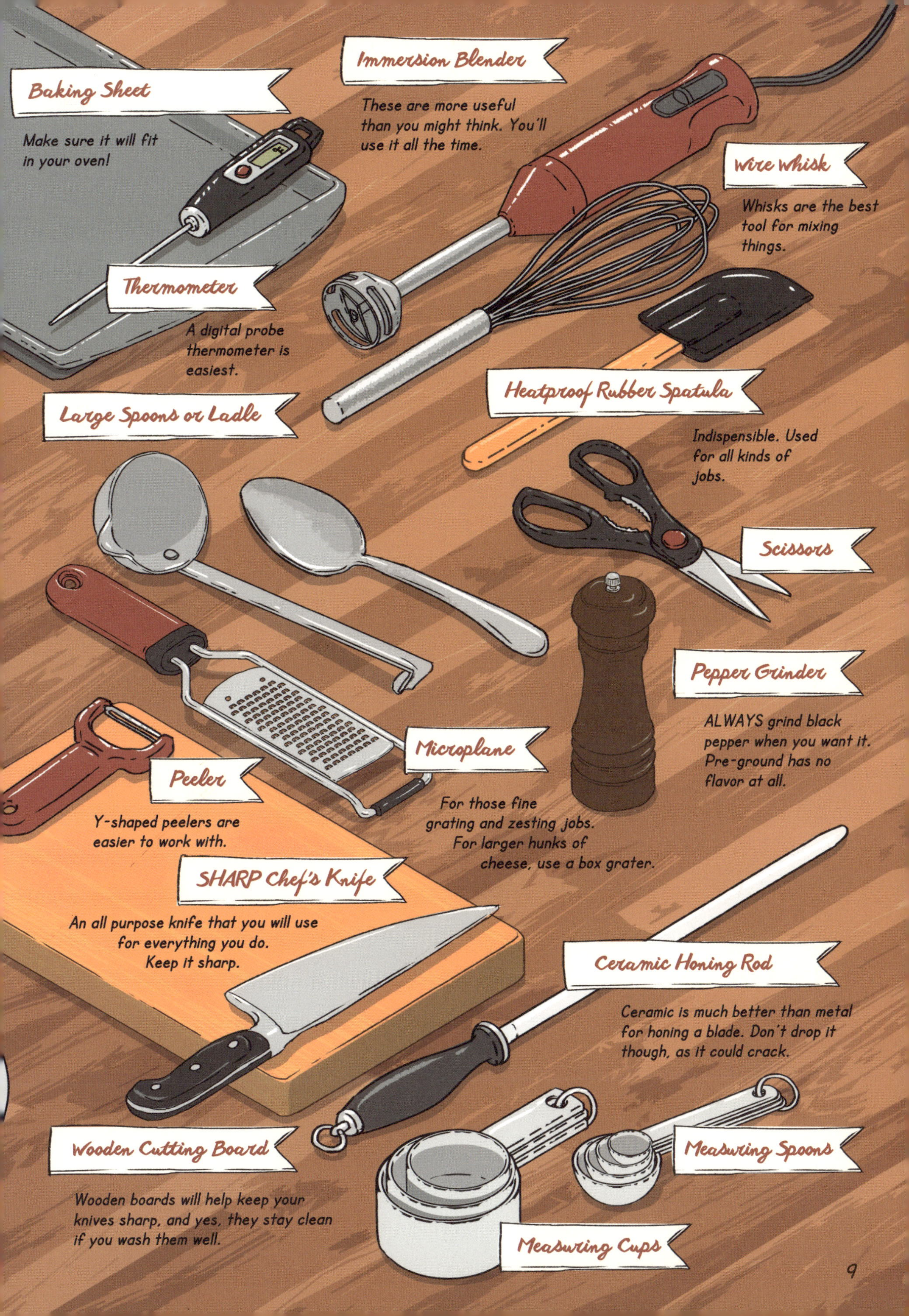
Baking Sheet
Make sure it will fit in your oven!
Immersion Blender
These are more useful than you might think. You'll use it all the time.
Wire Whisk
Whisks are the best tool for mixing things.
Thermometer
A digital probe thermometer is easiest.
Heatproof Rubber Spatula
Indispensible. Used for all kinds of jobs.
Large Spoons or Ladle
Scissors
Pepper Grinder
ALWAYS grind black pepper when you want it. Pre-ground has no flavor at all.
Microplane
For those fine grating and zesting jobs. For larger hunks of cheese, use a box grater.
Peeler
Y-shaped peelers are easier to work with.
SHARP Chef's Knife
An all purpose knife that you will use for everything you do. Keep it sharp.
Ceramic Honing Rod
Ceramic is much better than metal for honing a blade. Don't drop it though, as it could crack.
Wooden Cutting Board
Wooden boards will help keep your knives sharp, and yes, they stay clean if you wash them well.
Measuring Spoons
Measuring Cups

Pantry/ Groceries
to always have on hand

There are some things you will always want to have on hand. You will no doubt will add to this list, but this is a good staring point.

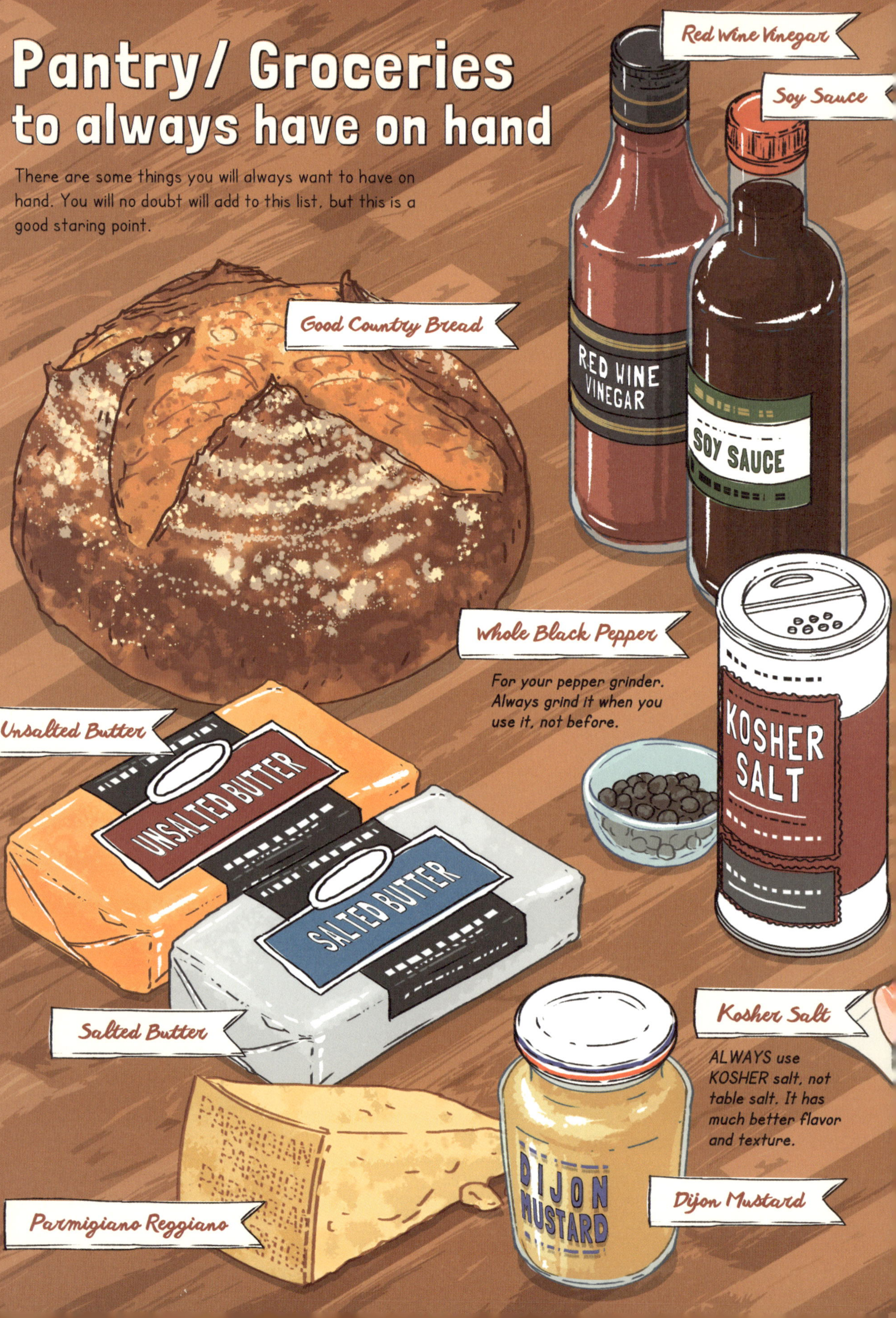
Red Wine Vinegar
Soy Sauce
RED WINE VINEGAR
SOY SAUCE
Good Country Bread
Whole Black Pepper
For your pepper grinder. Always grind it when you use it, not before.
KOSHER SALT
Unsalted Butter
UNSALTED BUTTER
SALTED BUTTER
Salted Butter
Kosher Salt
ALWAYS use KOSHER salt, not table salt. It has much better flavor and texture.
DIJON MUSTARD
Dijon Mustard
Parmigiano Reggiano

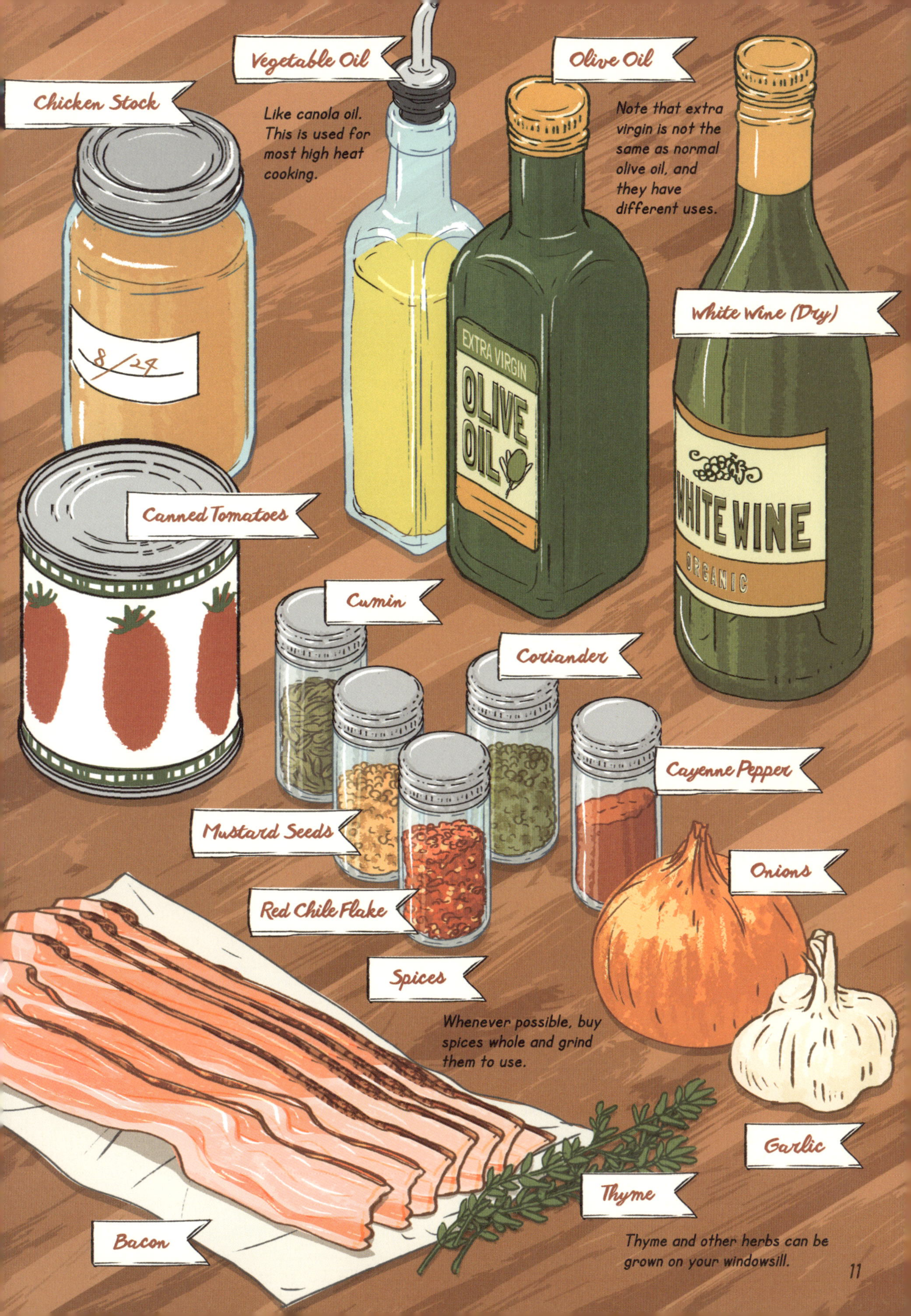
Vegetable Oil
Like canola oil. This is used for most high heat cooking.
Olive Oil
Note that extra virgin is not the same as normal olive oil, and they have different uses.
Chicken Stock
8/24
EXTRA VIRGIN
OLIVE OIL
White Wine (Dry)
WHITE WINE
ORGANIC
Canned Tomatoes
Cumin
Coriander
Cayenne Pepper
Mustard Seeds
Onions
Red Chile Flake
Spices
Whenever possible, buy spices whole and grind them to use.
Garlic
Thyme
Bacon
Thyme and other herbs can be grown on your windowsill.

BASIC SKILLS

Every single person who steps into a kitchen needs to have a solid understanding of the **basic techniques** that go into the dishes they want to make. Each dish, and each type of food, requires different techniques, so it would take a lifetime to learn them all. This book aims to teach you the basic skills and techniques that will enable you to feel comfortable enough to get creative in the kitchen.

Important!

Be Prepared!

This is, BY FAR, the most important thing you can learn about cooking. I cannot stress this enough. In French cooking this is called "mise en place," and it means that you need to have everything ready BEFORE you start cooking.

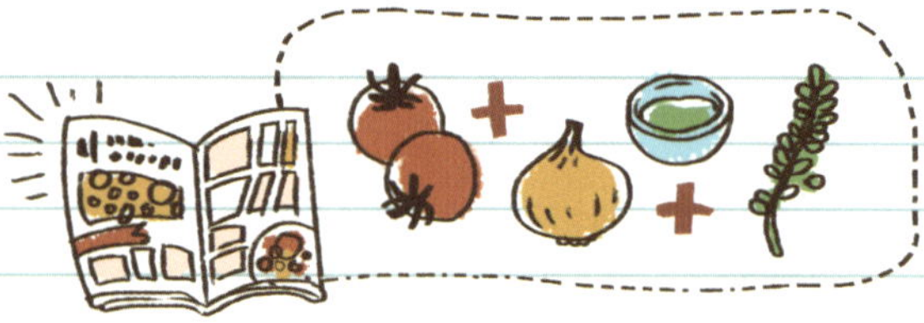

BEFORE you gather or shop for ingredients, read the recipe from beginning to end so you know what you need.

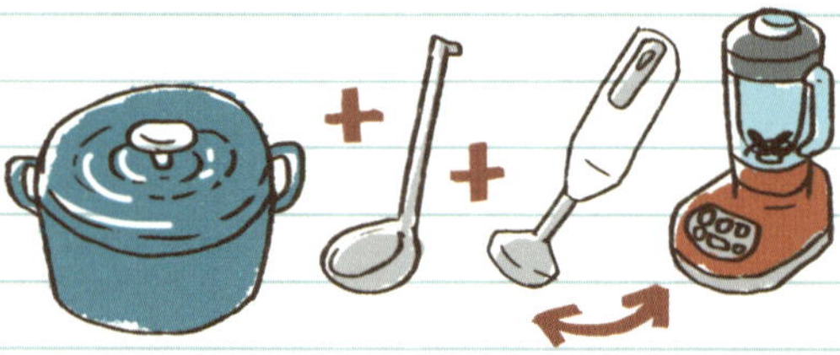

Make sure you have the necessary equipment BEFORE you start cooking. If you don't have the exact tool called for, can you find a substitute?

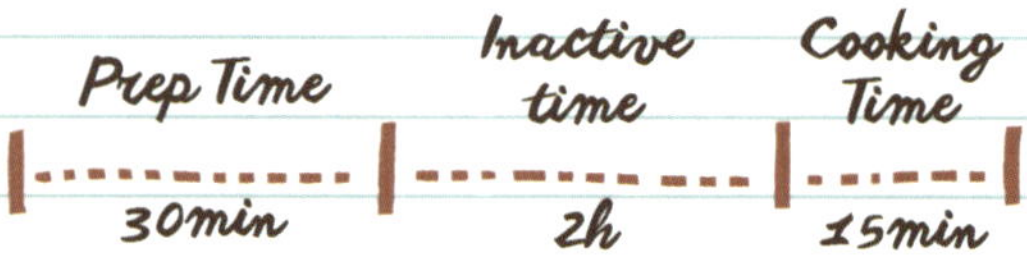
Prep Time
Inactive time
Cooking Time
30min
2h
15min

Make sure you have enough time! Pay attention to how much time you will need for the whole recipe and for each step. Don't forget to consider the inactive time.

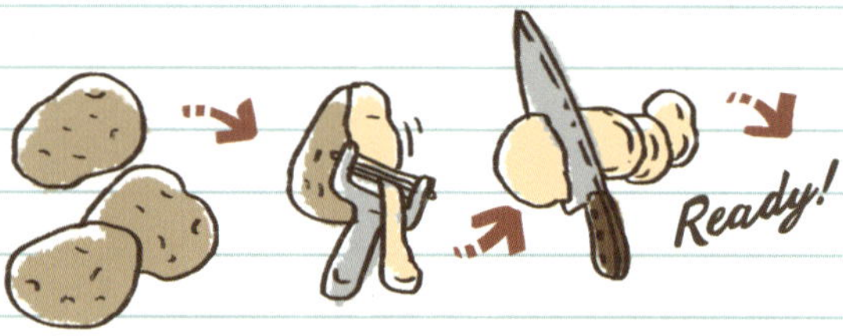
Ready!

Get your ingredients into the form the recipe calls for. Have everything chopped, peeled, sliced, and measured BEFORE you start cooking. You don't want to rush these tasks while you are trying to do something else!

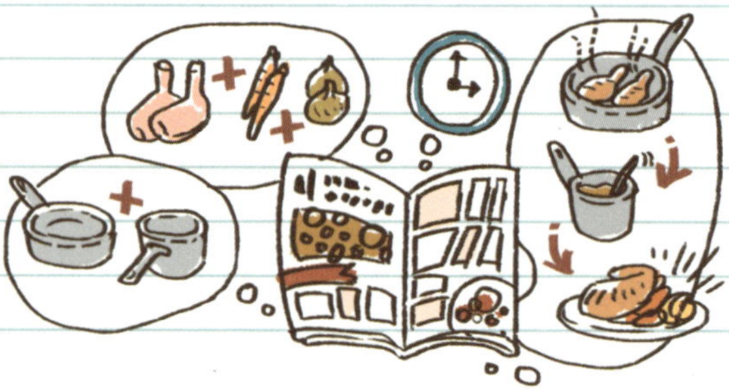

When everything else is ready, read the recipe one more time before you start to cook. Some recipes need you to pay close attention at every step. Some require multi-tasking. Some have long periods of time between tasks. Make sure you know what you are getting into!

Seasoning & Tasting

Properly seasoning your food with salt and pepper is the second most imporatant (and most neglected) skill you can learn. When in doubt, **TASTE YOUR FOOD!** Salt makes food taste more like itself. Getting the seasoning right is key!

As a rule, always use KOSHER salt and a grinder for black pepper.

When using a pepper grinder, try to flick your wrist when you turn the top. This will toss a cloud of pepper over the food. That is how you get a nice, even layer. DO NOT hold the grinder still and drop all your pepper in one pile. This takes a little practice.

6"~12"

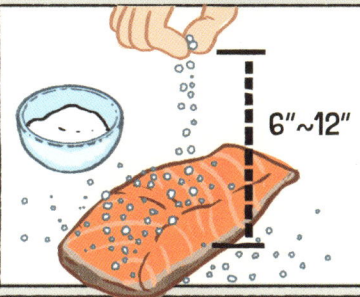

Season all proteins (meats) BEFORE cooking them. Season generously from 6 to 12 inches above the food and think of it as if you are 'dusting' the food. Place your food on a plate and grab a solid pinch of kosher salt in your fingers. Then sprinkle the salt so that falls all over the item evenly. The higher you hold the salt, the easier it is to coat the food evenly.Some of it will fall around the food or on the counter. Just sweep it up later.

Beginning
During cooking
Finishing

Don't just wait until the end to season, season throughout the cooking process. If you put onions in a pan, add a little salt with them. Taste things as you cook them and add a little salt and pepper if you think it needs it. Just be careful not to over salt.

Before you serve your food, ALWAYS TASTE IT! This is so simple, but so many people don't do it. Tasting before serving is your last chance to perfect the flavor a dish, don't miss it!

Slurp!

Sweating Vegetables

So many recipes involve sweating vegetables. It simple means to cook them a little, just until they turn **translucent**. This process draws a little water out of them and releases their flavor. Sweating does not brown the vegetables.

Add your vegetables to a cold pan.

Add a little fat (oil or butter) to the pan and place it over medium low heat.

Sprinkle the vegetable with a little kosher salt.

Stir the vegetables to prevent them from sticking to pan and burning or browning. You only want them to wilt and turn clear, not caramelize and turn brown.

The vegetables are ready when they are soft.

Knife Skills : Choose the Right Knife

There are only 2 knives that you MUST have in your kitchen, the **chef's knife** and the **paring knife**. Other knives are nice to have, and definately come in handy, but are not necessary for the home cook.

Chef's Knife
This is the workhorse of the kitchen, and you will use it for pretty much everything. 8-10 inches is ideal.

Paring Knife
This is small knife used for peeling vegetables or cutting little things in your hand, without a cutting board. You will find yourself using it all the time.

Slicing Knife
A long, thin blade used for cutting cooked proteins and butchering raw fish.

Bread Knife
A long knife with a serrated blade, making it much easier to cut bread.

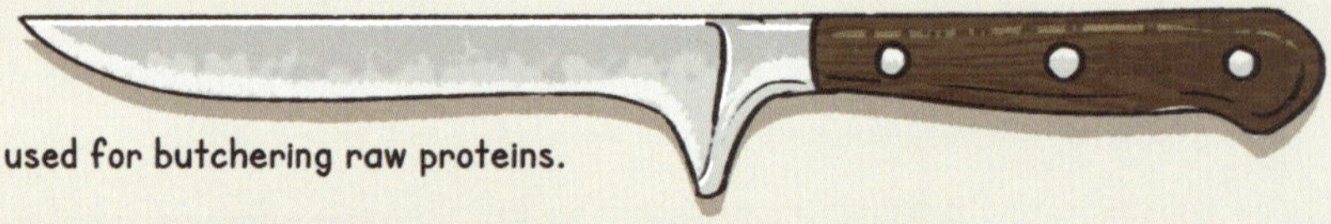

Boning Knife
A shorter knife with a thin, flexible blade used for butchering raw proteins.

Holding Knives

Don't be shy with your knife. The more comfortable you will become with it, the more you will use it properly and the less likely you will be to accidently cut yourself.

The Wrong Way

The Right Way
Hold the knife up near where the blade meeds the handle, and pinch the back of the blade between your thumb and index finger. You will find that this is a very stable way to control the blade.

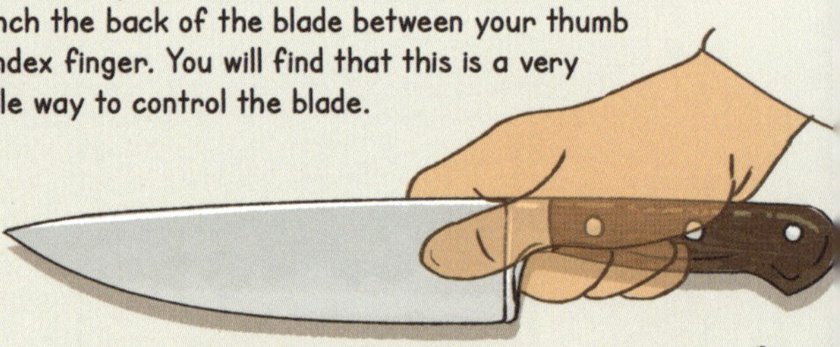

Maintaining Knives

Properly maintaining your knives is the key to keeping them in good shape for many years.

Keep your knives SHARP by honing them on a ceramic steel every time you use them.

Eventually your knife will not stay sharp after being honed. This is when it is time to get it professionally sharpened. You should only need to do this every few years or so.

Store your knives flat, on a towel (to protect the blade), in a drawer.

Always wash your knives by hand. NEVER put them in the dishwasher.

How to cut common foods
Cutting an Onion:

Onions need chopping all the time, and there is a specific way to do it easily. This method works for all layered vegetables, like shallots and fennel. **The sharper your knife, the less you will cry.**

Trim the end off the onion, but leave the root intact.

Cut the onion in half vertically, from top to bottom.

Peel the onion.

Place the flat side of the onion down on a cutting board.

Make vertical cuts with the grain as indicated, but do NOT cut through the root. The width of these cuts will be your dice size.

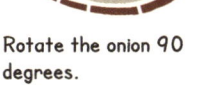
Rotate the onion 90 degrees.

Hold your knife parallel to the cutting board and make a few horizontal cuts through the onion. Don't cut through the root!

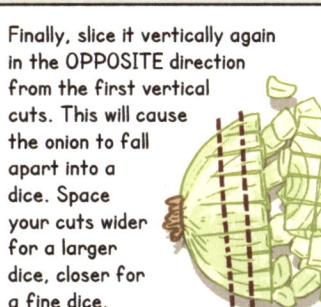
Finally, slice it vertically again in the OPPOSITE direction from the first vertical cuts. This will cause the onion to fall apart into a dice. Space your cuts wider for a larger dice, closer for a fine dice.

Discard the root, or save it for when you make stock.

Cutting a Tomato

Watch out for the core and skin of a tomato. Although the flesh of a tomato is soft and easy to cut through, the skin is not, so use a very sharp knife! If you don't have a **SHARP** knife, use a serrated bread knife.

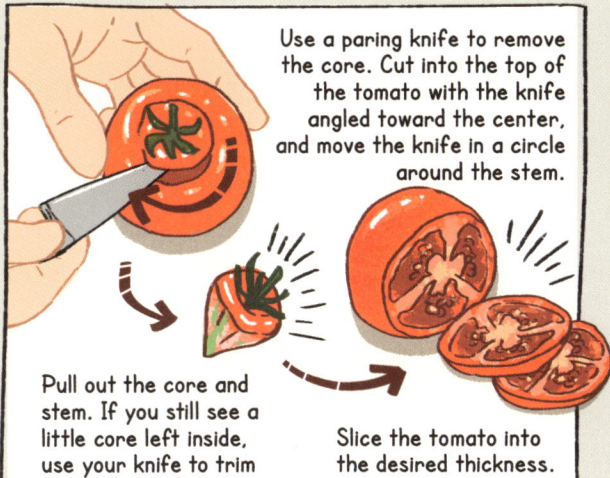

Use a paring knife to remove the core. Cut into the top of the tomato with the knife angled toward the center, and move the knife in a circle around the stem.

Pull out the core and stem. If you still see a little core left inside, use your knife to trim it out.

Slice the tomato into the desired thickness.

NOTE: A cherry tomato core is very small. Don't worry about it.

Slicing Meat

Slicing meat appropriately can be the difference between a tender bite and a tough bite. If your knife isn't very sharp, you can use a serrated bread knife.

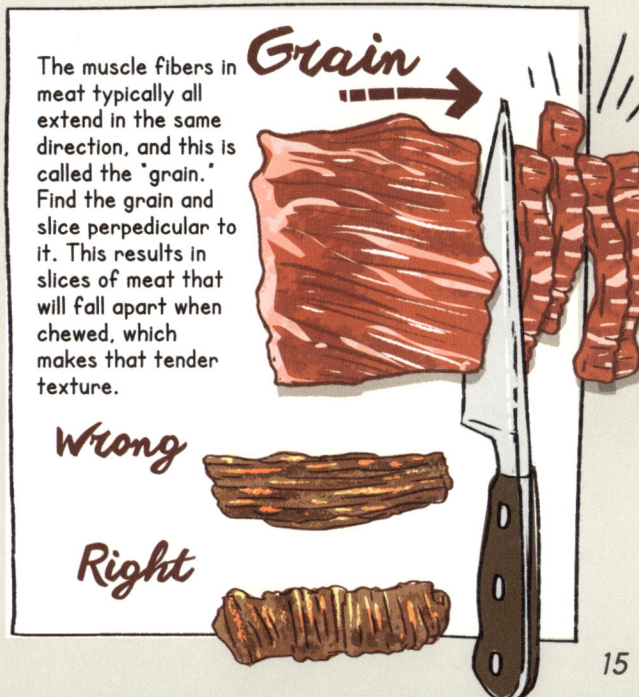

The muscle fibers in meat typically all extend in the same direction, and this is called the "grain." Find the grain and slice perpendicular to it. This results in slices of meat that will fall apart when chewed, which makes that tender texture.

Stock Making

Stock is the first thing that culinary students learn to make. That makes sense, because stock forms the base flavors of so many different dishes, and not just soups. A well made, flavorful stock can be the difference between a boring dish and great one. This chicken stock procedure works for beef, pork, or lamb stocks as well. Most grocery stores will sell bones for stock. Make the biggest batch you can and freeze it!

Equipment Necessary

- The largest pot you have
- Ladle or large spoon
- Fine Mesh strainer
- Cheese cloth (optional)
- Cooling rack (if you make a large amount of stock)

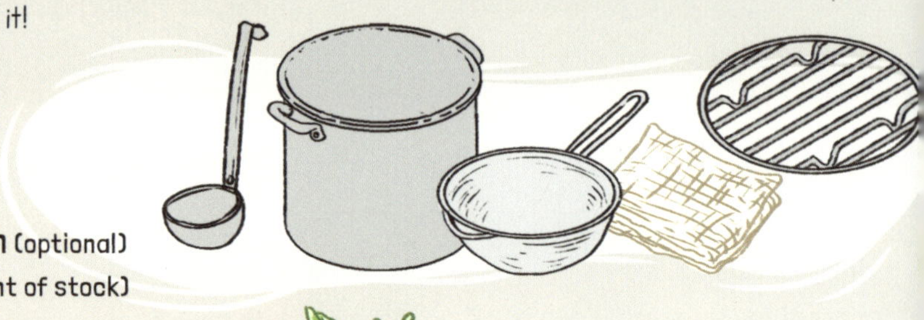

Chicken Stock

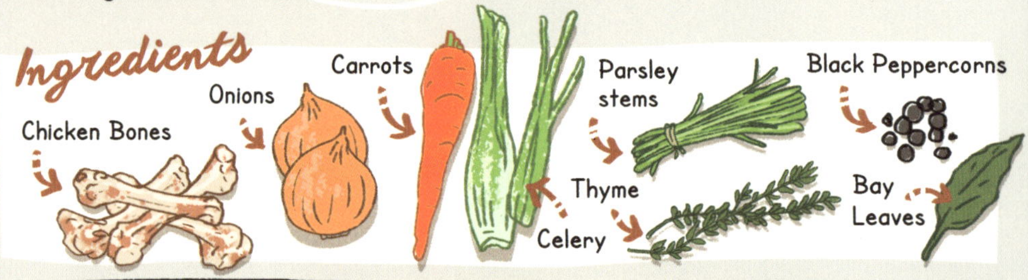

Ingredients
Chicken Bones
Onions
Carrots
Celery
Parsley stems
Thyme
Black Peppercorns
Bay Leaves

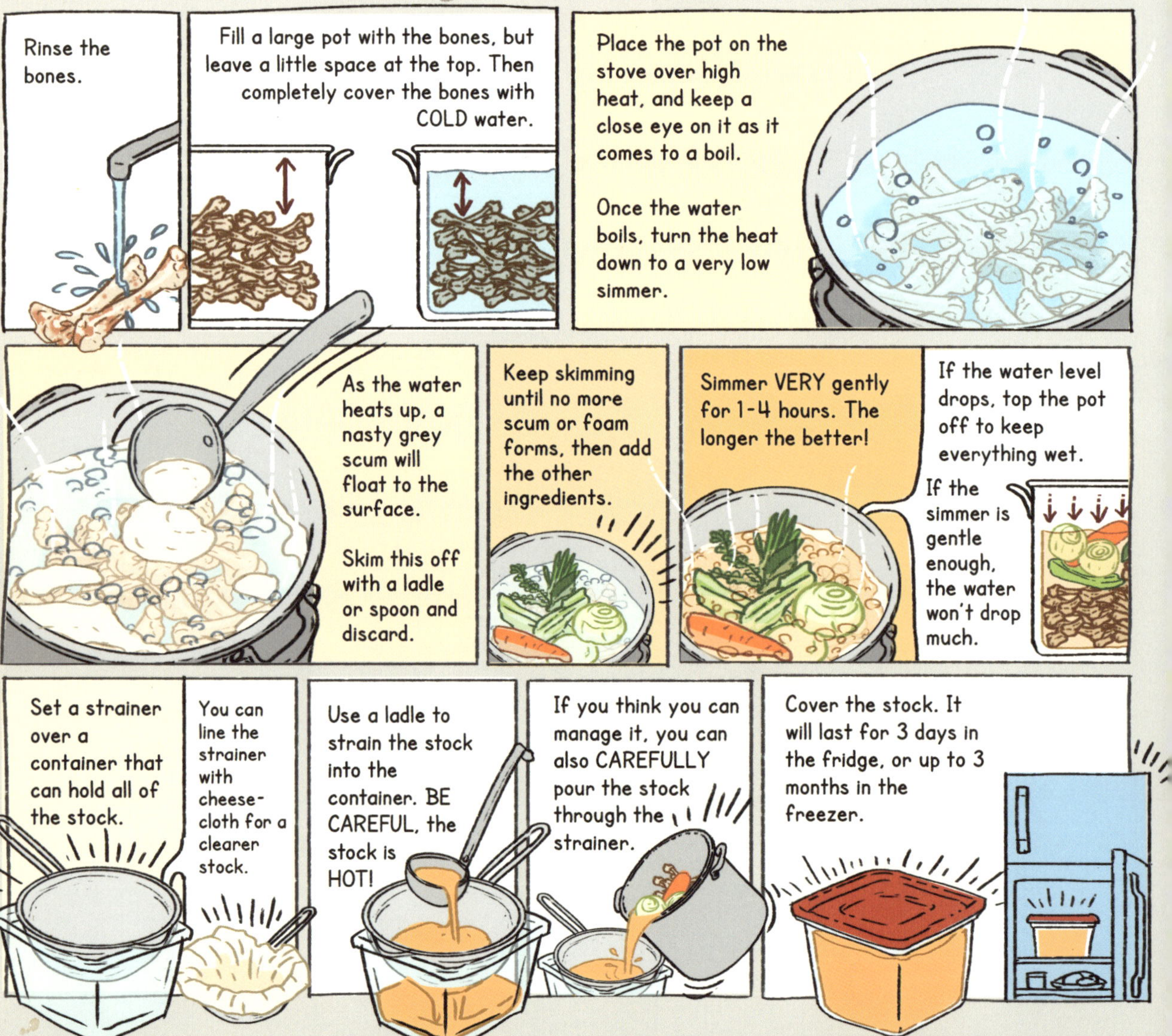

Rinse the bones.
Fill a large pot with the bones, but leave a little space at the top. Then completely cover the bones with COLD water.
Place the pot on the stove over high heat, and keep a close eye on it as it comes to a boil.
Once the water boils, turn the heat down to a very low simmer.
As the water heats up, a nasty grey scum will float to the surface.
Skim this off with a ladle or spoon and discard.
Keep skimming until no more scum or foam forms, then add the other ingredients.
Simmer VERY gently for 1-4 hours. The longer the better!
If the water level drops, top the pot off to keep everything wet.
If the simmer is gentle enough, the water won't drop much.
Set a strainer over a container that can hold all of the stock.
You can line the strainer with cheese-cloth for a clearer stock.
Use a ladle to strain the stock into the container. BE CAREFUL, the stock is HOT!
If you think you can manage it, you can also CAREFULLY pour the stock through the strainer.
Cover the stock. It will last for 3 days in the fridge, or up to 3 months in the freezer.

Vegetable Stock

You can use almost any vegetables to make a stock, but if you use a strong tasting vegetable, your stock is going to taste like that vegetable. No matter what vegetable stock I'm making, I use very little carrot. Carrots have an overpowering flavor, and they will completely take over any stock you put them in. Think about the vegetable flavors that go into the stock, and match them to the sort of dish you want to make! This recipe is for a basic, versatile, vegetable stock.

Ingredients

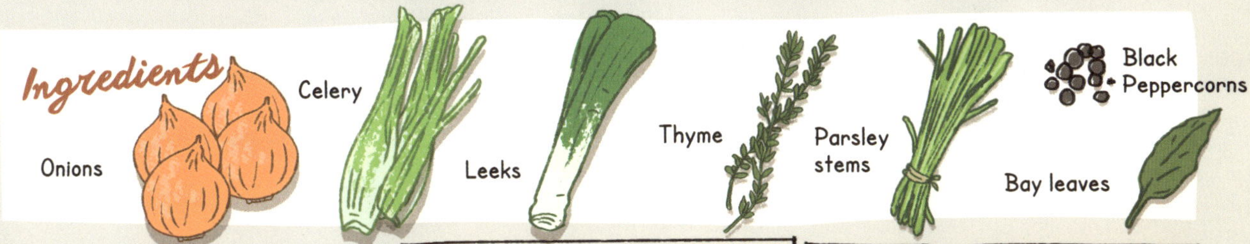

Onions
Celery
Leeks
Thyme
Parsley stems
Black Peppercorns
Bay leaves

Fill a large pot with the vegetables and cover with cold water.

Set over high heat.

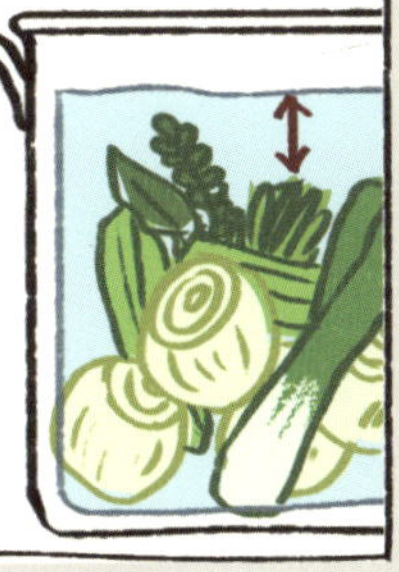

When the water comes to a boil turn the heat down to maintain a very gentle simmer. It should not boil.

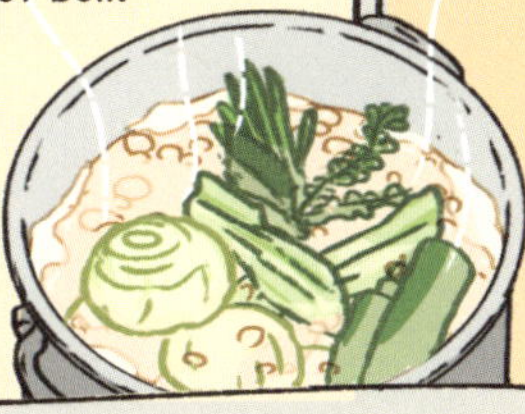

Simmer for 30-60 minutes.

Ladle the stock through a strainer and store.

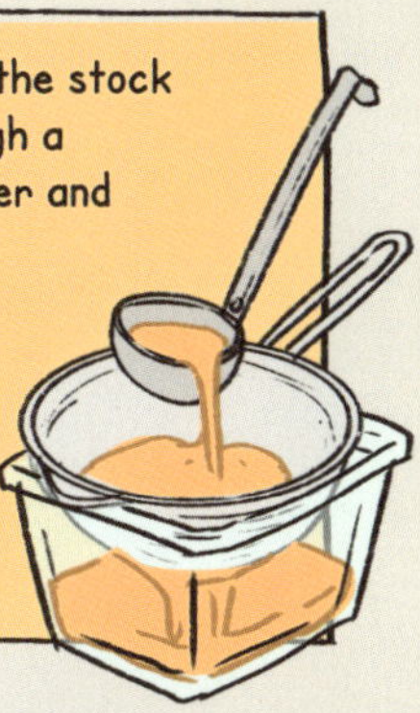

Safety Tips for straining a stock

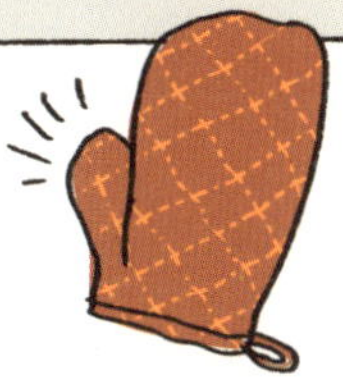

Use thick oven mitts or heavy towels to hold the pot when you are straining.

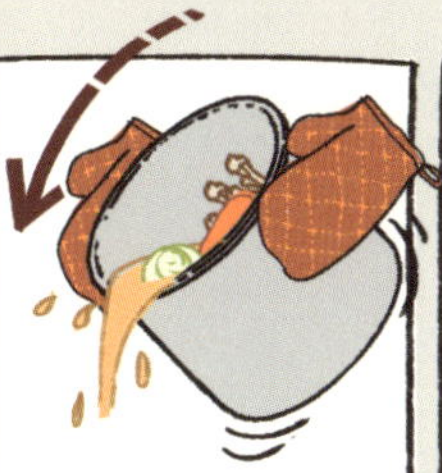

Always pour away from yourself.

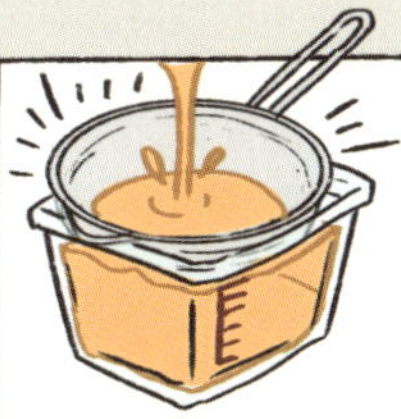

Make sure your container is big enough to hold the stock.

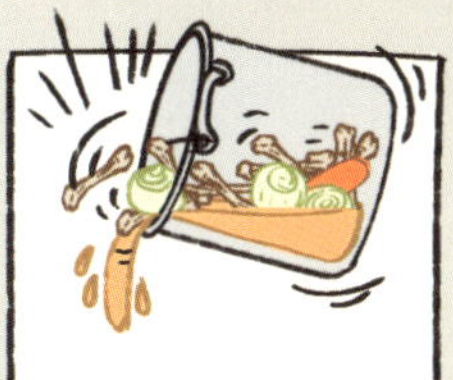

Don't let the bones or vegetables splash out of the pot!

Cooling Stocks

Cooling your stock **quickly** will help preserve the flavors and extend the shelf life. There are a few ways to cool a stock down safely. Decide from the following methods based on how much time you have.

The shallow pan method

A wide, shallow pan will cool down much quicker in the refridgerator. Just fill shallow pans with stock and place in the fridge to cool.

Once the stock is cool, transfer it to whatever storage container you like.

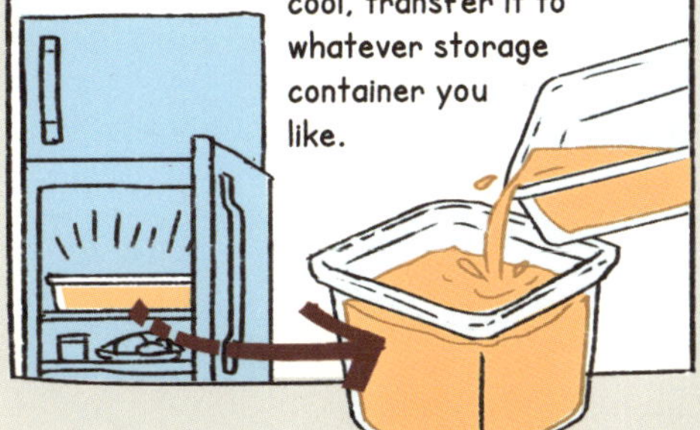

Put it in the freezer

Fill shallow pans with stock and put them in the freezer, uncovered. Wait until they are frozen to cover them.

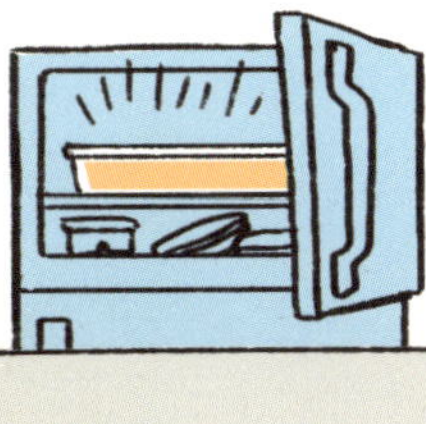

The ice-bath method

If you have made more stock than will fit easily in the fridge, good for you! You will want to cool it with ice water in the sink. Just plug the drain and set a cooling rack over it. Set the hot pot of stock on the rack. Fill the area around the pot with ice, then turn on the water. Let it cool surrounded by the ice water, and stir occasionally. When the stock is cold, transfer to a storage container.

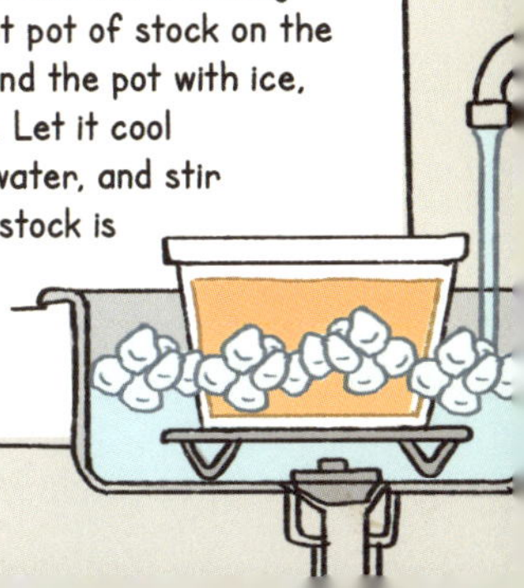

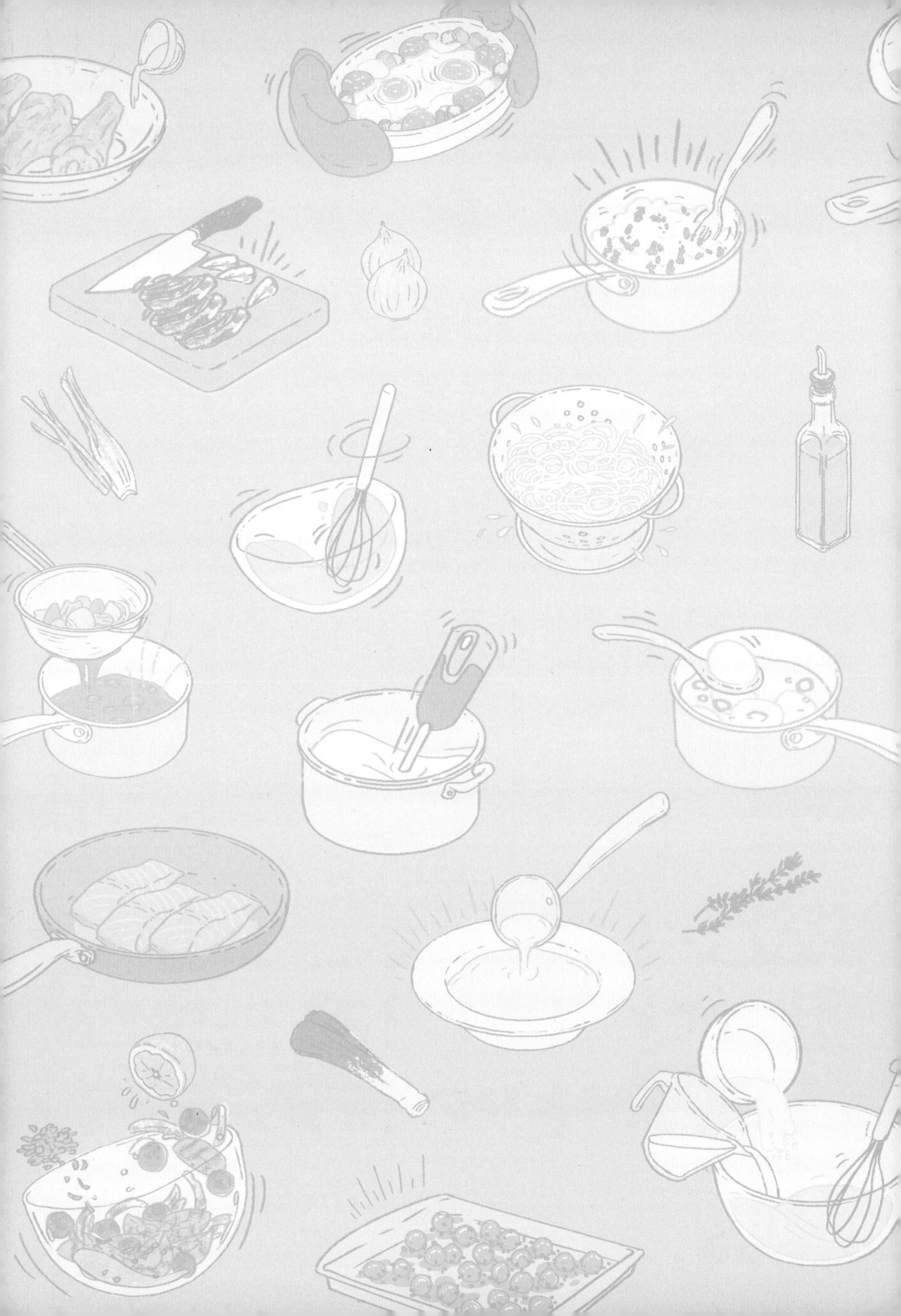

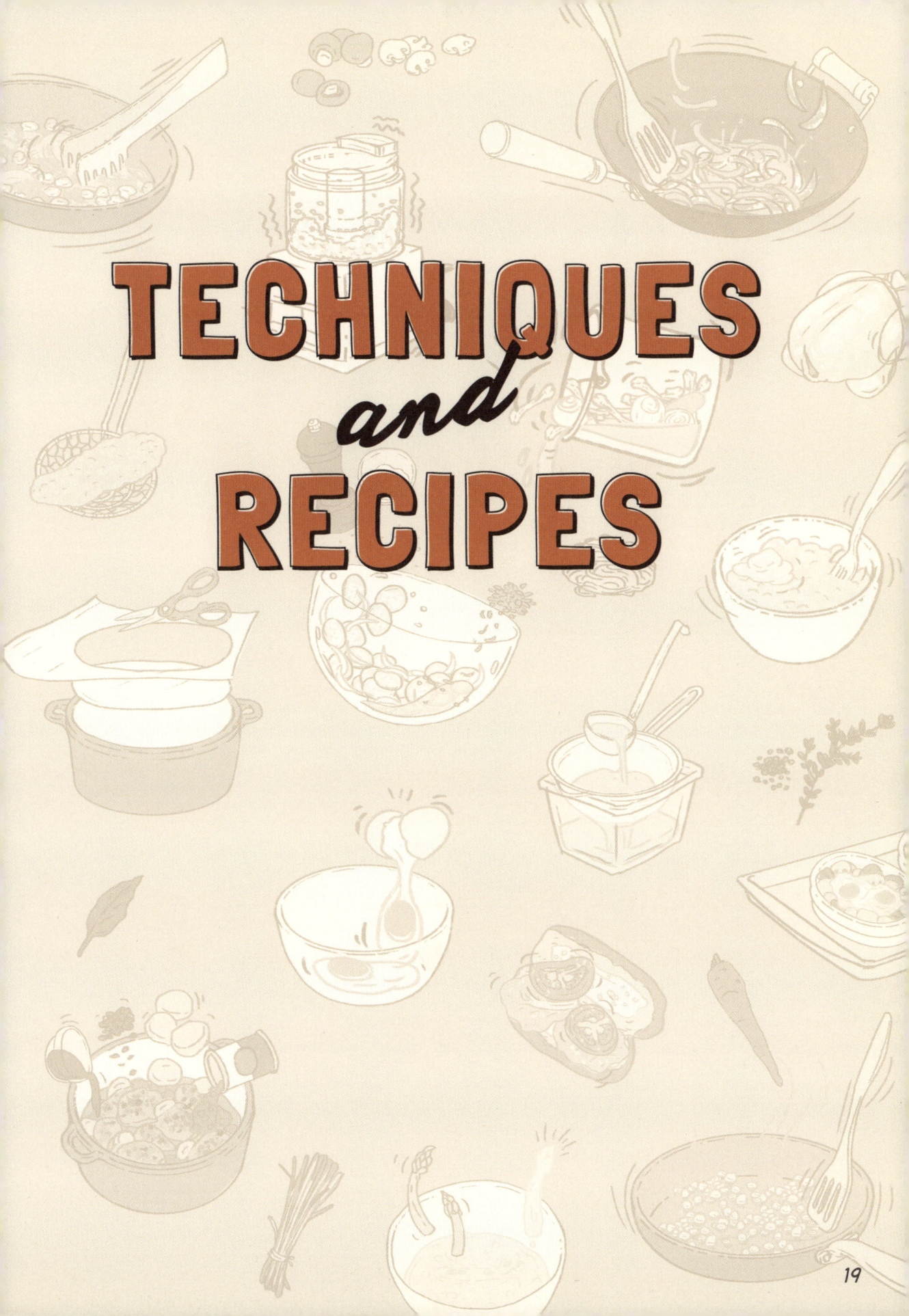

TECHNIQUES and RECIPES

Technique 1

SOUPS

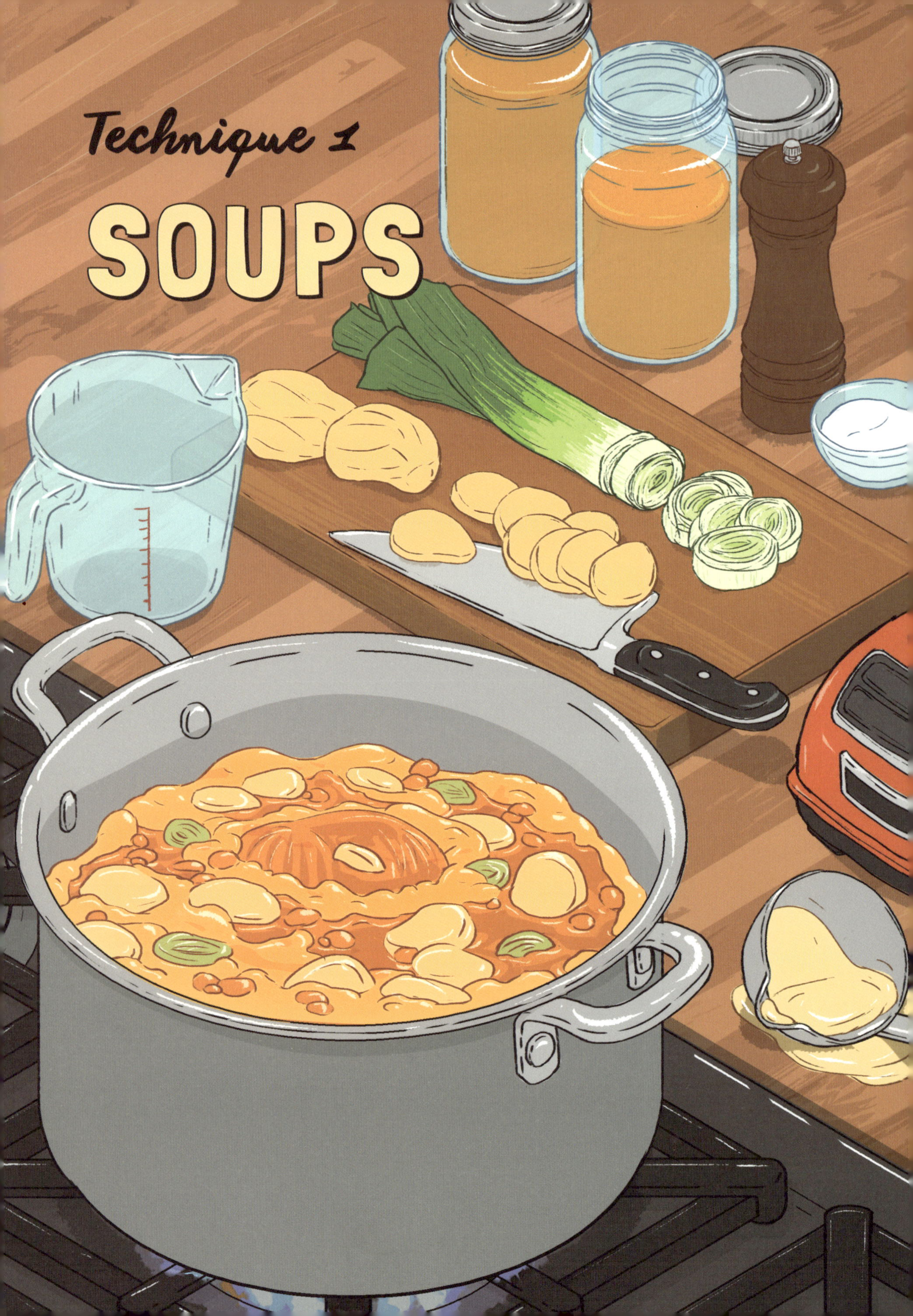

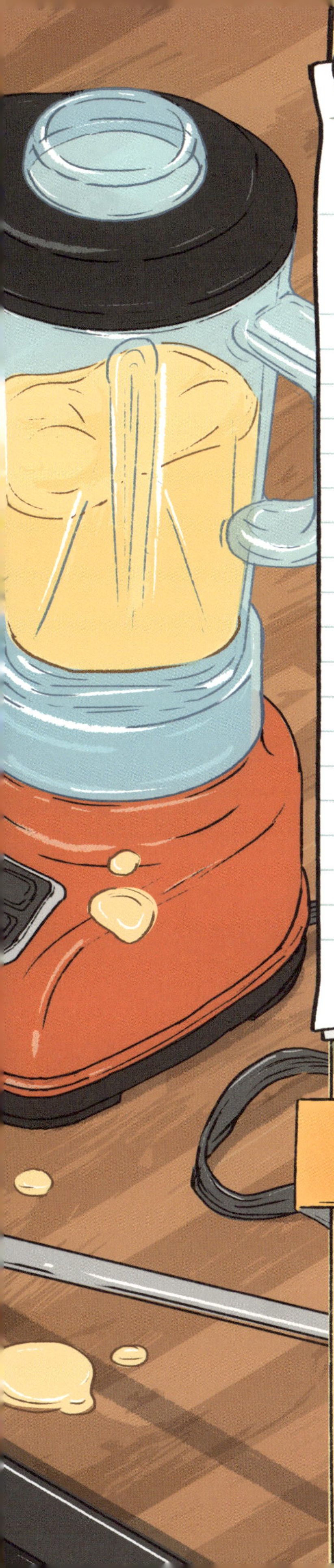

Chef's Note

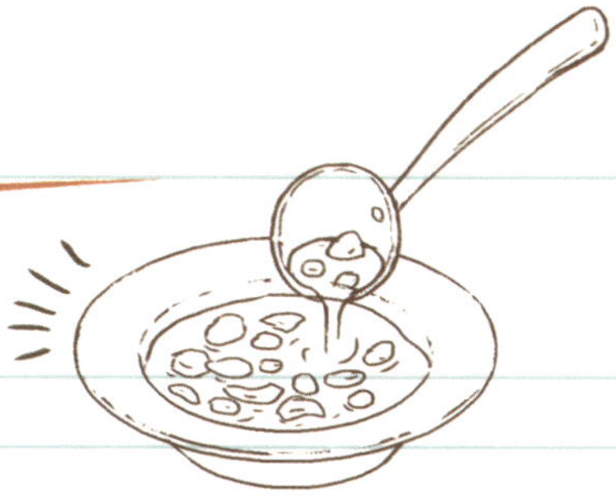

Soups are some of the easiest and most diverse kinds of food out there. Nearly all cultures have some kind of soup in their cuisine, from a delicately prepared French consommé, to a quick Italian minestrone, a lovingly cared for Vietnamese pho, or a rich Japanese ramen.

They aren't just easy—they're super efficient. Sometimes you find a few ingredients in the fridge that couldn't be a meal on their own, but throw them together in a soup and you've got something delicious and special. But soups are not limited cleaning out the fridge. They can also be an amazing start to a gourmet meal. Soups are as simple or as complex as you want to make them, but they are always delicious soul-warming.

SKILL BADGES

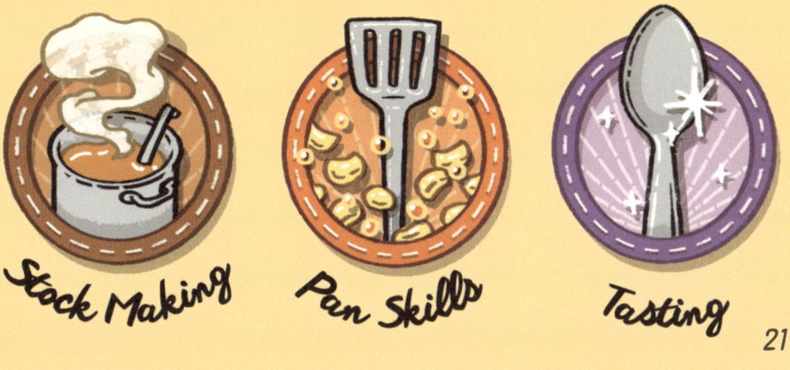

Stock Making
Pan Skills
Tasting

Light and Luscious Broth Soups

The most important ingredient in a broth-based soup is the **broth** itself, which is directly related to the quality of the **stock** you start with. You can make your own stock (see page 16) or you can just buy one. Even professional chefs buy stock sometimes. Regardless, it needs to taste good on its own before you can make a soup from it. Once you have a good broth to work with, you can flavor it by simmering aromatics in the broth until it takes on those favors. Always be sure to **taste** your broth along the way so that you know when your broth is flavored enough. Next, add the solid ingredients (like pastas, meats, or vegetables) to the broth. They will need to cook through before the soup is ready, so make sure you take into account the time they will need.

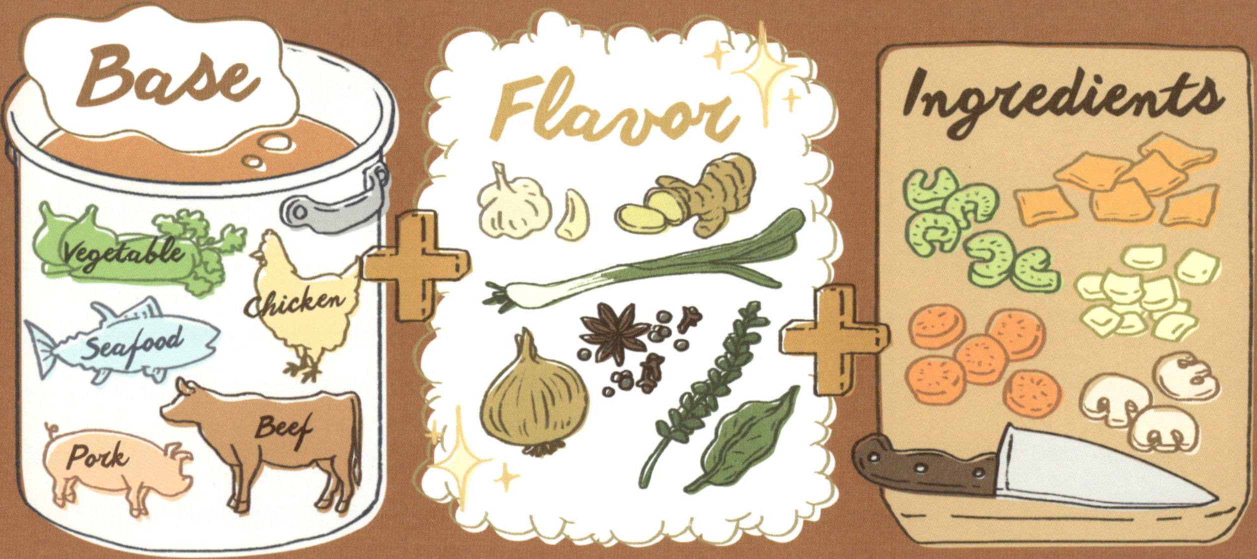

Base
Vegetable
Chicken
Seafood
Beef
Pork
Flavor
Ingredients

Basic broth soup technique

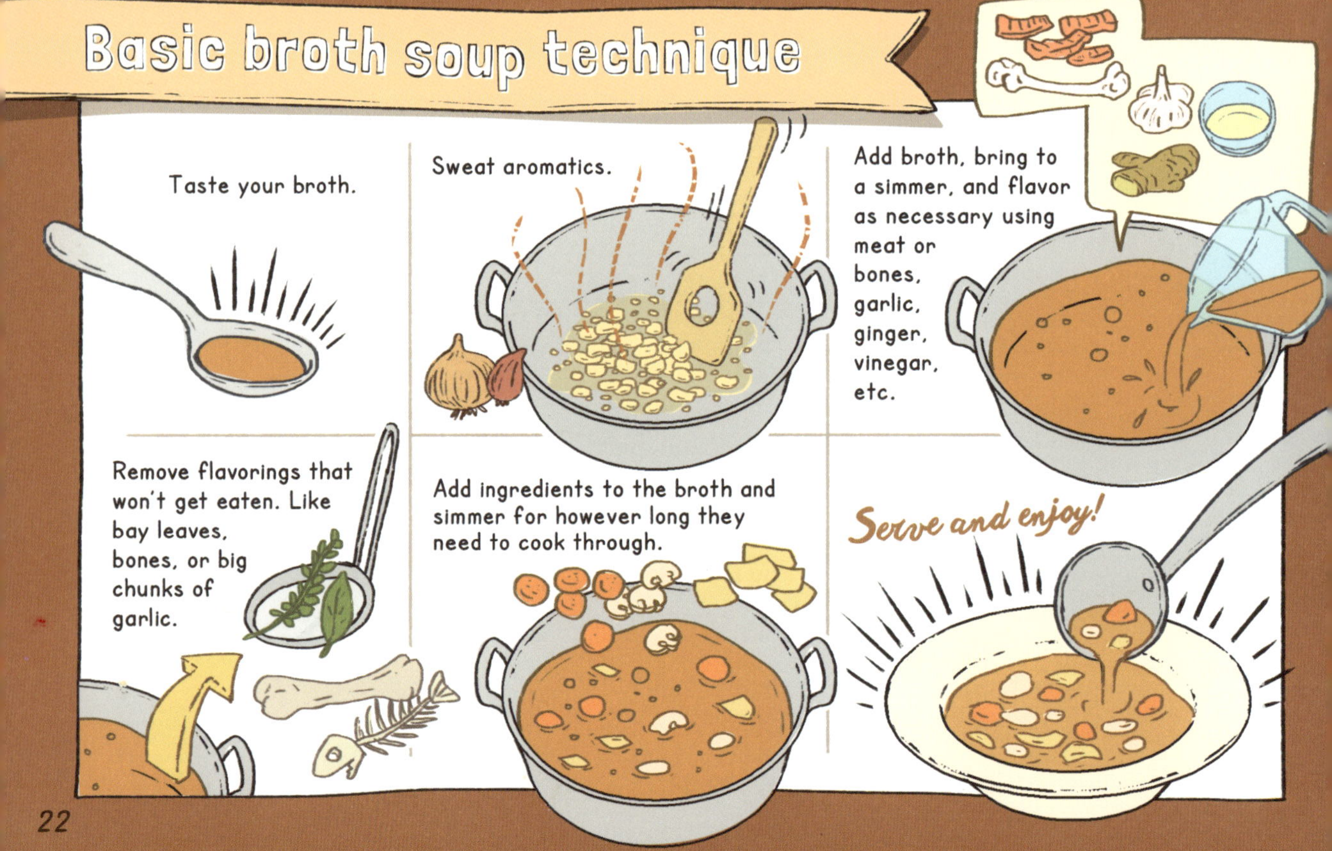

Taste your broth.

Sweat aromatics.

Add broth, bring to a simmer, and flavor as necessary using meat or bones, garlic, ginger, vinegar, etc.

Remove flavorings that won't get eaten. Like bay leaves, bones, or big chunks of garlic.

Add ingredients to the broth and simmer for however long they need to cook through.

Serve and enjoy!

Hearty, Heavier, Creamy Soups

Creamier, heavier soups are made with ingredients that are usually cooked until they are soft and then **puréed**. Once the base ingredients are cooked, they are puréed with their cooking liquid until the mixture reaches the desired consistency, which is up to you. You can make them silky **smooth**, or leave them with a little texture.

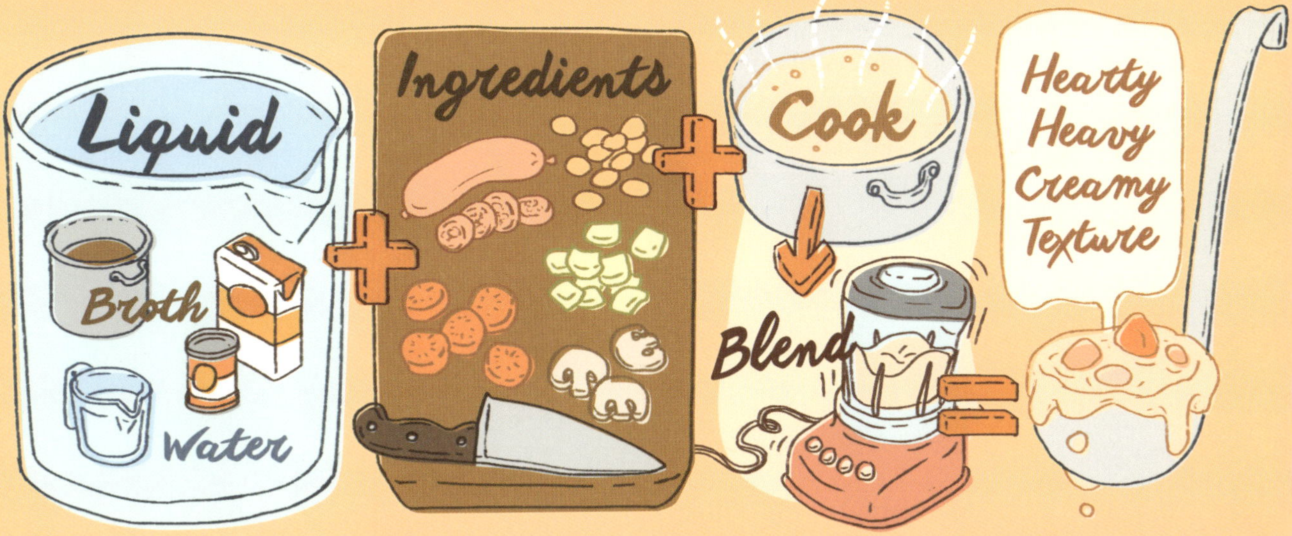

Liquid
Broth
Water
Ingredients
Cook
Blend
Hearty Heavy Creamy Texture

Basic puréed soup technique

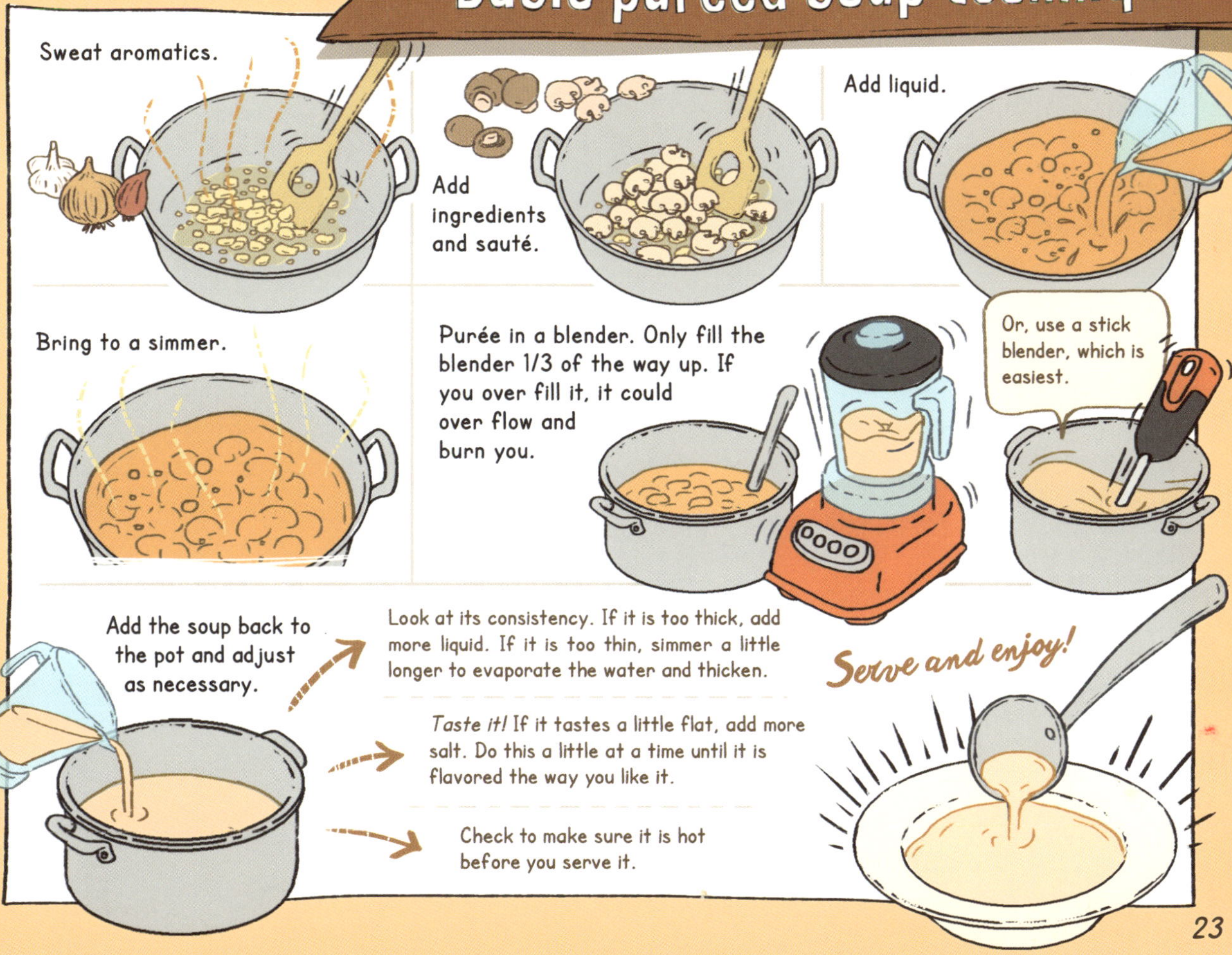

Sweat aromatics.
Add ingredients and sauté.
Add liquid.
Bring to a simmer.
Purée in a blender. Only fill the blender 1/3 of the way up. If you over fill it, it could over flow and burn you.
Or, use a stick blender, which is easiest.
Add the soup back to the pot and adjust as necessary.
Look at its consistency. If it is too thick, add more liquid. If it is too thin, simmer a little longer to evaporate the water and thicken.
Taste it! If it tastes a little flat, add more salt. Do this a little at a time until it is flavored the way you like it.
Check to make sure it is hot before you serve it.
Serve and enjoy!

Recipe 1

Potato Leek Soup with Brown Butter

Also known as "vichyssois," this is a **classic** French soup that is as **simple** as it is delicious. A drizzle of **brown butter** before serving brings the soup to another level, but if you're pressed for time you can omit it.

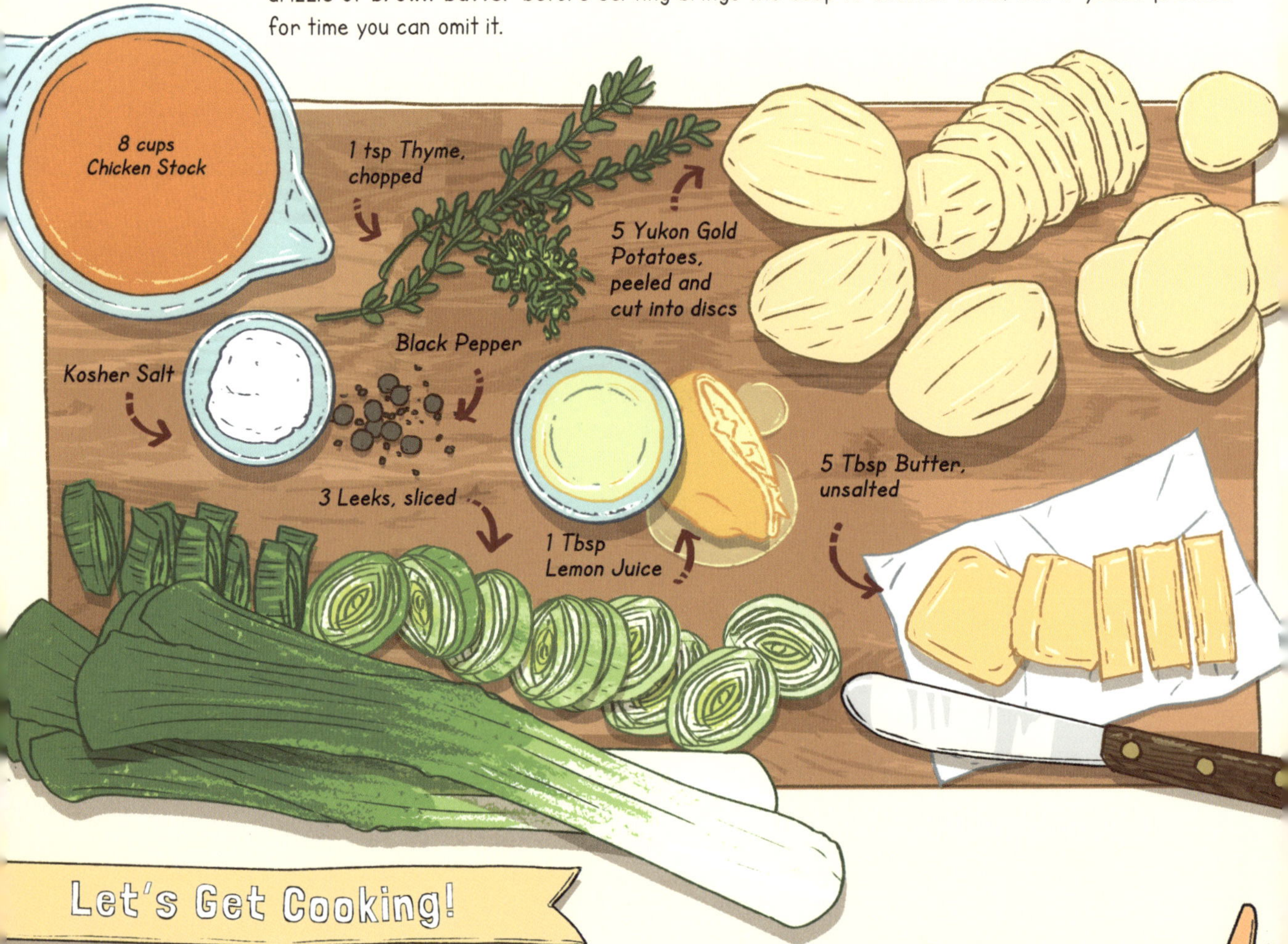
8 cups Chicken Stock
1 tsp Thyme, chopped
5 Yukon Gold Potatoes, peeled and cut into discs
Kosher Salt
Black Pepper
3 Leeks, sliced
1 Tbsp Lemon Juice
5 Tbsp Butter, unsalted

Let's Get Cooking!

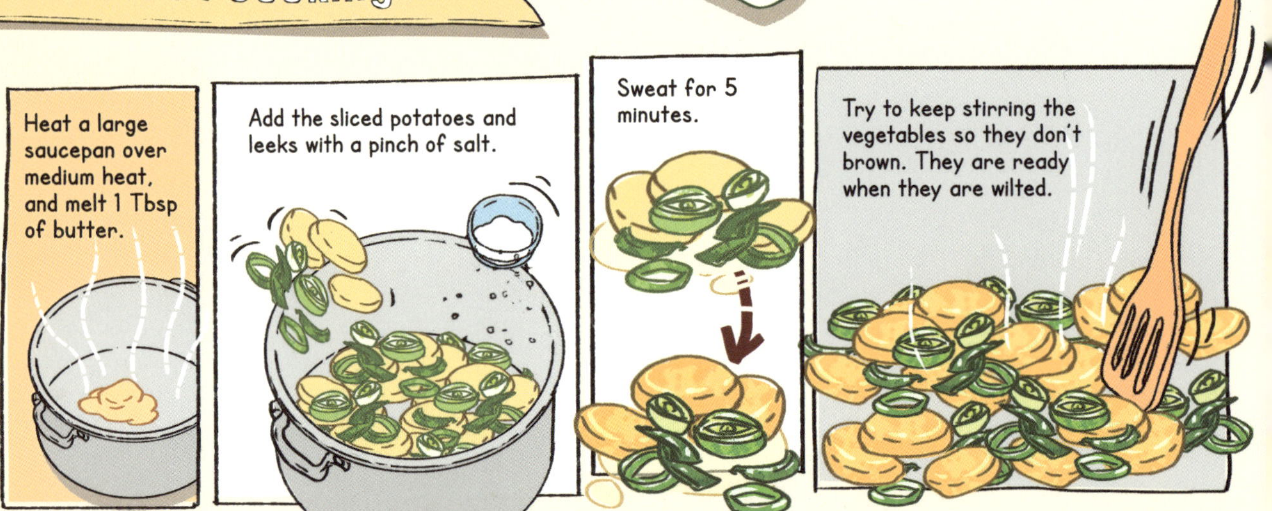
Heat a large saucepan over medium heat, and melt 1 Tbsp of butter.
Add the sliced potatoes and leeks with a pinch of salt.
Sweat for 5 minutes.
Try to keep stirring the vegetables so they don't brown. They are ready when they are wilted.

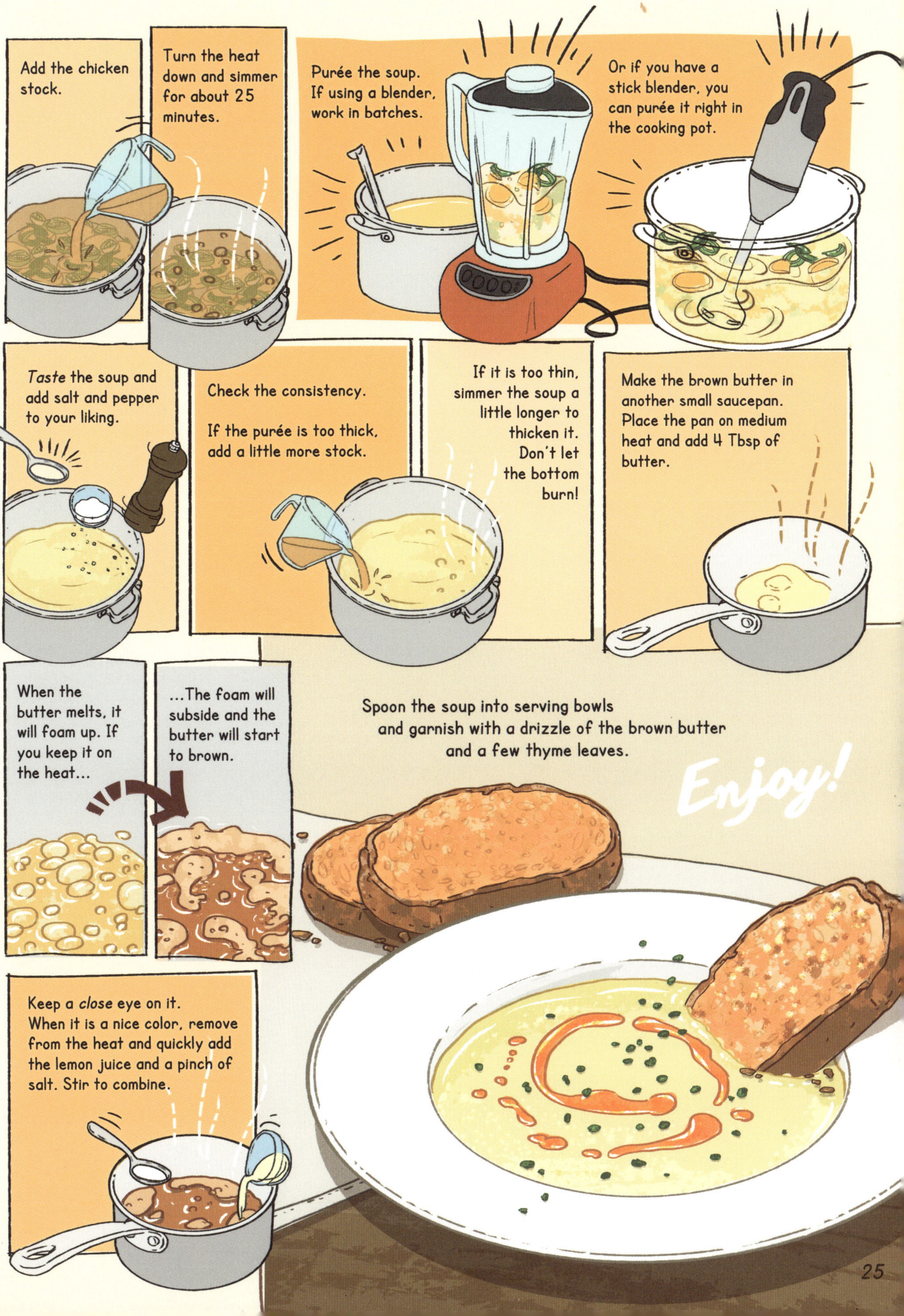
Add the chicken stock.
Turn the heat down and simmer for about 25 minutes.
Purée the soup. If using a blender, work in batches.
Or if you have a stick blender, you can purée it right in the cooking pot.
Taste the soup and add salt and pepper to your liking.
Check the consistency.
If the purée is too thick, add a little more stock.
If it is too thin, simmer the soup a little longer to thicken it. Don't let the bottom burn!
Make the brown butter in another small saucepan. Place the pan on medium heat and add 4 Tbsp of butter.
When the butter melts, it will foam up. If you keep it on the heat...
...The foam will subside and the butter will start to brown.
Keep a *close* eye on it. When it is a nice color, remove from the heat and quickly add the lemon juice and a pinch of salt. Stir to combine.
Spoon the soup into serving bowls and garnish with a drizzle of the brown butter and a few thyme leaves.
Enjoy!

Recipe 2

Sausage with Beans, Pimenton & Crème Friache

This broth-based soup is rich, **hearty**, and filling. **Pimenton** does not get nearly enough love. A good quality smoked paprika can really elevate a dish, and this soup shows it off nicely. If you don't have any, a normal paprika will work just fine.

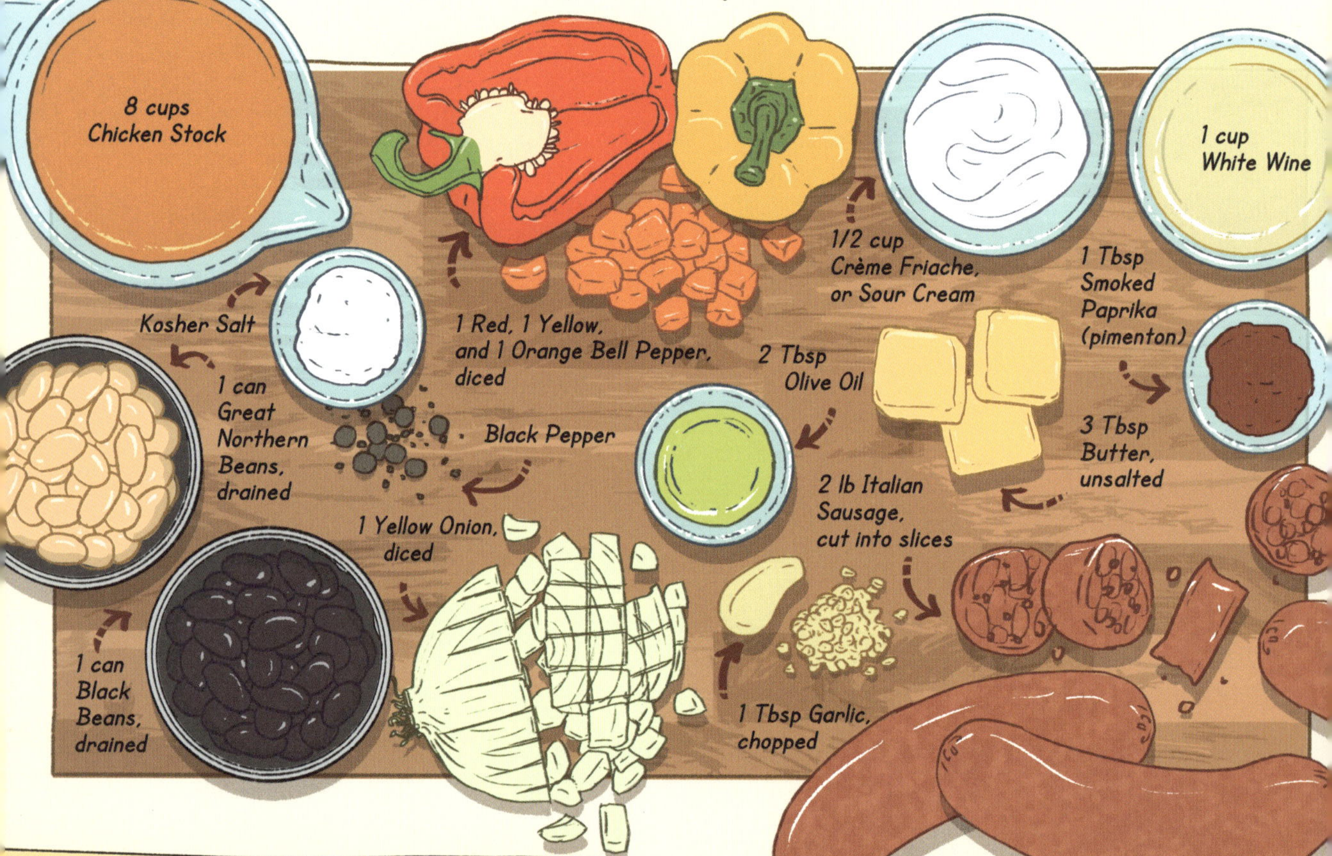
8 cups Chicken Stock
1 cup White Wine
1/2 cup Crème Friache, or Sour Cream
1 Tbsp Smoked Paprika (pimenton)
Kosher Salt
1 Red, 1 Yellow, and 1 Orange Bell Pepper, diced
2 Tbsp Olive Oil
1 can Great Northern Beans, drained
Black Pepper
3 Tbsp Butter, unsalted
2 lb Italian Sausage, cut into slices
1 Yellow Onion, diced
1 can Black Beans, drained
1 Tbsp Garlic, chopped

Let's Get Cooking!

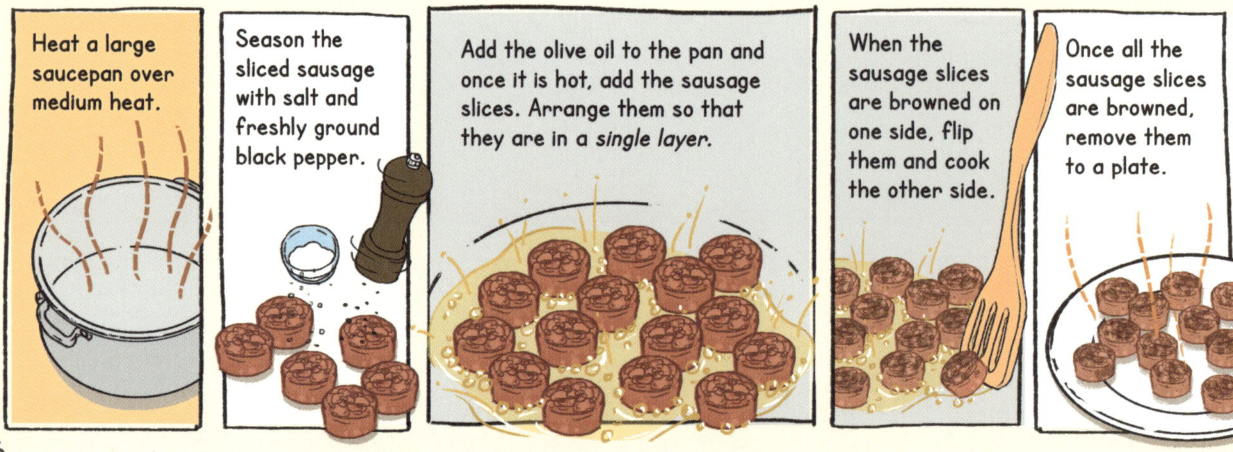
Heat a large saucepan over medium heat.
Season the sliced sausage with salt and freshly ground black pepper.
Add the olive oil to the pan and once it is hot, add the sausage slices. Arrange them so that they are in a *single layer*.
When the sausage slices are browned on one side, flip them and cook the other side.
Once all the sausage slices are browned, remove them to a plate.

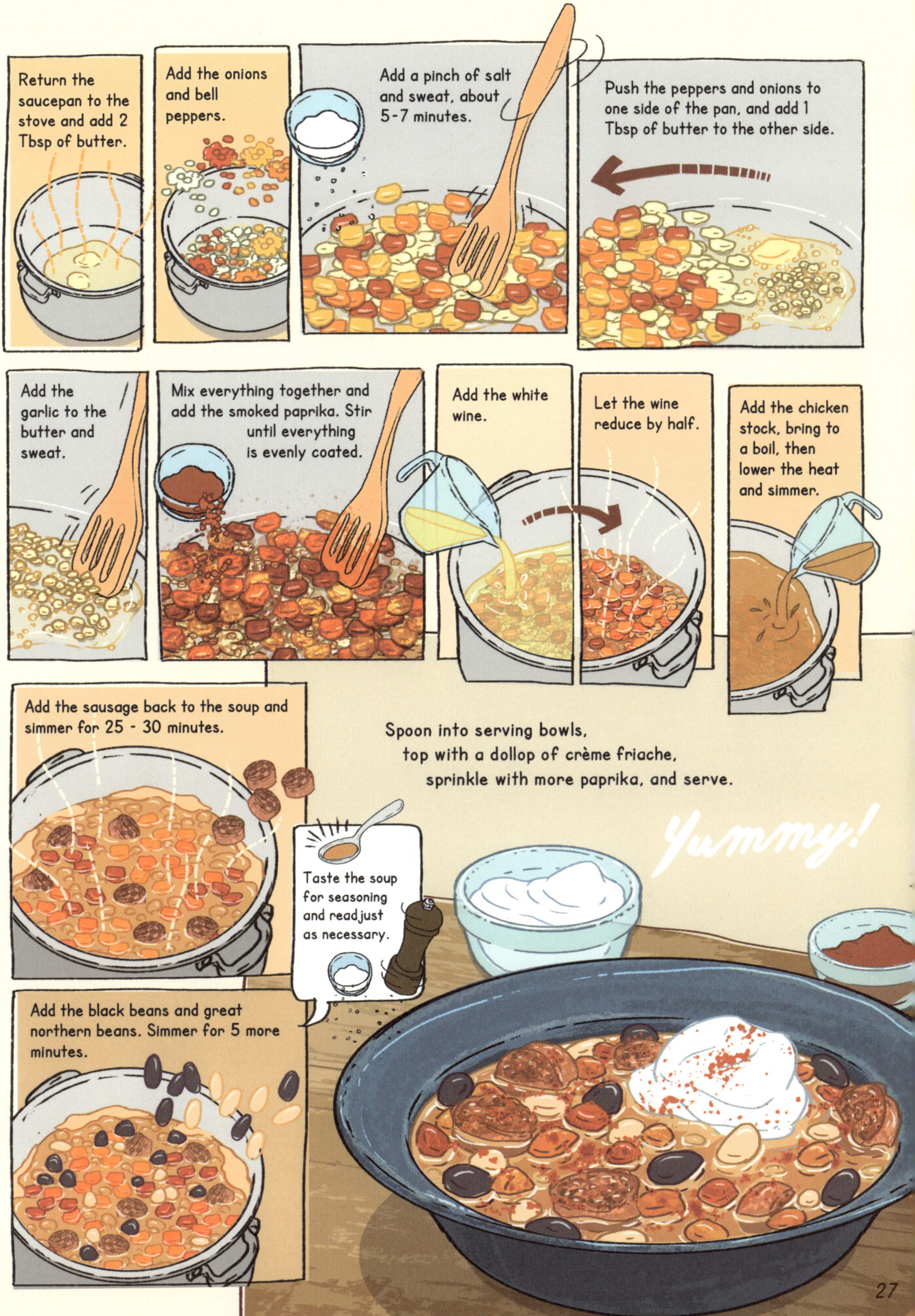

Return the saucepan to the stove and add 2 Tbsp of butter.
Add the onions and bell peppers.
Add a pinch of salt and sweat, about 5-7 minutes.
Push the peppers and onions to one side of the pan, and add 1 Tbsp of butter to the other side.
Add the garlic to the butter and sweat.
Mix everything together and add the smoked paprika. Stir until everything is evenly coated.
Add the white wine.
Let the wine reduce by half.
Add the chicken stock, bring to a boil, then lower the heat and simmer.
Add the sausage back to the soup and simmer for 25 - 30 minutes.
Add the black beans and great northern beans. Simmer for 5 more minutes.
Taste the soup for seasoning and readjust as necessary.
Spoon into serving bowls, top with a dollop of crème friache, sprinkle with more paprika, and serve.
Yummy!

Technique 2

SALADS

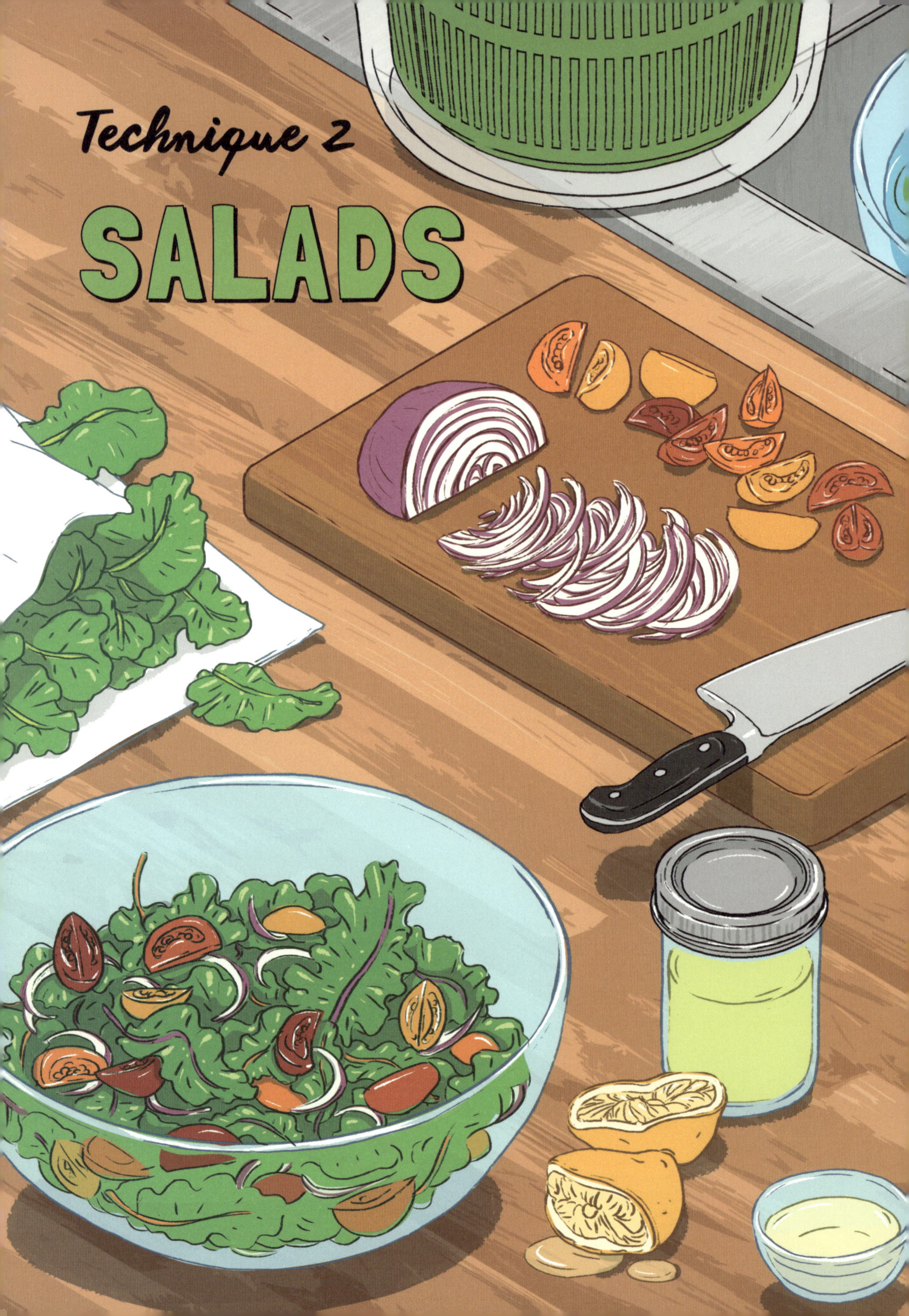

Chef's Note

Few things are more satisfying than a well made salad. Some people treat salads as if they don't matter, but when they are crisp and dressed well, a salad can easily be the best thing on the table. "Crisp" and "dressed well" are important though. What's worse than a soggy, floppy, wet, or flavorless salad? Haven't you turned your nose up at a wilted salad? Or at a flavorless bowl of dry leaves?

Salads are the place to let your creativity shine. They don't have to be made of lettuces and leaves. Some of my favorites salads are made from beans, or pastas, or hearty root veggies. Pretty much anything can work in the right salad.

Just remember: a really well made salad highlights its ingredients, brings them together and makes them pop!

SKILL BADGES

Knife Skills

Dressing

Tasting

SALAD TECHNIQUES

Dressings

Dressings are the **stars** of the salad world. It's very easy to buy a bottle of dressing at the store, and honestly everyone does it sometimes. But you miss out on so much with bottled dressings! The flavors are muted and dull because they have been sitting in a jar for ages. The vinegars lost their punch long ago, the herbs have lost their fragrant essential oils, and what you end up getting is a boring dressing with no personality. Don't settle for that, **make your own**!

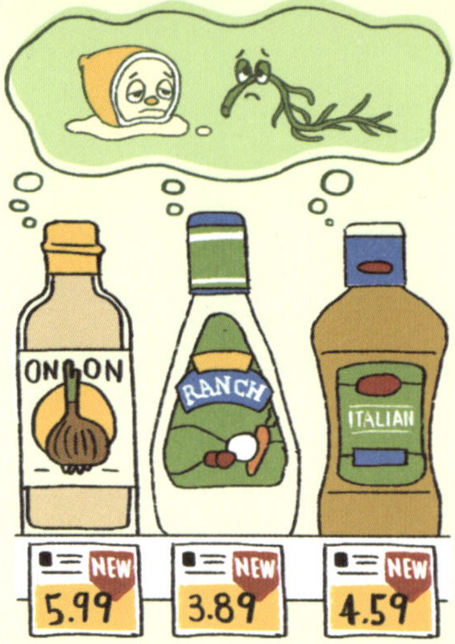
ONION
RANCH
ITALIAN
NEW 5.99
NEW 3.89
NEW 4.59

Making your own vinaigrette is easy!

Just think: 3 to 1.

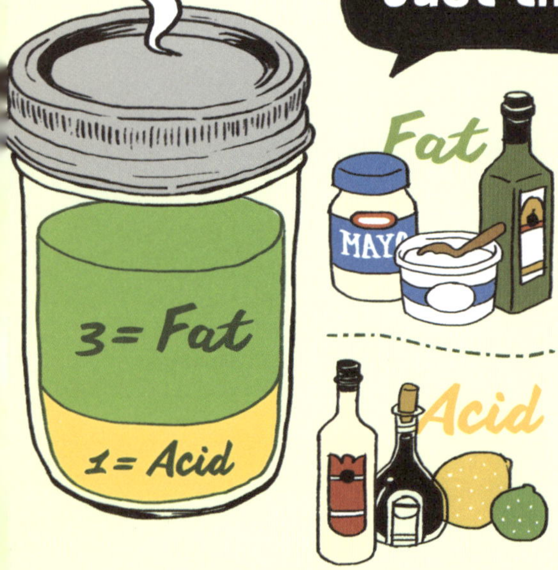
Fat
MAYO
3 = Fat
1 = Acid
Acid

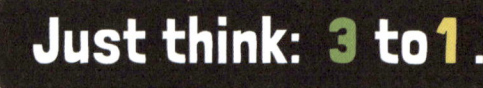

The "3" stands for whatever **fat** you are using, which could be anything from olive oil to crème friache to mayonnaise. The "1" stands for the **acid**, which could be anything from citrus juice to vinegar, anything that has a puckery punch! Just remember the golden rule: **taste it before you use it**. You're looking for balance between the fat and the acid. The fat adds body to the dressing and cuts the harshness of the acid. The acid is there for pop or brightness and keeps dressing feeling **light**. They work together to enhance and compliment the ingrediants in the salad. Whenever you make a vinaigrette, make enough to fill a jar and keep it in your refrigerator. That way you'll have a dressing ready when you want it, and it will be cheaper **and** more flavorful than any you will buy.

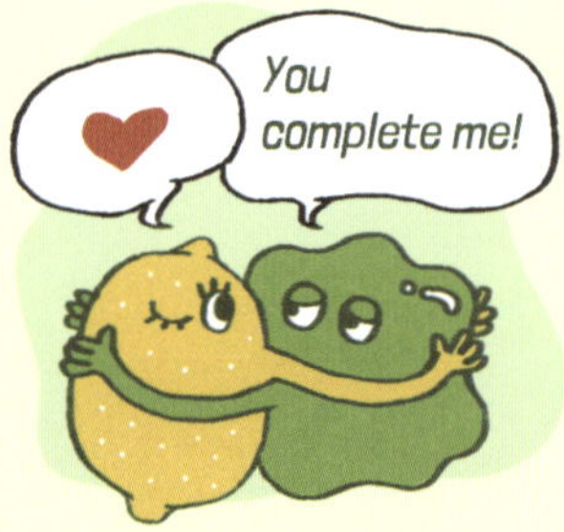
You complete me!

How to make a Vinaigrette

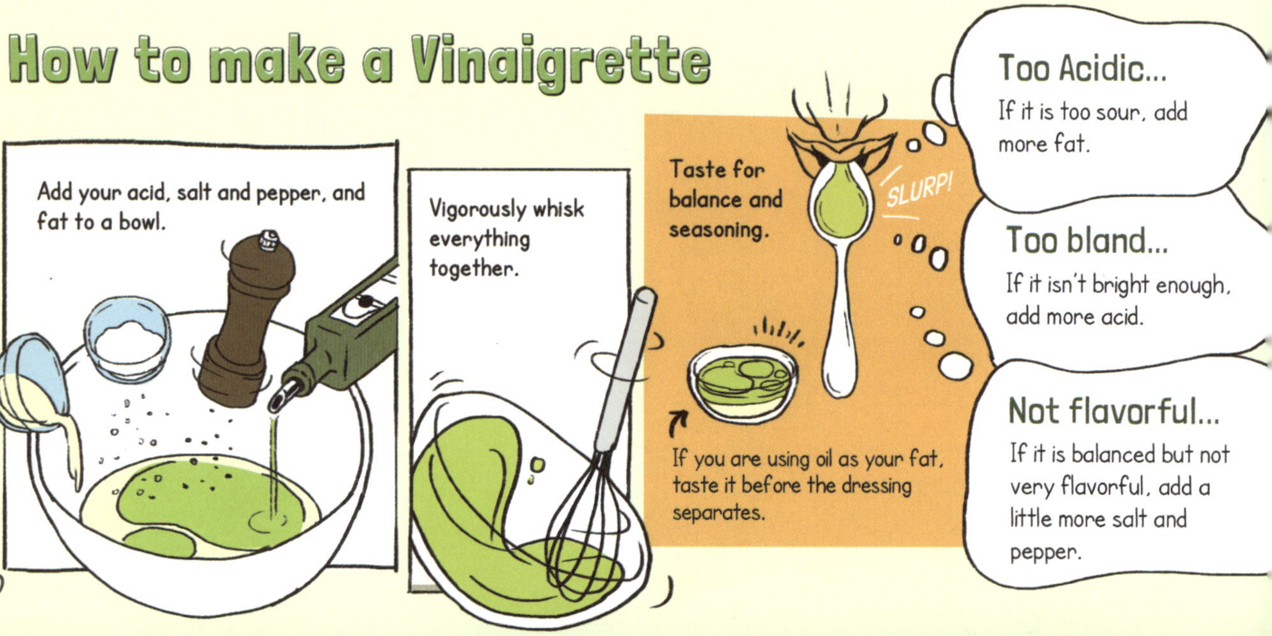
Add your acid, salt and pepper, and fat to a bowl.
Vigorously whisk everything together.
Taste for balance and seasoning.
SLURP!
If you are using oil as your fat, taste it before the dressing separates.
Too Acidic...
If it is too sour, add more fat.
Too bland...
If it isn't bright enough, add more acid.
Not flavorful...
If it is balanced but not very flavorful, add a little more salt and pepper.

Washing greens

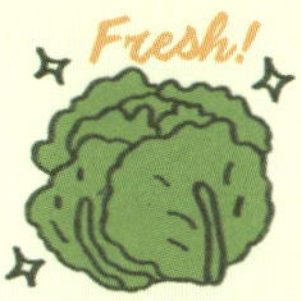
Fresh!

Buy your lettuces **whole**. Yes, sometimes it's easier to buy a bag of salad mix, but lettuce starts to wilt the moment it's cut, and that bag might have been on the shelf for a long time. Buy it whole to keep it **crunchy**!

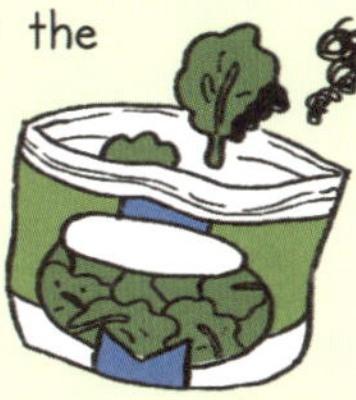

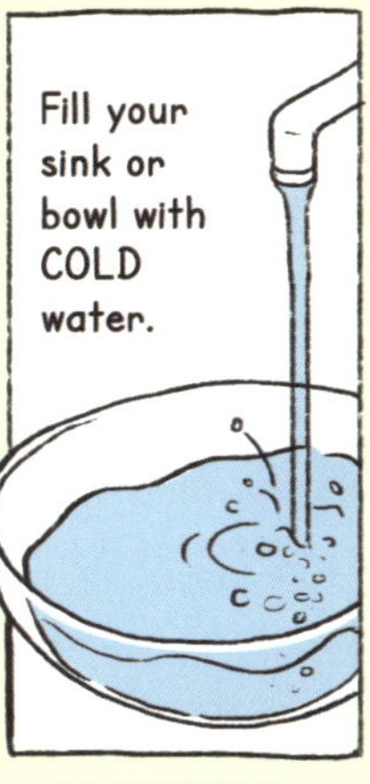
Fill your sink or bowl with COLD water.

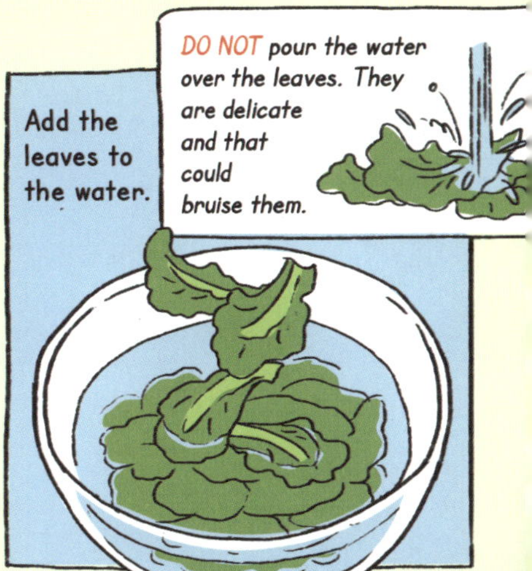
Add the leaves to the water.
DO NOT pour the water over the leaves. They are delicate and that could bruise them.

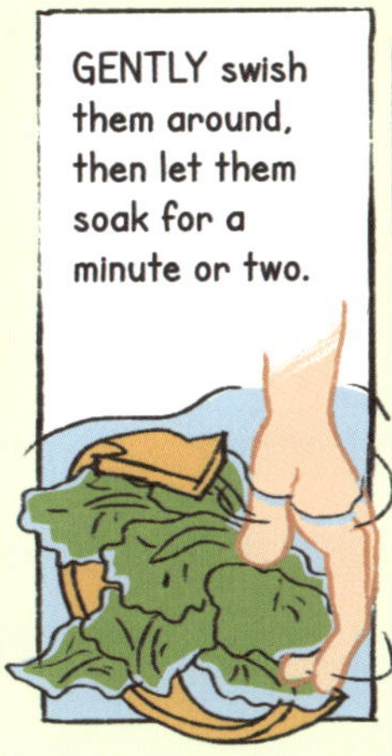
GENTLY swish them around, then let them soak for a minute or two.

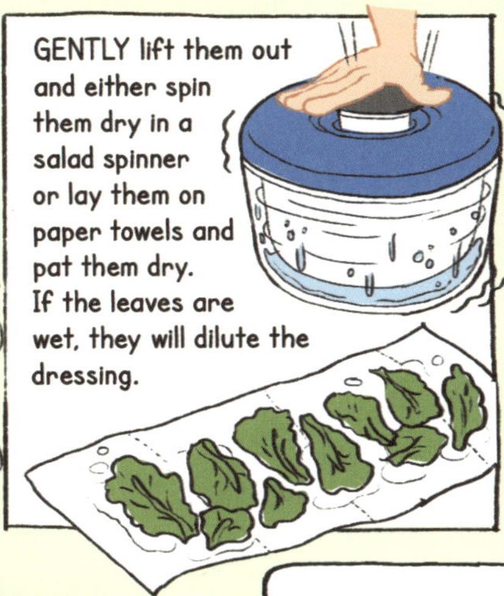
GENTLY lift them out and either spin them dry in a salad spinner or lay them on paper towels and pat them dry. If the leaves are wet, they will dilute the dressing.

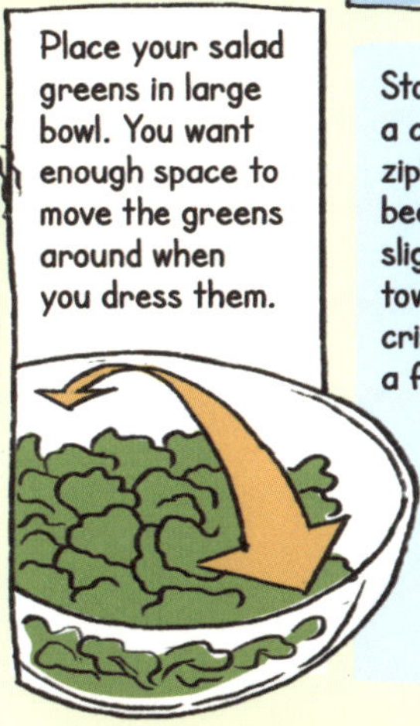
Place your salad greens in large bowl. You want enough space to move the greens around when you dress them.

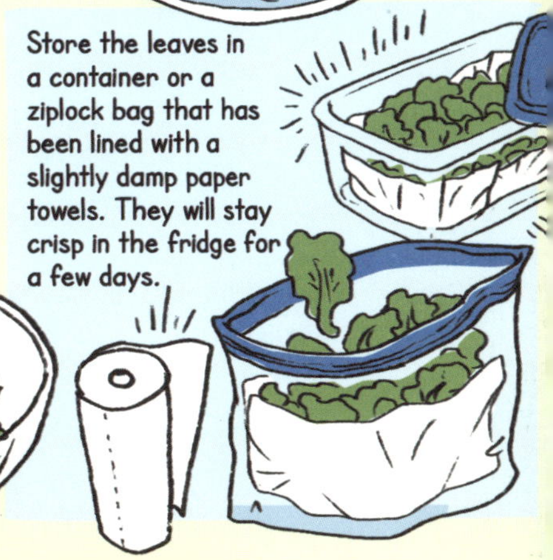
Store the leaves in a container or a ziplock bag that has been lined with a slightly damp paper towels. They will stay crisp in the fridge for a few days.

Dressing your greens

Dressing your greens properly is important. You don't want too much or too little dressing, and you want that dressing evenly distributed. The following tips make it easy to get it right.

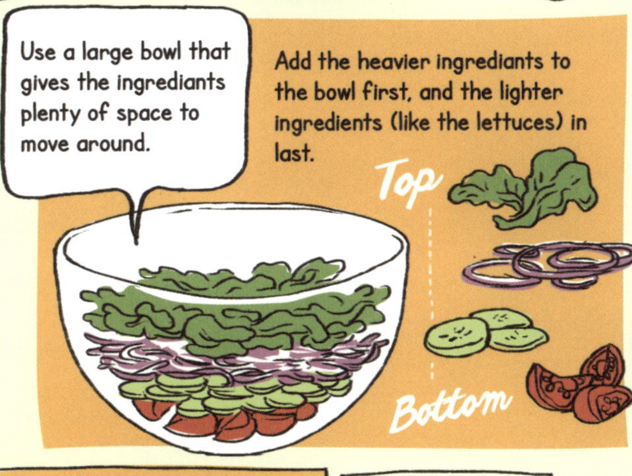
Use a large bowl that gives the ingrediants plenty of space to move around.
Add the heavier ingrediants to the bowl first, and the lighter ingredients (like the lettuces) in last.
Top
Bottom

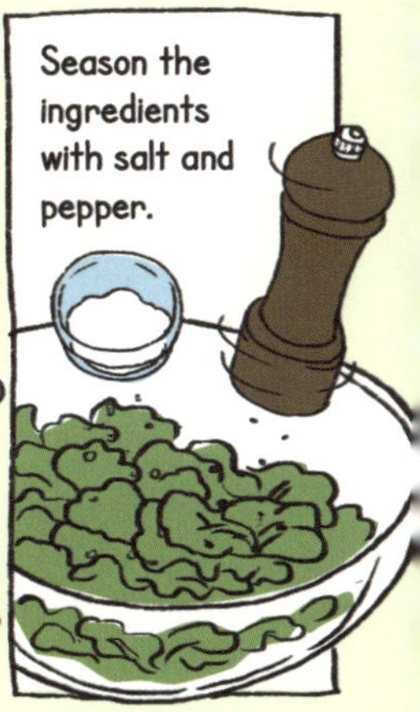
Season the ingredients with salt and pepper.

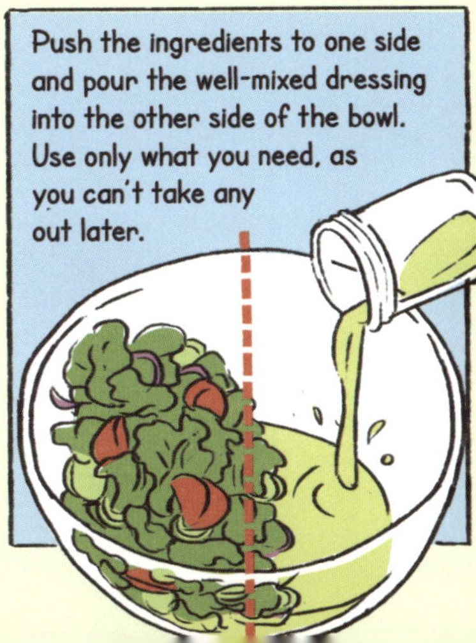
Push the ingredients to one side and pour the well-mixed dressing into the other side of the bowl. Use only what you need, as you can't take any out later.

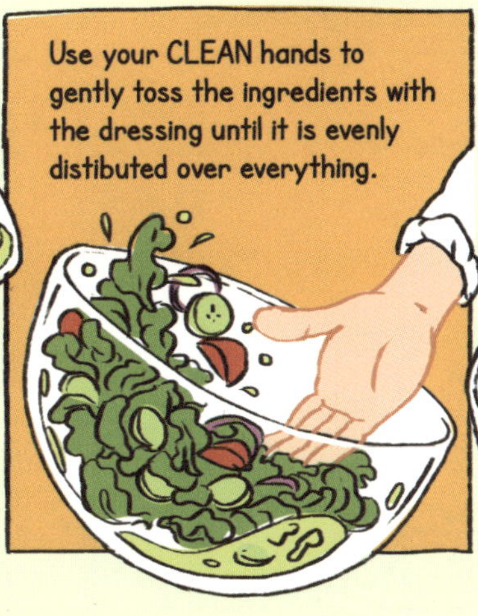
Use your CLEAN hands to gently toss the ingredients with the dressing until it is evenly distibuted over everything.

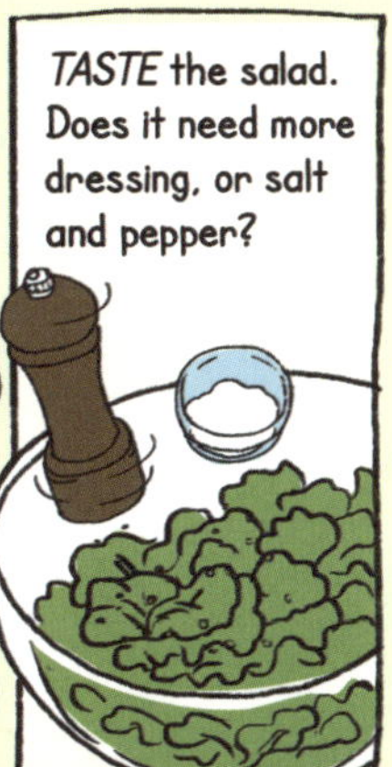
TASTE the salad. Does it need more dressing, or salt and pepper?

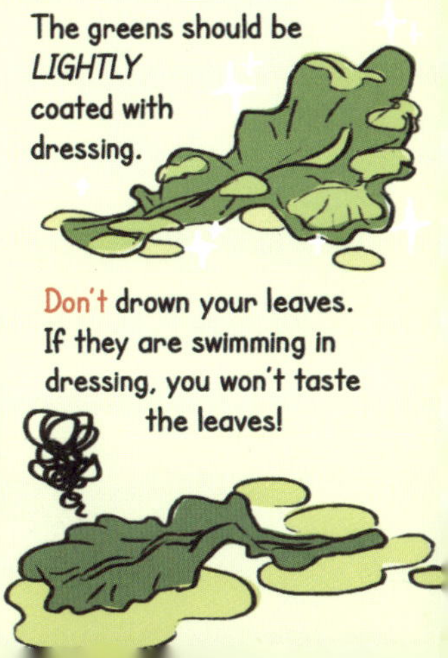
The greens should be LIGHTLY coated with dressing.
Don't drown your leaves. If they are swimming in dressing, you won't taste the leaves!

Recipe 3

Bitter Greens with Bacon & Honey Vinaigrette

Many lettuces have **unique** flavors to play with. Some are sweet, some are spicy, and others are bitter. The bitter lettuces are very **crunchy** and **hearty** and they make a wonderful salad when combined with the right vinaigrette.

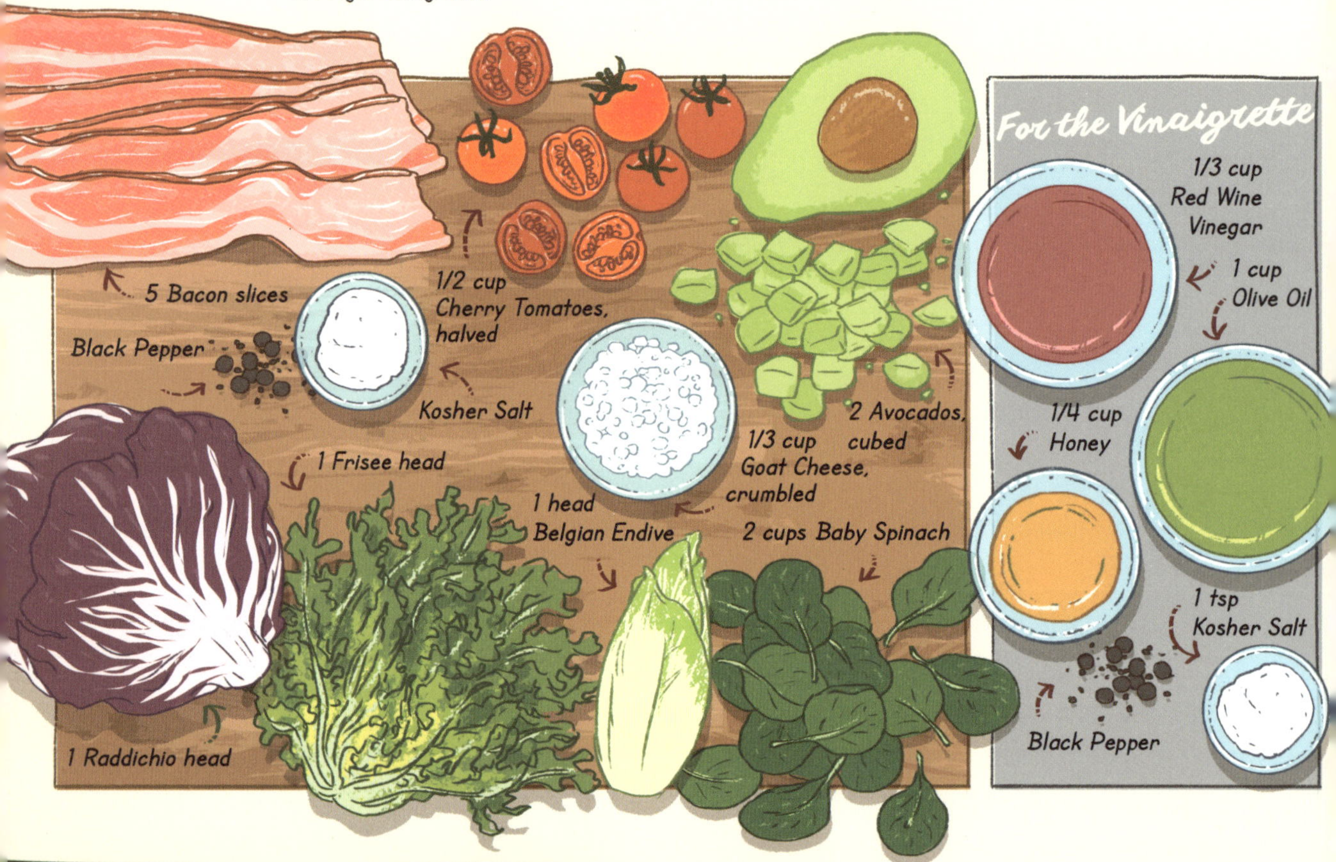

5 Bacon slices
Black Pepper
1/2 cup Cherry Tomatoes, halved
Kosher Salt
2 Avocados, cubed
1/3 cup Goat Cheese, crumbled
1 Frisee head
1 head Belgian Endive
2 cups Baby Spinach
1 Raddichio head
For the Vinaigrette
1/3 cup Red Wine Vinegar
1 cup Olive Oil
1/4 cup Honey
1 tsp Kosher Salt
Black Pepper

Let's Get Cooking!

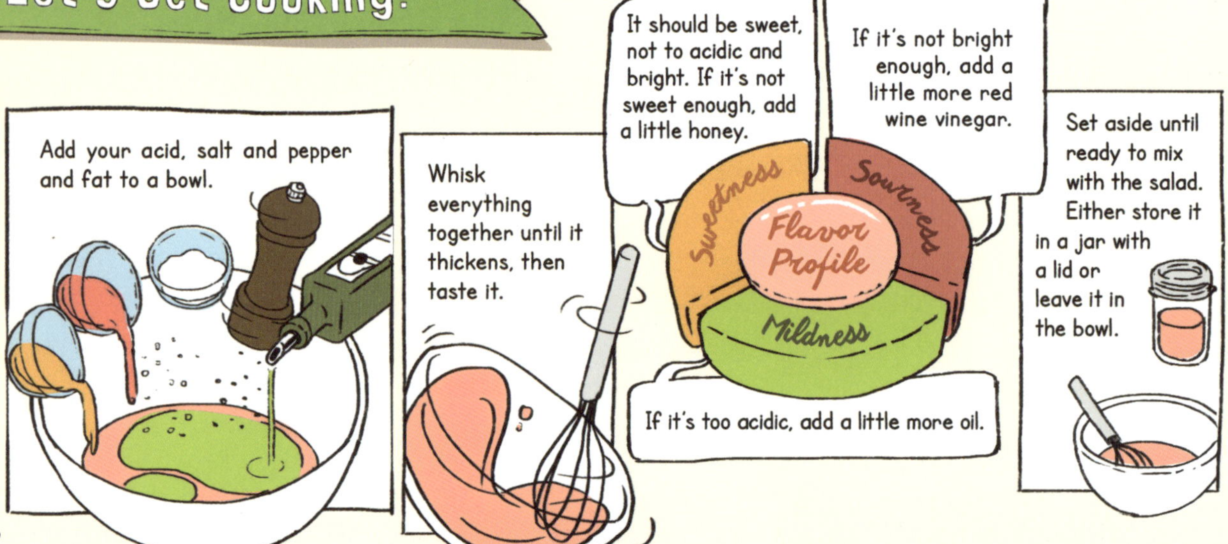

Add your acid, salt and pepper and fat to a bowl.
Whisk everything together until it thickens, then taste it.
It should be sweet, not to acidic and bright. If it's not sweet enough, add a little honey.
If it's not bright enough, add a little more red wine vinegar.
Sweetness
Sourness
Flavor Profile
Mildness
If it's too acidic, add a little more oil.
Set aside until ready to mix with the salad. Either store it in a jar with a lid or leave it in the bowl.

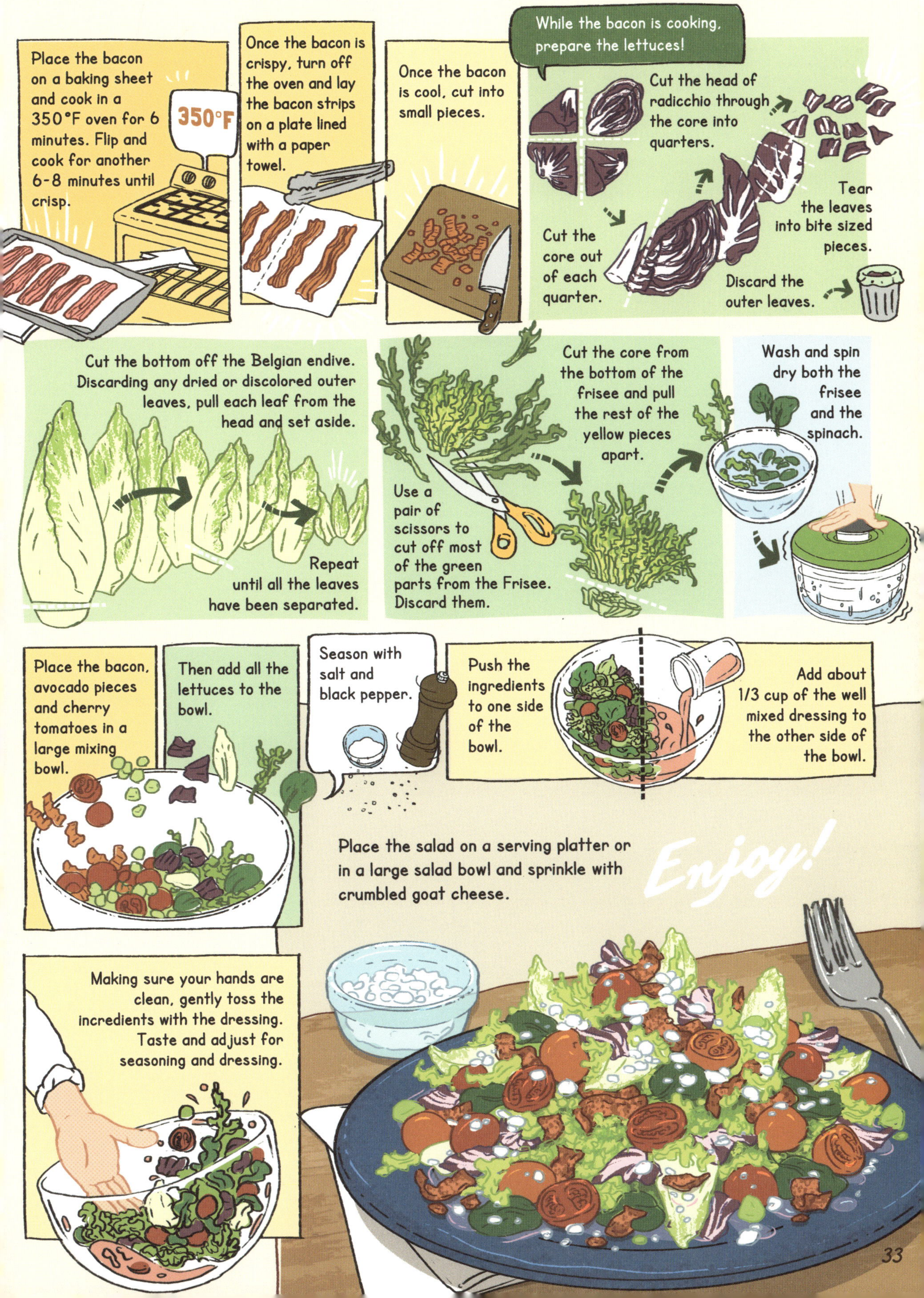
Place the bacon on a baking sheet and cook in a 350°F oven for 6 minutes. Flip and cook for another 6-8 minutes until crisp.
350°F
Once the bacon is crispy, turn off the oven and lay the bacon strips on a plate lined with a paper towel.
Once the bacon is cool, cut into small pieces.
While the bacon is cooking, prepare the lettuces!
Cut the head of radicchio through the core into quarters.
Cut the core out of each quarter.
Tear the leaves into bite sized pieces.
Discard the outer leaves.
Cut the bottom off the Belgian endive. Discarding any dried or discolored outer leaves, pull each leaf from the head and set aside.
Repeat until all the leaves have been separated.
Use a pair of scissors to cut off most of the green parts from the Frisee. Discard them.
Cut the core from the bottom of the frisee and pull the rest of the yellow pieces apart.
Wash and spin dry both the frisee and the spinach.
Place the bacon, avocado pieces and cherry tomatoes in a large mixing bowl.
Then add all the lettuces to the bowl.
Season with salt and black pepper.
Push the ingredients to one side of the bowl.
Add about 1/3 cup of the well mixed dressing to the other side of the bowl.
Making sure your hands are clean, gently toss the incredients with the dressing. Taste and adjust for seasoning and dressing.
Place the salad on a serving platter or in a large salad bowl and sprinkle with crumbled goat cheese.
Enjoy!

Recipe 4

Shaved Root Vegetables with Arugula, Rosemary & Lemon

Salads don't have to be made of lettuce. Anything can work in a delicious salad. In this dish, the arugula is there to lighten it up, but it's the shaved vegetables that are the real stars. Their **warm flavors** and contrasting textures make a delicious salad that will stand out on any dinner table!

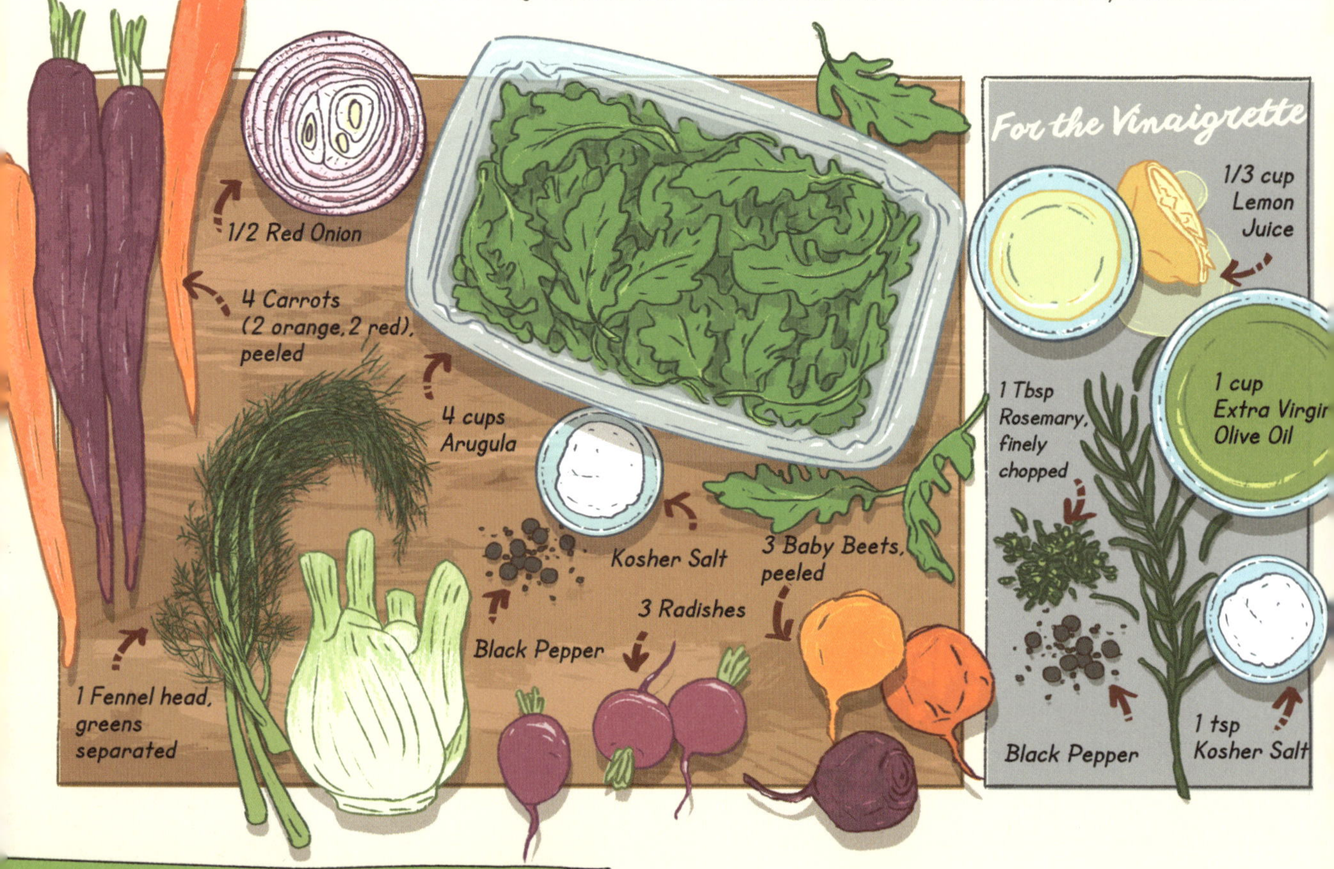

1/2 Red Onion
4 Carrots (2 orange, 2 red), peeled
4 cups Arugula
Kosher Salt
3 Baby Beets, peeled
3 Radishes
Black Pepper
1 Fennel head, greens separated
For the Vinaigrette
1/3 cup Lemon Juice
1 cup Extra Virgin Olive Oil
1 Tbsp Rosemary, finely chopped
Black Pepper
1 tsp Kosher Salt

Let's Get Cooking!

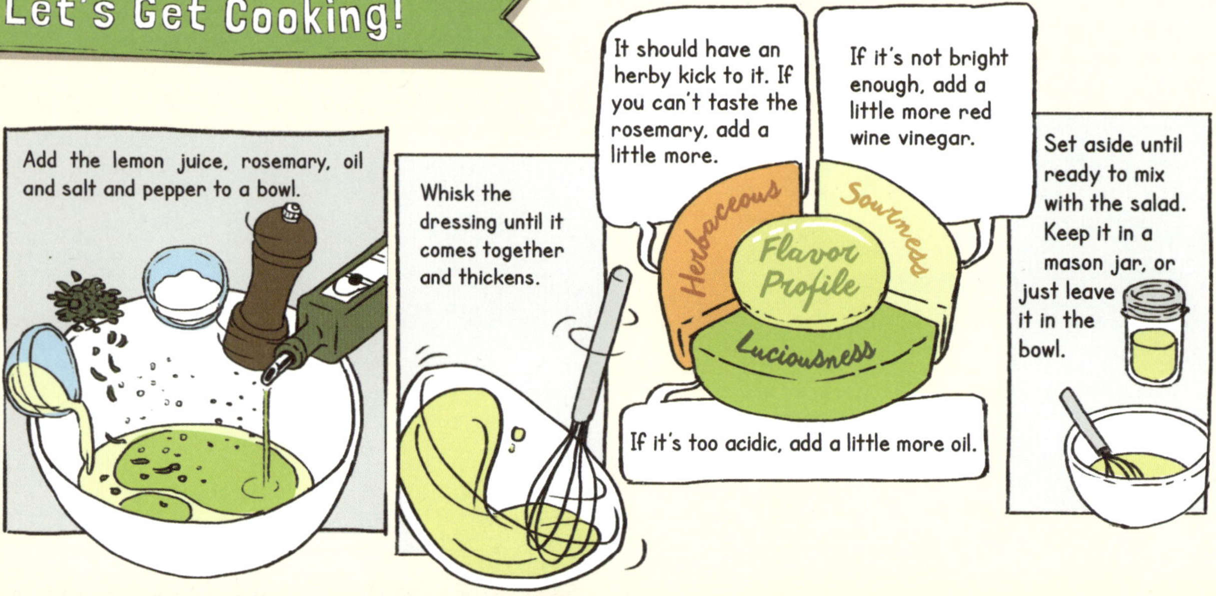

Add the lemon juice, rosemary, oil and salt and pepper to a bowl.
Whisk the dressing until it comes together and thickens.
It should have an herby kick to it. If you can't taste the rosemary, add a little more.
If it's not bright enough, add a little more red wine vinegar.
Herbaceous
Sourness
Flavor Profile
Luciousness
If it's too acidic, add a little more oil.
Set aside until ready to mix with the salad. Keep it in a mason jar, or just leave it in the bowl.

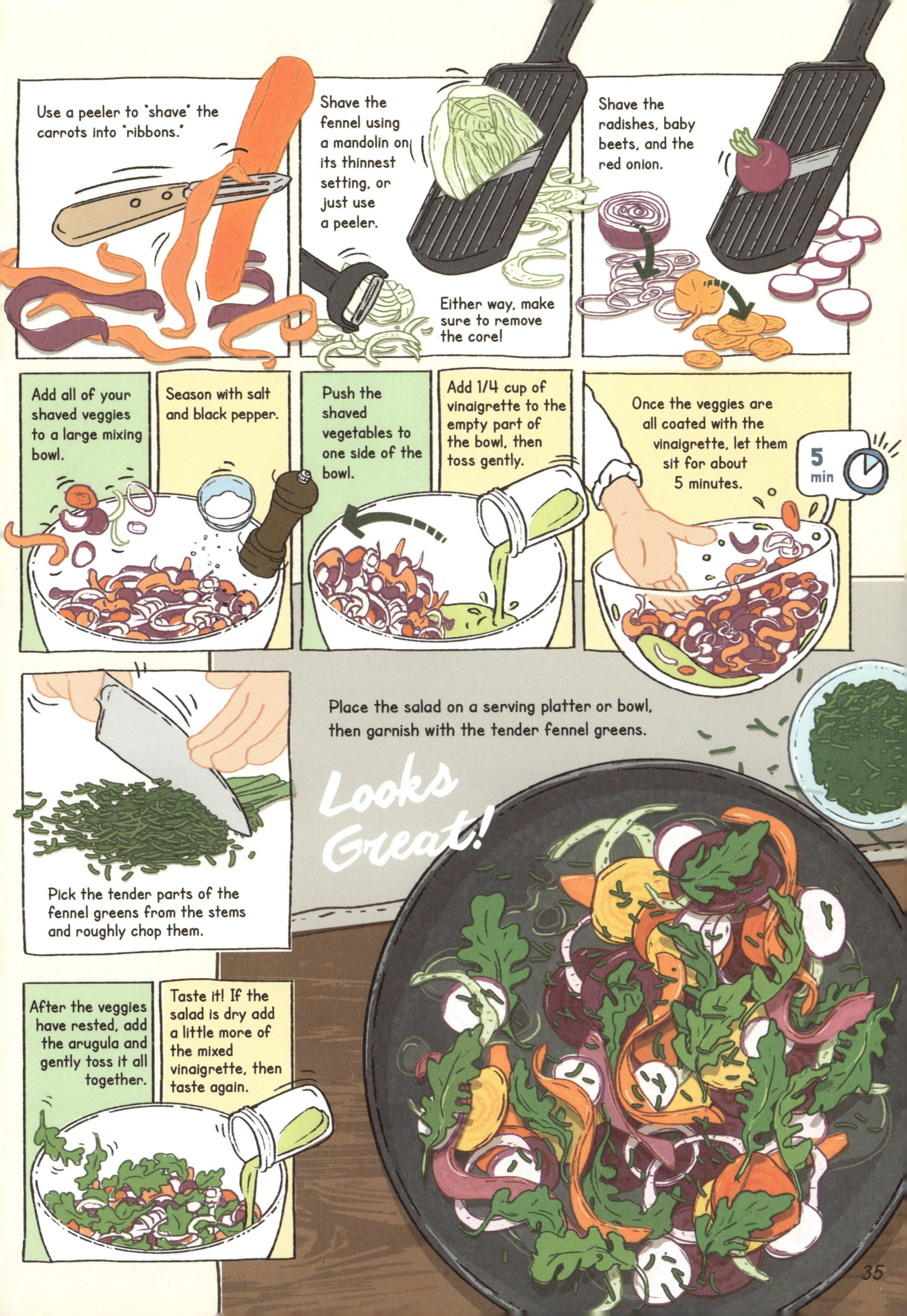
Use a peeler to "shave" the carrots into "ribbons."
Shave the fennel using a mandolin on its thinnest setting, or just use a peeler.
Either way, make sure to remove the core!
Shave the radishes, baby beets, and the red onion.
Add all of your shaved veggies to a large mixing bowl.
Season with salt and black pepper.
Push the shaved vegetables to one side of the bowl.
Add 1/4 cup of vinaigrette to the empty part of the bowl, then toss gently.
Once the veggies are all coated with the vinaigrette, let them sit for about 5 minutes.
5 min
Pick the tender parts of the fennel greens from the stems and roughly chop them.
Place the salad on a serving platter or bowl, then garnish with the tender fennel greens.
Looks Great!
After the veggies have rested, add the arugula and gently toss it all together.
Taste it! If the salad is dry add a little more of the mixed vinaigrette, then taste again.

Technique 3

EGGS

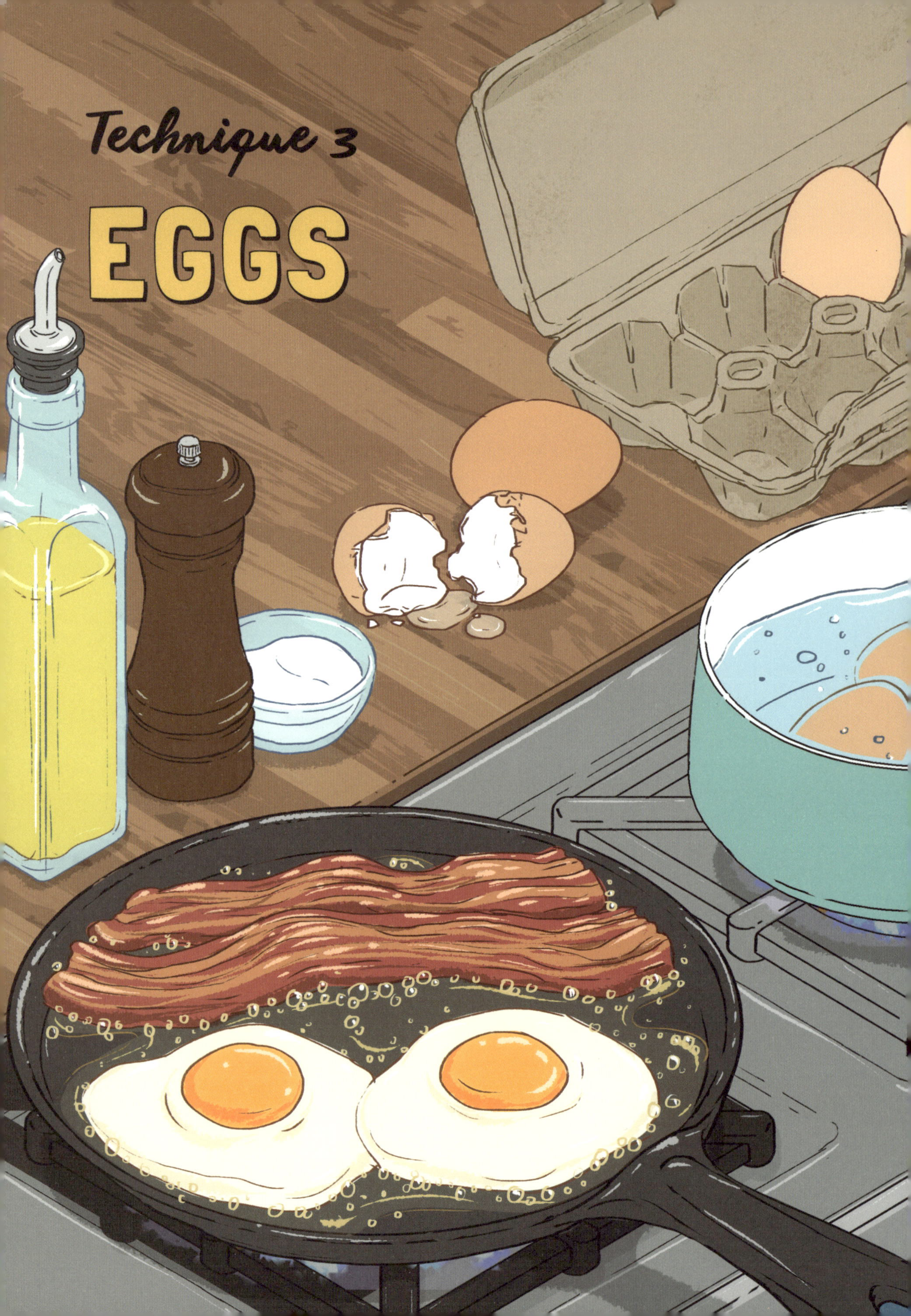

Chef's Note

It's a safe bet that everyone out there knows at least one way to cook an egg. Scrambled eggs were probably one of the first things I learned to cook as a child. All these years later, and I still reach for eggs at breakfast time. These days I tend to prefer baked, or "shirred," eggs. They are even easier to make than scrambled eggs! Eggs are one of the most versatile, easy, and delicious ingredients out there. Once you learn a few more ways of cooking them, you'll see that they can stand out in any meal, and don't need to be stuck relegated to the breakfast table.

This section will teach you many ways to cook an egg, and each one is appropriate for different uses. Eggs can play a back up role a dish, or they can be the star of the meal. How you use them is up to you!

SKILL BADGES

Boiling

Pan Skills

Oven Skills

EGG BASICS

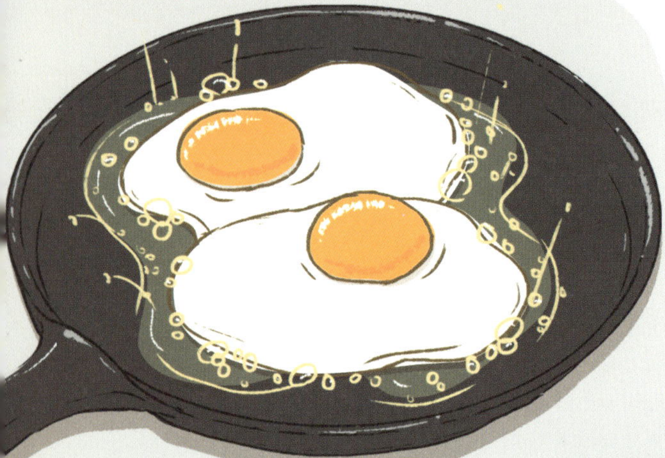

Tips for cooking eggs

The *t* cook much faster than the *yolk*.

Be careful if you want the yolk to stay *runny*, they can overcook very quickly!

It takes more salt than you think to properly season an egg.

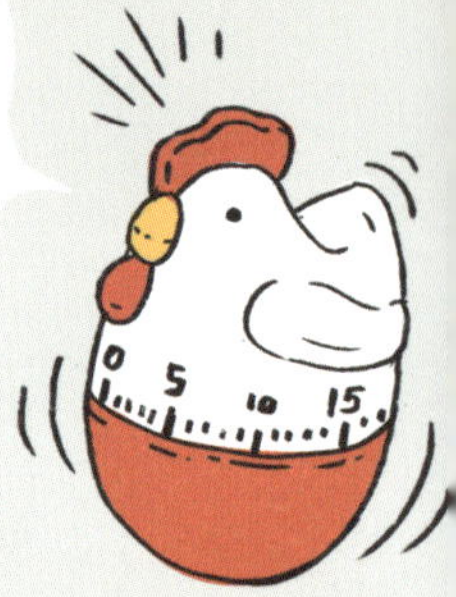
0 5 10 15

Fried Eggs

Fried eggs are actually sautéed eggs. Honestly, they are much easier to fry up if you use a non-stick sauté pan. If you have a well-seasoned cast iron griddle, that will also work as a nonstick surface. If you only have a normal sauté pan, don't worry! Its easy to fry an egg in any pan, provided you use enough oil or butter to keep it from sticking!

1. Sunny Side Up

The whites are cooked, but the yolk is completely runny.

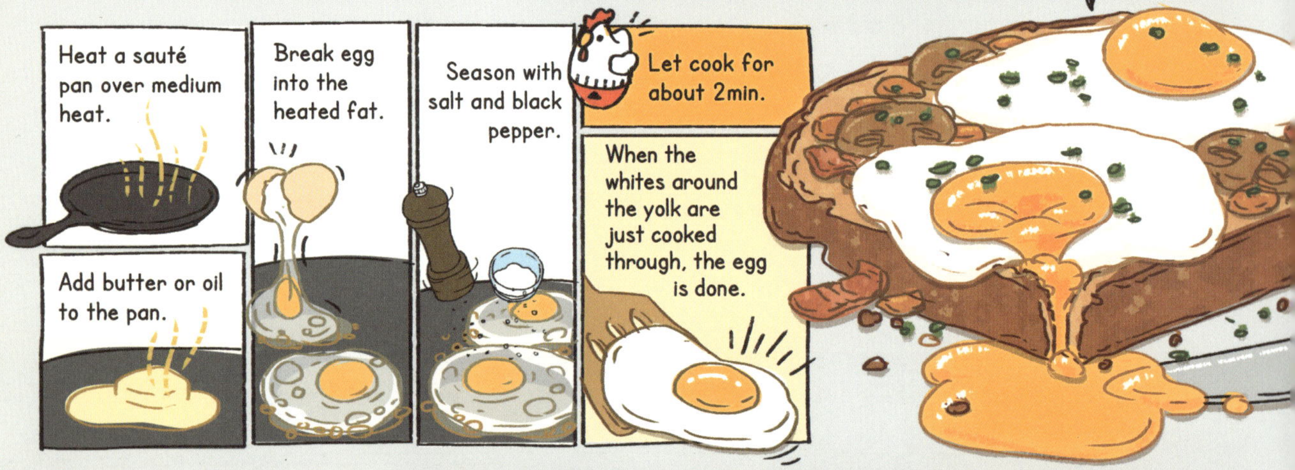
Heat a sauté pan over medium heat.
Add butter or oil to the pan.
Break egg into the heated fat.
Season with salt and black pepper.
Let cook for about 2min.
When the whites around the yolk are just cooked through, the egg is done.

2. Over easy

The whites are cooked AND the covering of the yolk is also cooked.

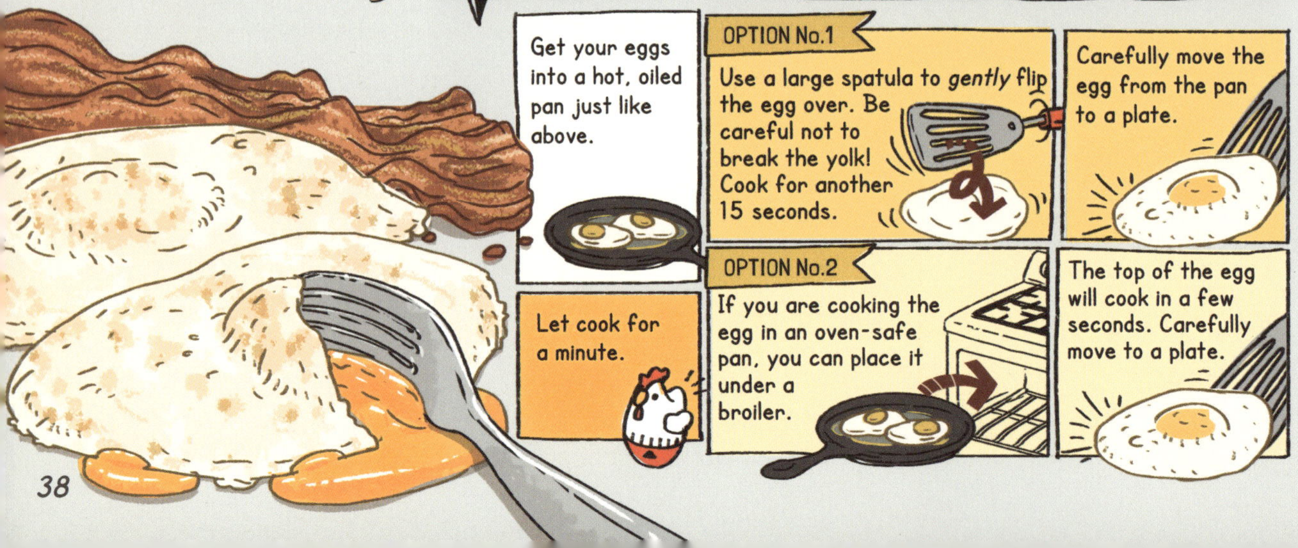
Get your eggs into a hot, oiled pan just like above.
Let cook for a minute.
OPTION No.1
Use a large spatula to *gently* flip the egg over. Be careful not to break the yolk! Cook for another 15 seconds.
Carefully move the egg from the pan to a plate.
OPTION No.2
If you are cooking the egg in an oven-safe pan, you can place it under a broiler.
The top of the egg will cook in a few seconds. Carefully move to a plate.

3. Over hard

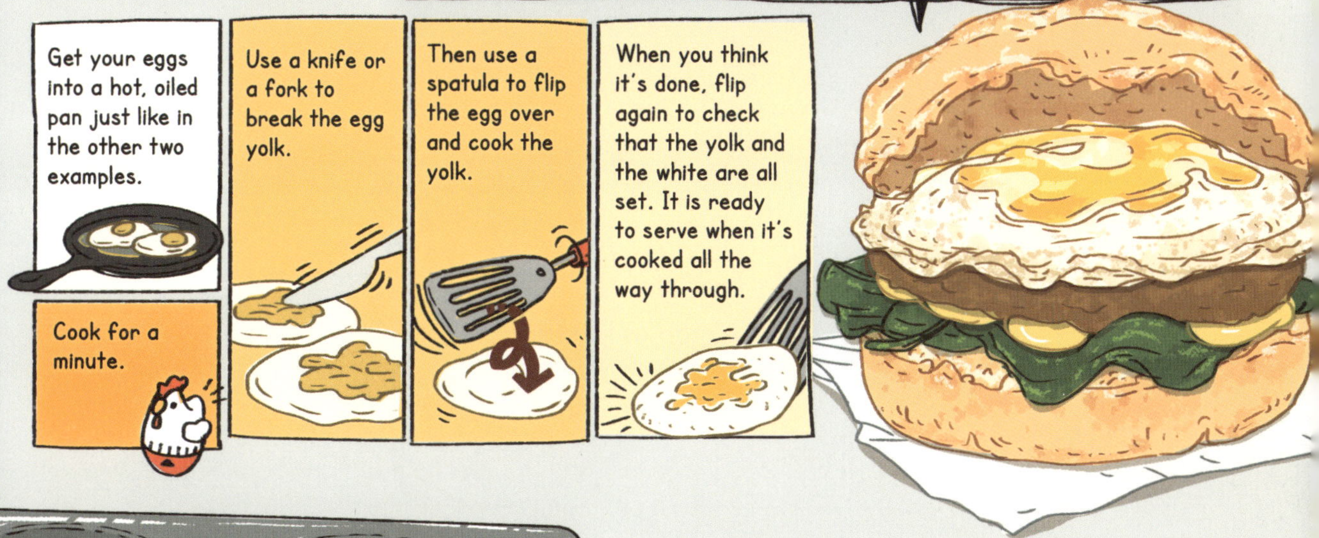

The whites AND the yolk are cooked until set and nothing runs.
Get your eggs into a hot, oiled pan just like in the other two examples.
Cook for a minute.
Use a knife or a fork to break the egg yolk.
Then use a spatula to flip the egg over and cook the yolk.
When you think it's done, flip again to check that the yolk and the white are all set. It is ready to serve when it's cooked all the way through.

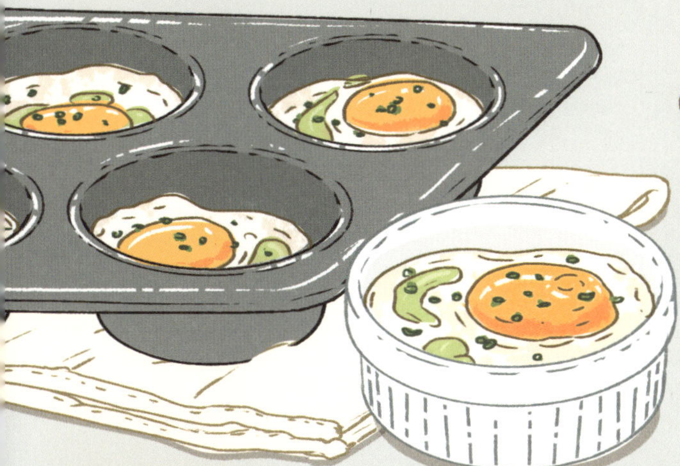

4. Baked Eggs

Baking eggs is one of the easiest ways to prepare them. To mimic the various ways eggs can be fried, you only need to change how long you bake them. The best part of this method is how **easy** it is. All you have to do is pop them in the oven and set a timer. You can add whatever ingredients you want to the eggs and end up with a whole meal cooked all at once in one dish!

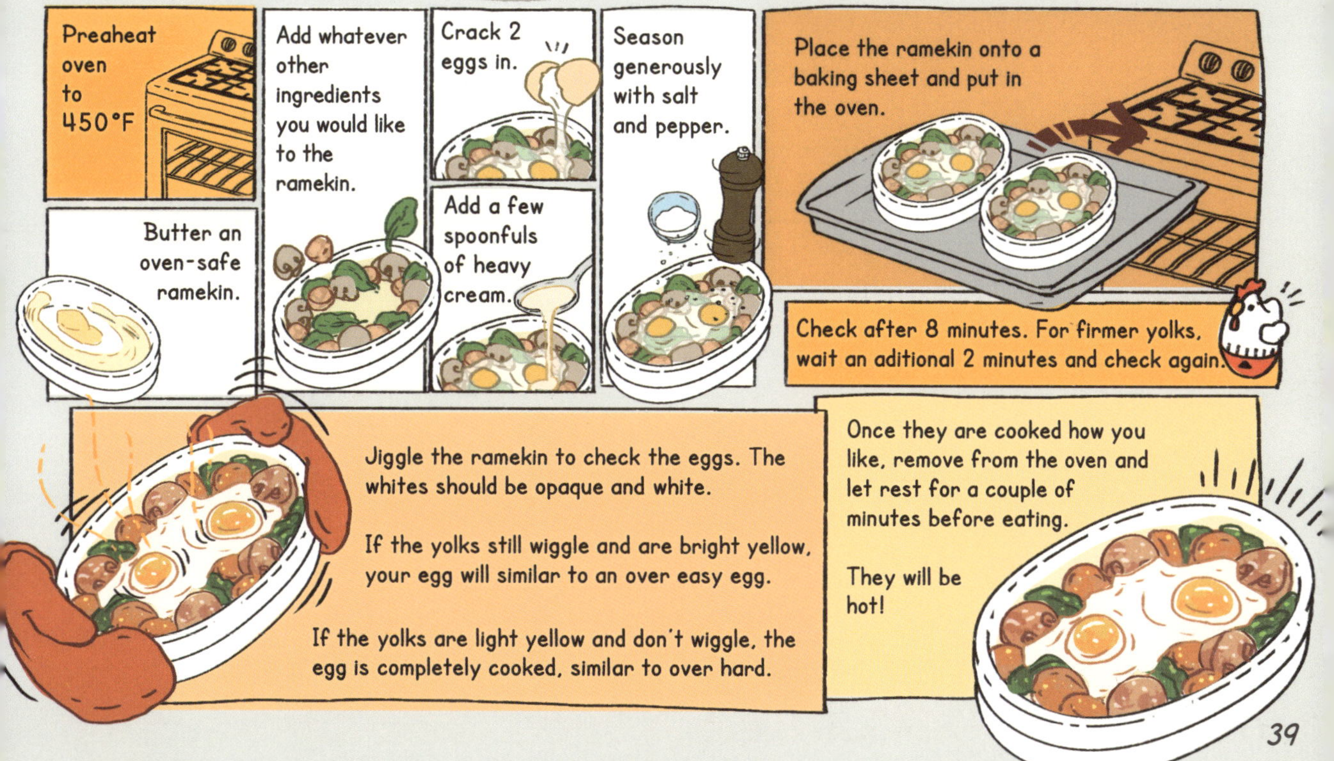

Preheat oven to 450°F
Butter an oven-safe ramekin.
Add whatever other ingredients you would like to the ramekin.
Crack 2 eggs in.
Add a few spoonfuls of heavy cream.
Season generously with salt and pepper.
Place the ramekin onto a baking sheet and put in the oven.
Check after 8 minutes. For firmer yolks, wait an aditional 2 minutes and check again.
Jiggle the ramekin to check the eggs. The whites should be opaque and white.
If the yolks still wiggle and are bright yellow, your egg will similar to an over easy egg.
If the yolks are light yellow and don't wiggle, the egg is completely cooked, similar to over hard.
Once they are cooked how you like, remove from the oven and let rest for a couple of minutes before eating.
They will be hot!

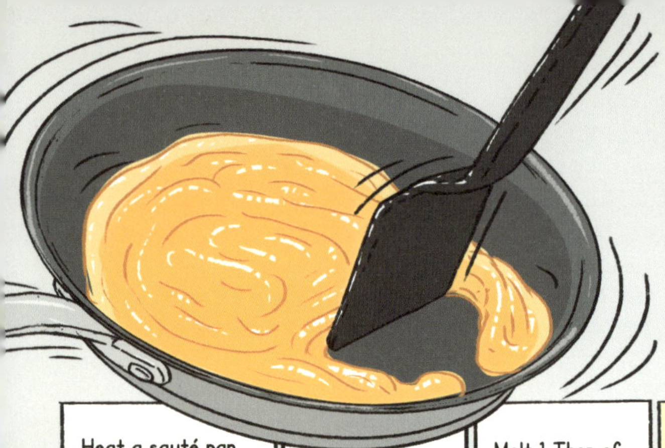

Scrambled Eggs

Professional chefs are always debating the best way to cook scrambled eggs. Should you add milk or cream? Cook them slowly or quickly? Use a whisk or a spatula? Scrambled eggs can be as complicated as you like, but this method is simple and produces great results.

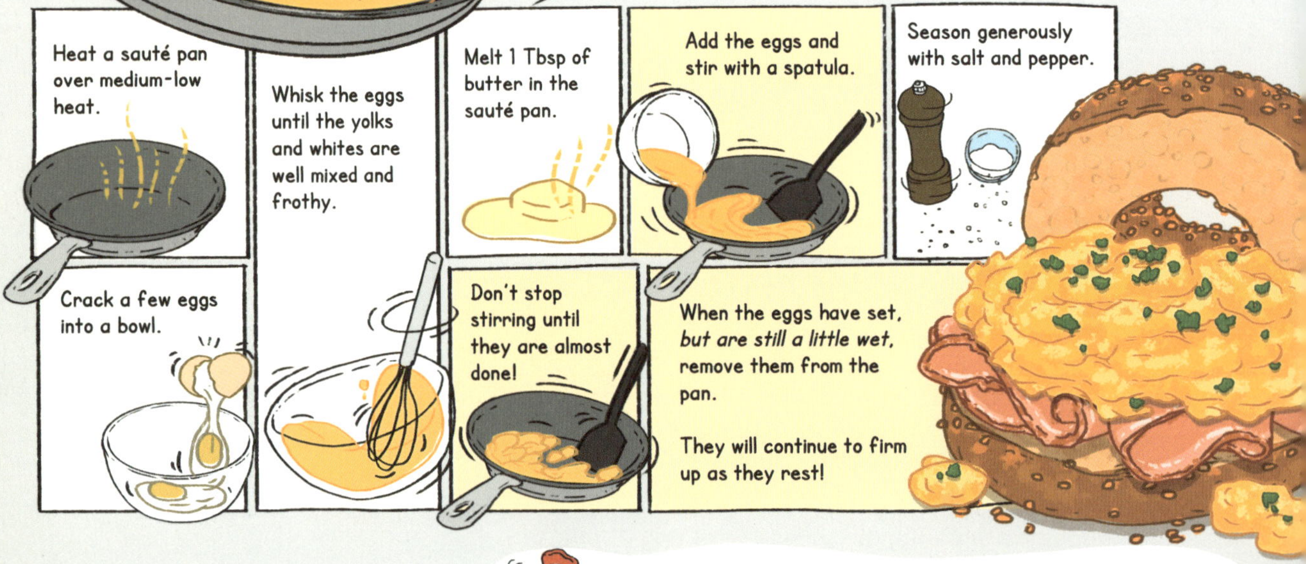

Heat a sauté pan over medium-low heat.
Crack a few eggs into a bowl.
Whisk the eggs until the yolks and whites are well mixed and frothy.
Melt 1 Tbsp of butter in the sauté pan.
Add the eggs and stir with a spatula.
Don't stop stirring until they are almost done!
Season generously with salt and pepper.
When the eggs have set, *but are still a little wet*, remove them from the pan.
They will continue to firm up as they rest!

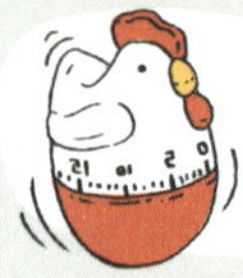

Note: If they stay in the pan too long, they will get dry and start to leach water. At that point, the eggs are overcooked and will have a rubbery texture.

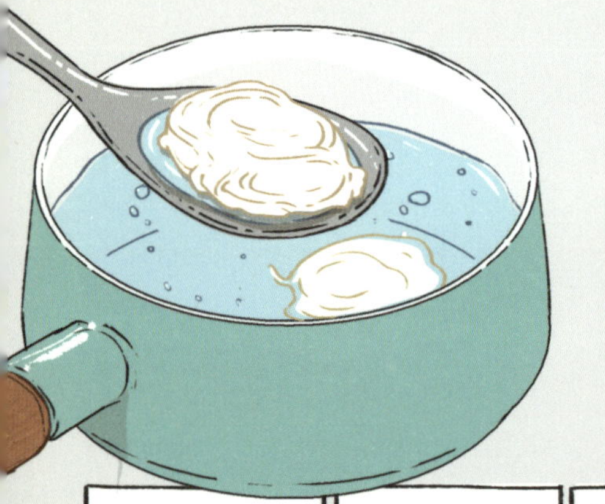

Poached Eggs

Poached eggs are very **delicate** and satisfying. The whites are fully set, but cooking them in liquid leaves them tender and moist compared to other methods. The whites wrap around the yolk like a package, and the yolk cooks gently inside.

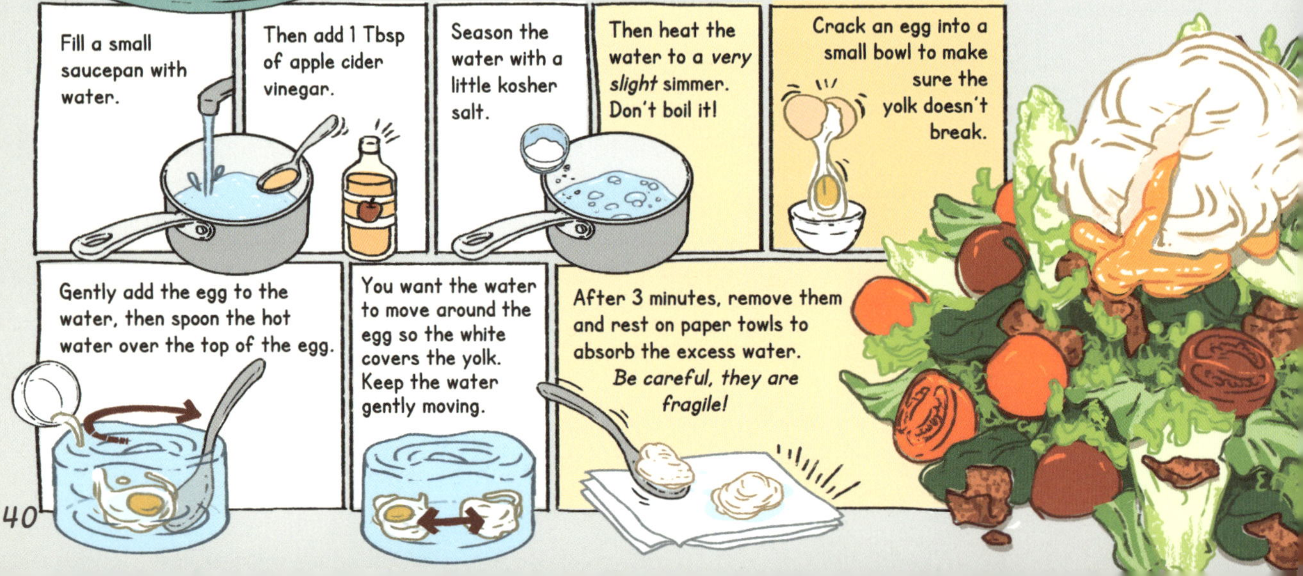

Fill a small saucepan with water.
Then add 1 Tbsp of apple cider vinegar.
Season the water with a little kosher salt.
Then heat the water to a *very slight* simmer. Don't boil it!
Crack an egg into a small bowl to make sure the yolk doesn't break.
Gently add the egg to the water, then spoon the hot water over the top of the egg.
You want the water to move around the egg so the white covers the yolk. Keep the water gently moving.
After 3 minutes, remove them and rest on paper towls to absorb the excess water.
Be careful, they are fragile!

Boiled Eggs

Eggs boiled right in their shells are a key part of all sorts of dishes. On one hand, they can serve as the main ingredient of a meal (think deviled eggs, or egg salad). On the other hand, they make a great snack. However you want to eat them, knowing how to properly boil an egg is an essential skill to have in your arsenal of cooking skills.

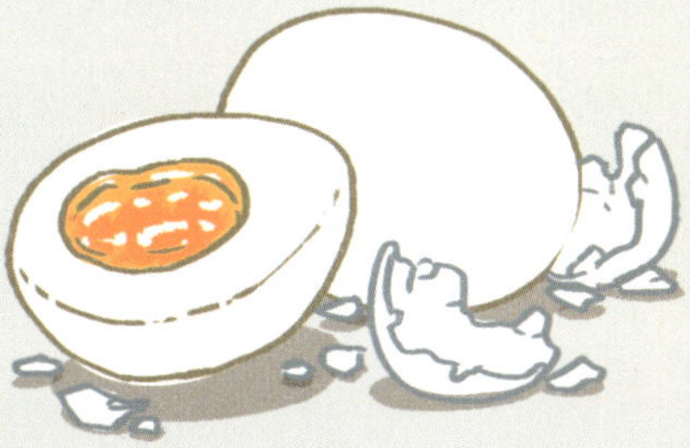

Soft Boiled eggs

When I was a kid, I ate soft boiled eggs for breakfast all the time. Now I make them for my own children. Kids (and adults) love to eat them with cut toast "soldiers," but they work fantastically well in all kinds of dishes. I love them in a bowl of ramen, or congee, or just served simply with a piece of toast and a pinch of salt and pepper.

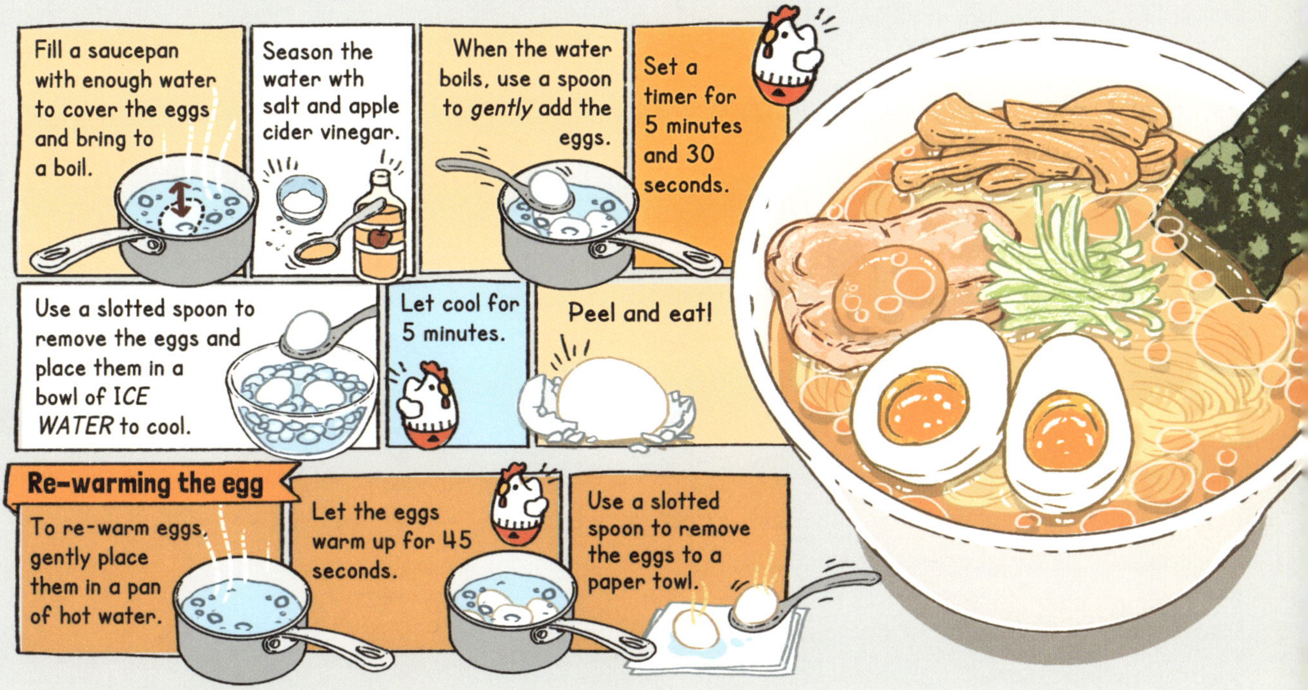
Fill a saucepan with enough water to cover the eggs and bring to a boil.
Season the water wth salt and apple cider vinegar.
When the water boils, use a spoon to *gently* add the eggs.
Set a timer for 5 minutes and 30 seconds.
Use a slotted spoon to remove the eggs and place them in a bowl of *ICE WATER* to cool.
Let cool for 5 minutes.
Peel and eat!
Re-warming the egg
To re-warm eggs, gently place them in a pan of hot water.
Let the eggs warm up for 45 seconds.
Use a slotted spoon to remove the eggs to a paper towl.

Hard Boiled eggs

It seems like every year since I started cooking, I run into a new method for hard boiling eggs. It's not that any of these are definitively better than the others, or that getting it right is very difficult at all. You just don't want to overcook them. This method works well no matter how many eggs you are cooking, and always produces consistent results.

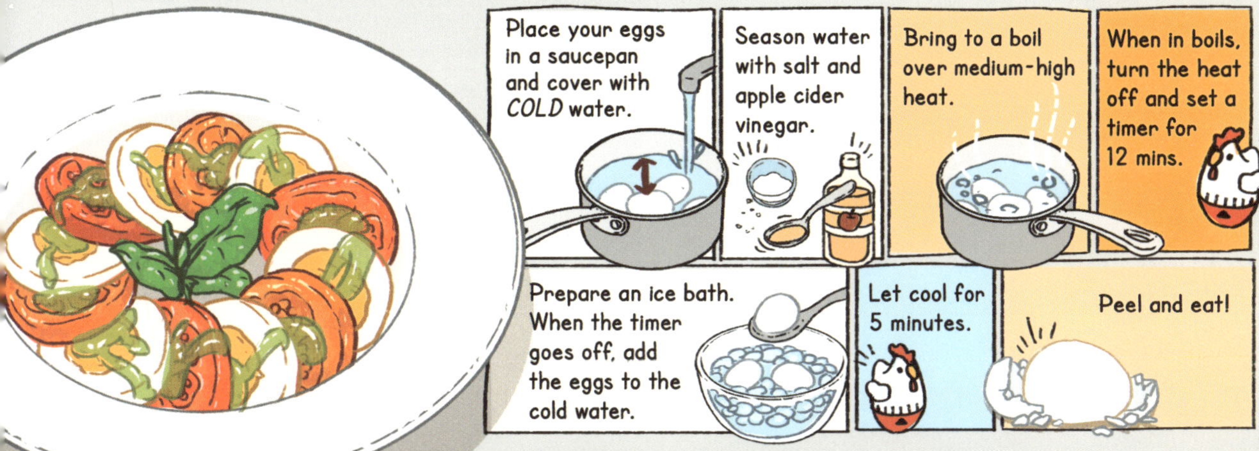
Place your eggs in a saucepan and cover with *COLD* water.
Season water with salt and apple cider vinegar.
Bring to a boil over medium-high heat.
When in boils, turn the heat off and set a timer for 12 mins.
Prepare an ice bath. When the timer goes off, add the eggs to the cold water.
Let cool for 5 minutes.
Peel and eat!

Recipe 5

Baked Eggs with Asparagus Cherry Tomatoes & Bacon

Baked eggs are **super easy** to make. You can whip up a balanced meal in a few minutes! The other ingredients in this dish are added raw, so all you need to do is chop them. This recipe is only a suggestion. Remember, you can add anything to these! **Get creative**!

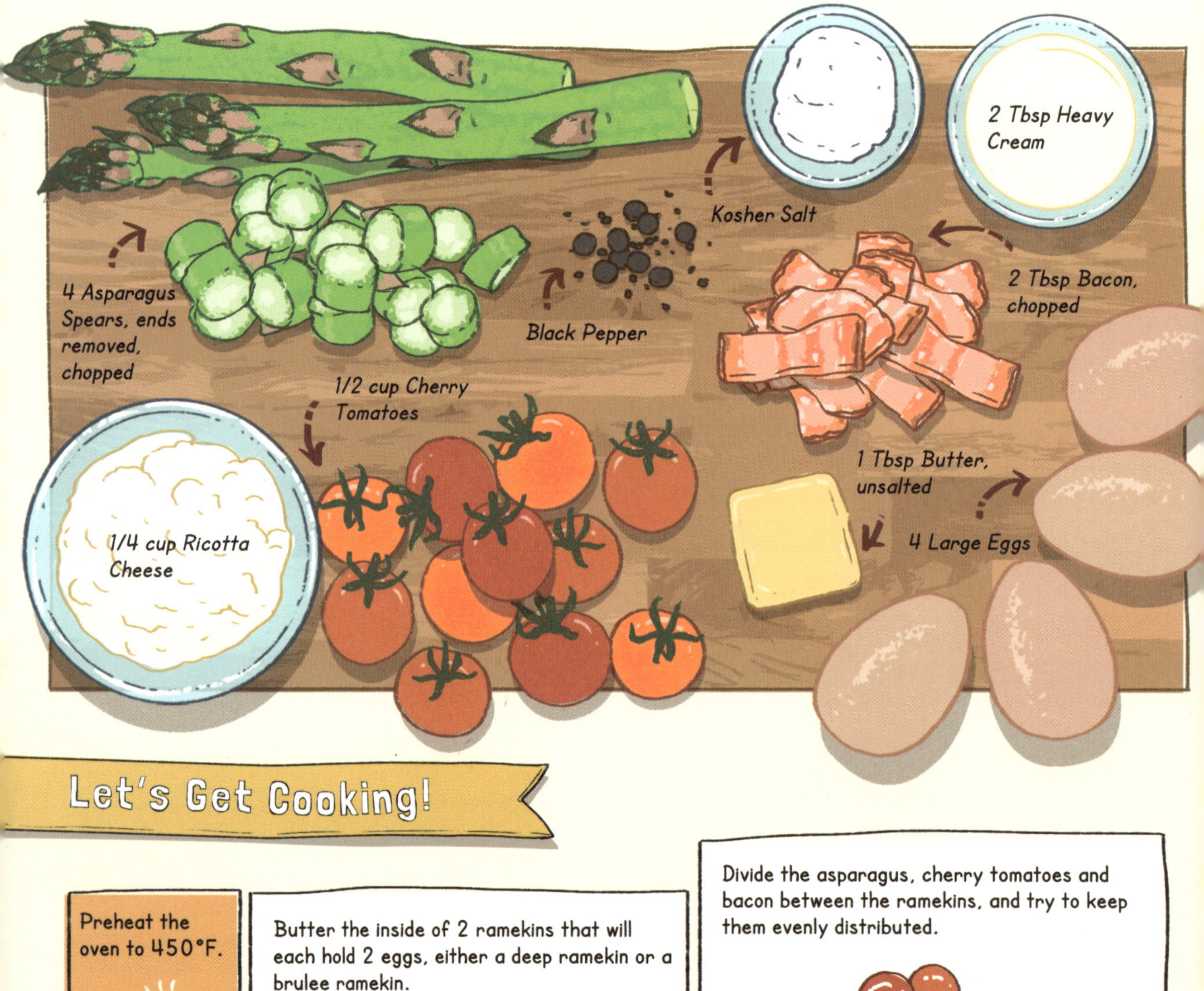

Kosher Salt
2 Tbsp Heavy Cream
4 Asparagus Spears, ends removed, chopped
Black Pepper
2 Tbsp Bacon, chopped
1/2 cup Cherry Tomatoes
1 Tbsp Butter, unsalted
4 Large Eggs
1/4 cup Ricotta Cheese

Let's Get Cooking!

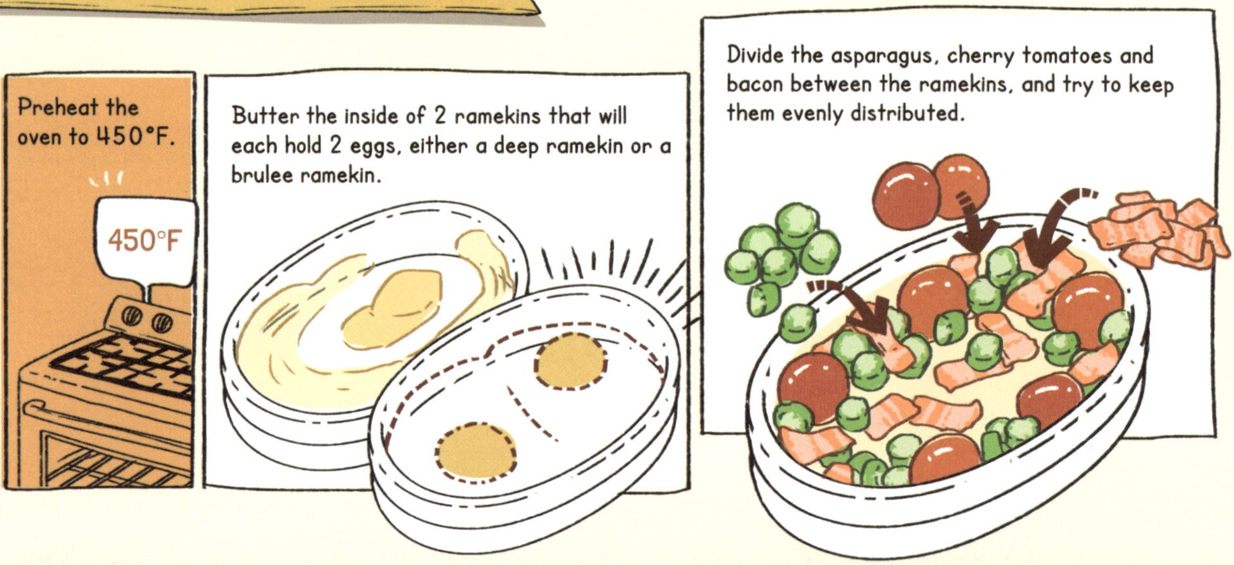

Preheat the oven to 450°F.
450°F
Butter the inside of 2 ramekins that will each hold 2 eggs, either a deep ramekin or a brulee ramekin.
Divide the asparagus, cherry tomatoes and bacon between the ramekins, and try to keep them evenly distributed.

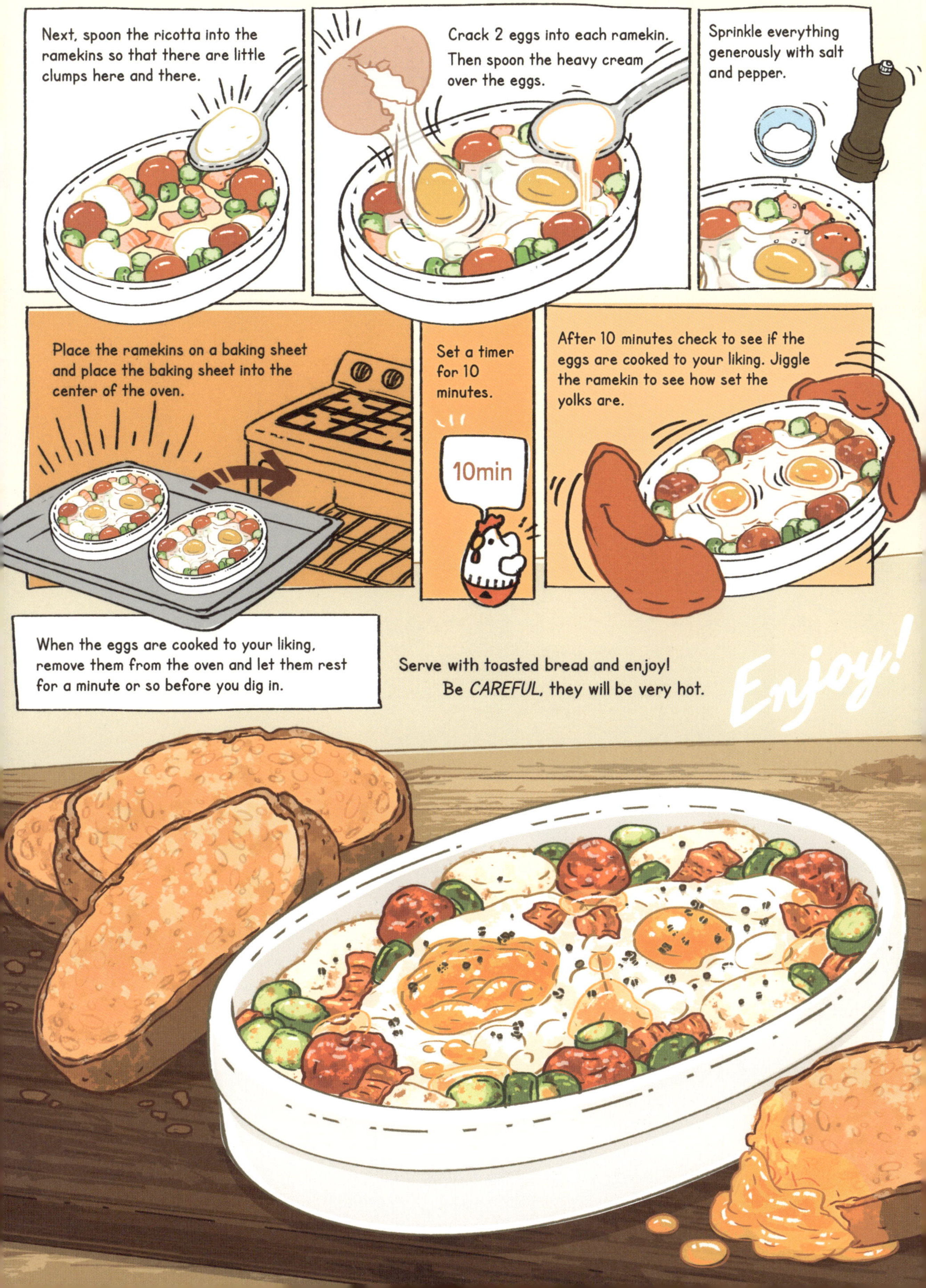
Next, spoon the ricotta into the ramekins so that there are little clumps here and there.
Crack 2 eggs into each ramekin. Then spoon the heavy cream over the eggs.
Sprinkle everything generously with salt and pepper.
Place the ramekins on a baking sheet and place the baking sheet into the center of the oven.
Set a timer for 10 minutes.
10min
After 10 minutes check to see if the eggs are cooked to your liking. Jiggle the ramekin to see how set the yolks are.
When the eggs are cooked to your liking, remove them from the oven and let them rest for a minute or so before you dig in.
Serve with toasted bread and enjoy!
Be *CAREFUL*, they will be very hot.
Enjoy!

Technique 4

PASTA

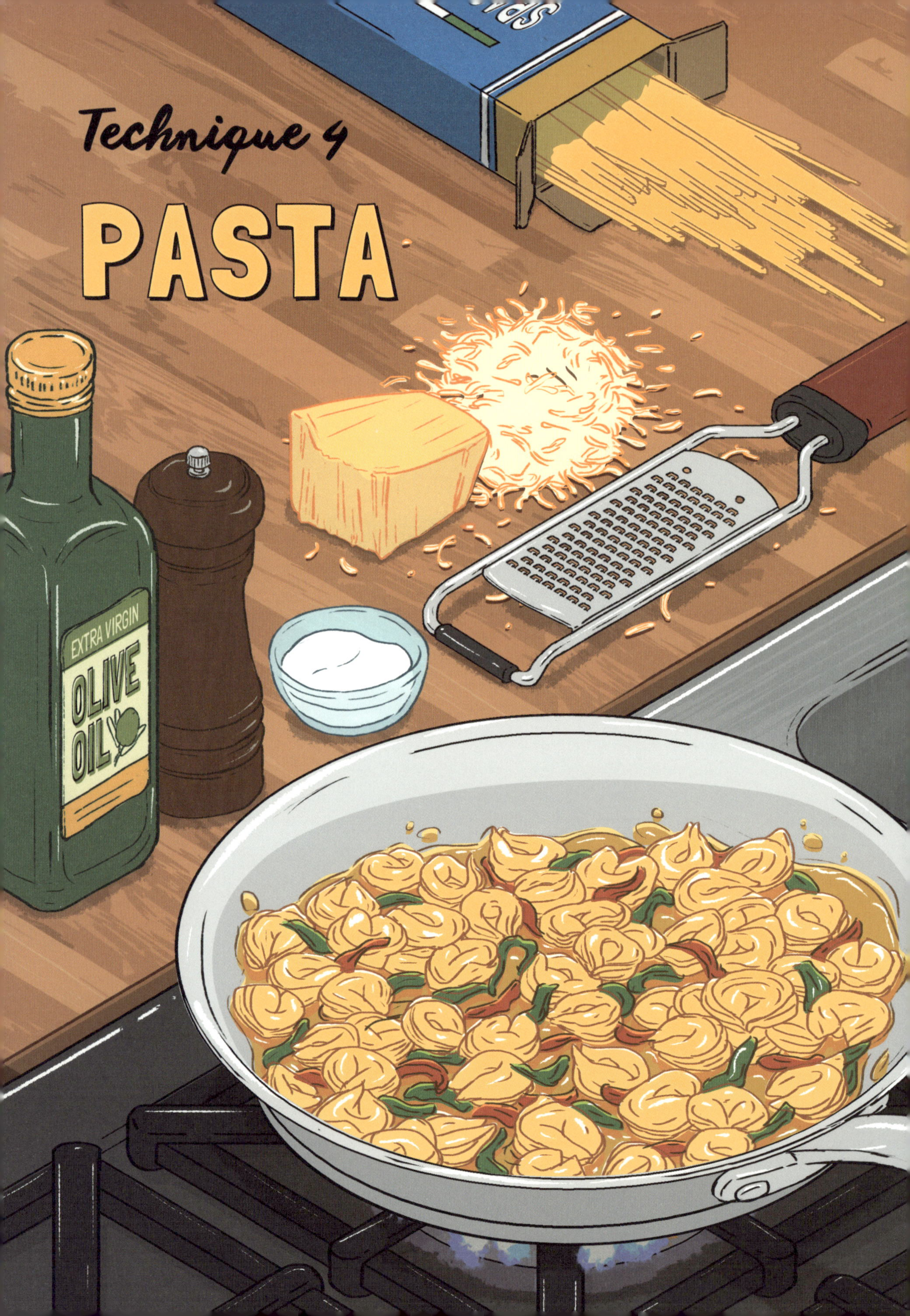
EXTRA VIRGIN
OLIVE OIL

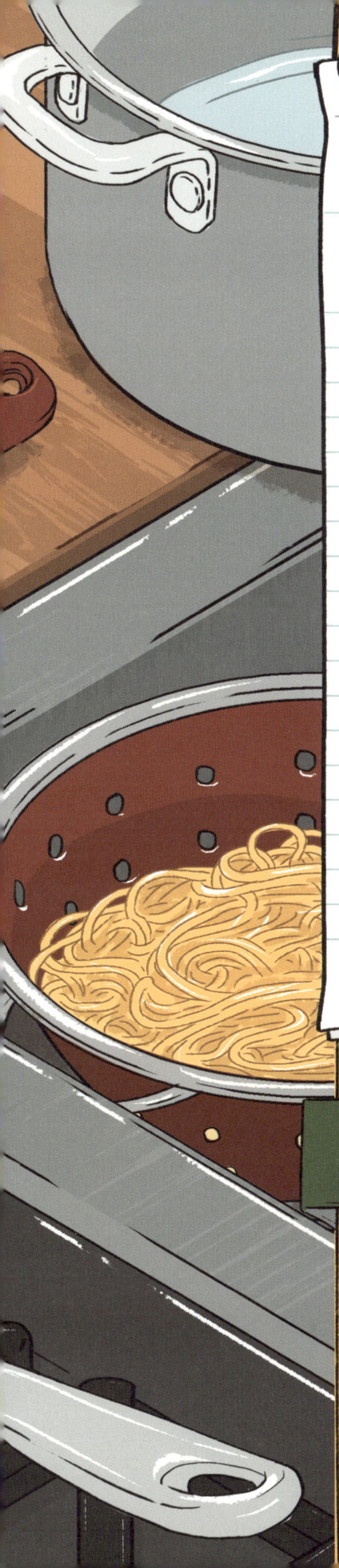

Chef's Note

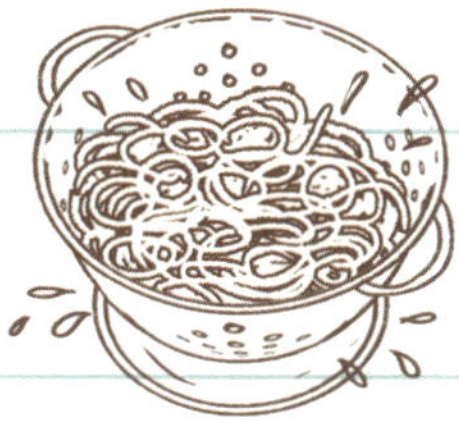

Everyone knows how to make Spaghetti, or at least they think they do. Spaghetti might be the go-to dish for every teenager in the world, but there really is a lot more to cooking pasta than boiling spaghetti, draining it, and dumping a jar of tomato sauce on top.

Pasta can be heavenly, and you really don't need much. With a little know how, your spaghetti dinners will be ten times better—and there is a whole world of pasta out there besides spaghetti! There are hundreds of different shapes, there are fresh and dry pastas, and a dizzying array of sauces. Not to mention the categories of pasta that don't even require a pot of boiling water!

Volumes have been written on all the nuances of pasta cooking and making, but in this chapter we're going to focus on the basics you need to get going.

SKILL BADGES

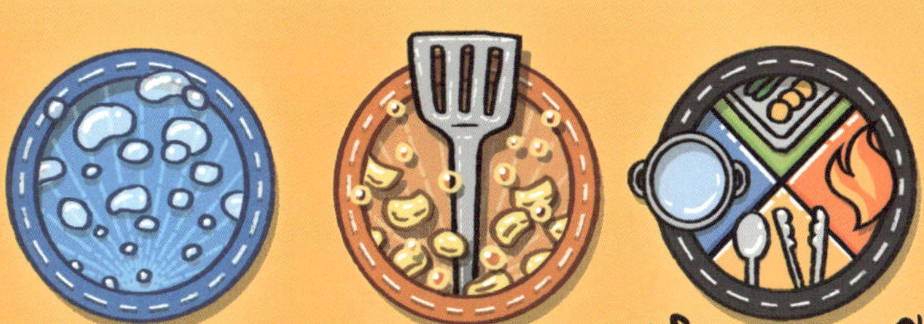

Bouiling Pan Skills Station Set up

PASTA TECHNIQUE

Equipment Necessary

- Large pot
- Large strainer or colander
- Large Saute pan
- Tongs or Pasta spoon

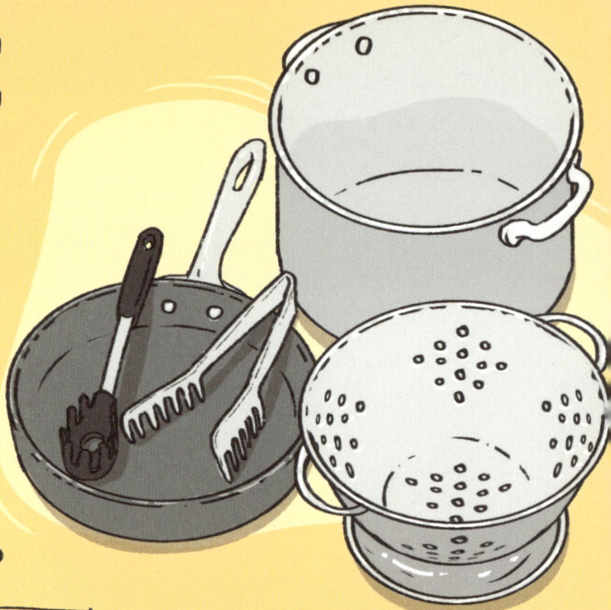

Get Your Water Ready

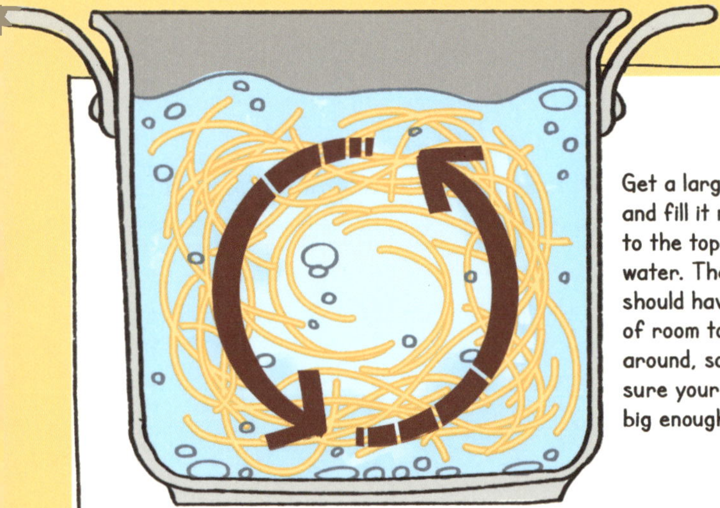

Get a large pot and fill it nearly to the top with water. The pasta should have a lot of room to move around, so make sure your pot is big enough!

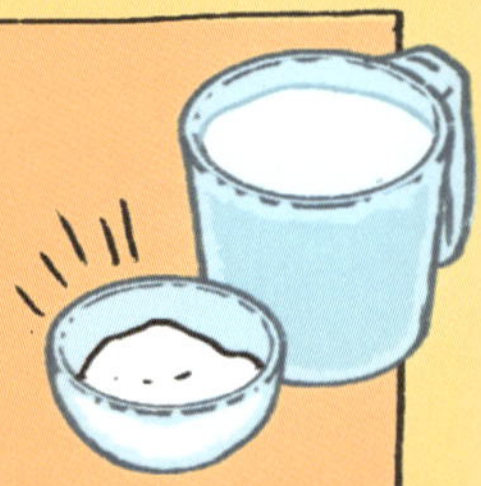

SALT YOUR WATER! Add enough salt to the water so that it tastes salty.

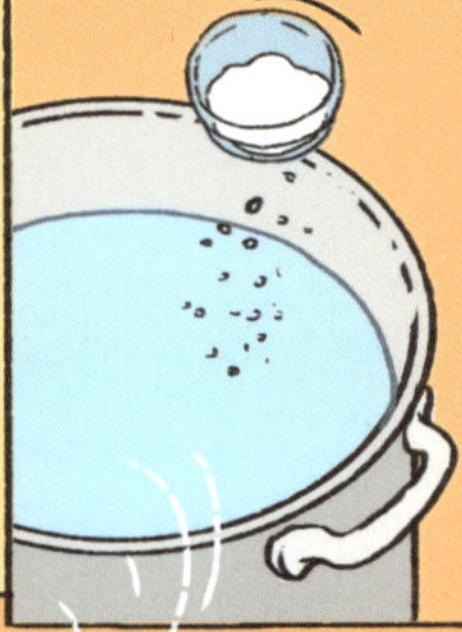

There is a lot of water in the pot, so it is harder to over salt then you might expect. Remember to taste *AFTER* it dissolves!

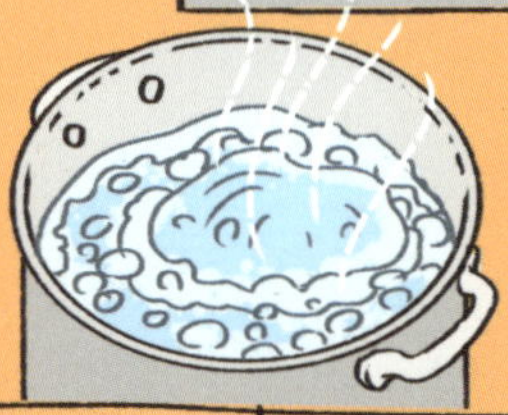

Bring the water to a rolling boil.

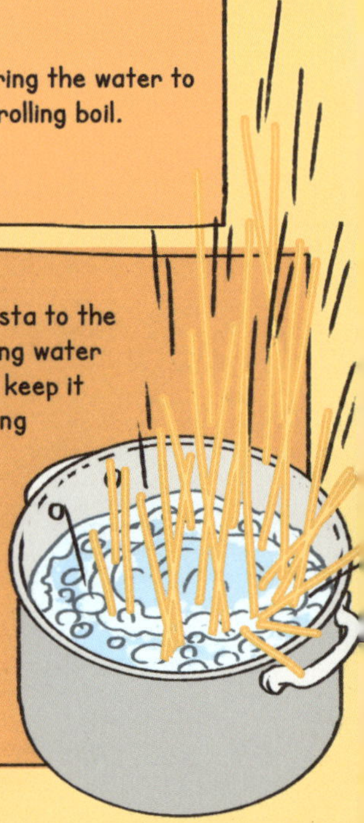

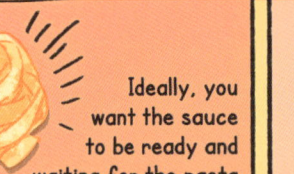

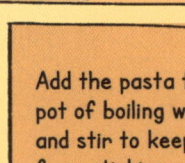

Add the pasta to the pot of boiling water and stir to keep it from sticking together.

Make sure your sauce is ready or almost ready...

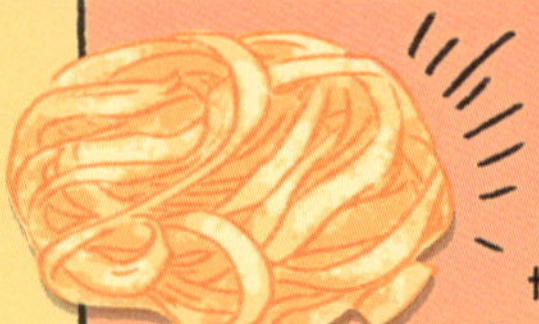

Ideally, you want the sauce to be ready and waiting for the pasta to come out of the water.

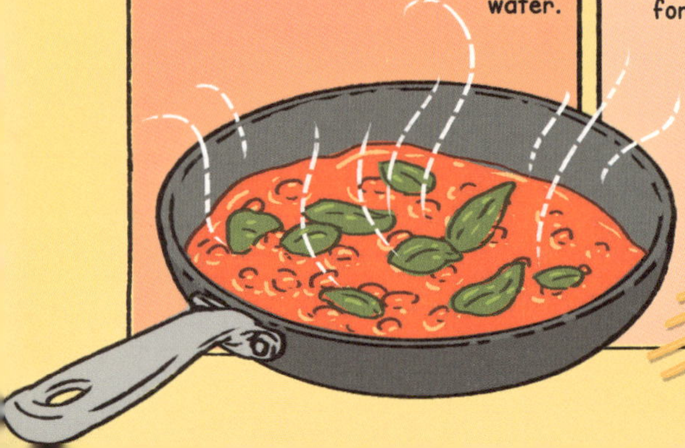

Fresh pasta cooks faster than dried pasta, so keep that in mind when judging how much time you need for your sauce.

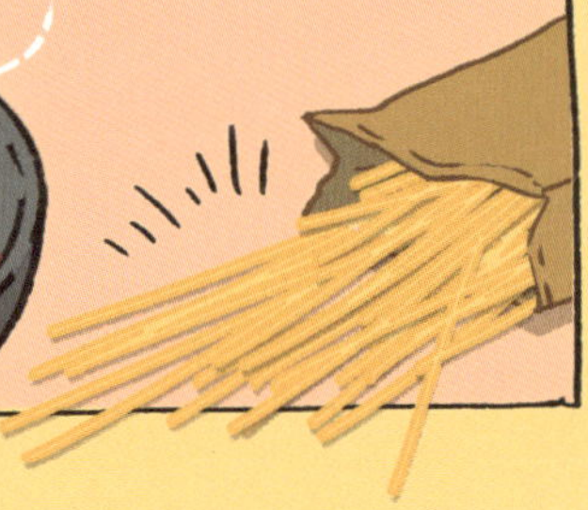

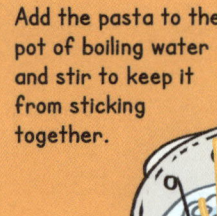

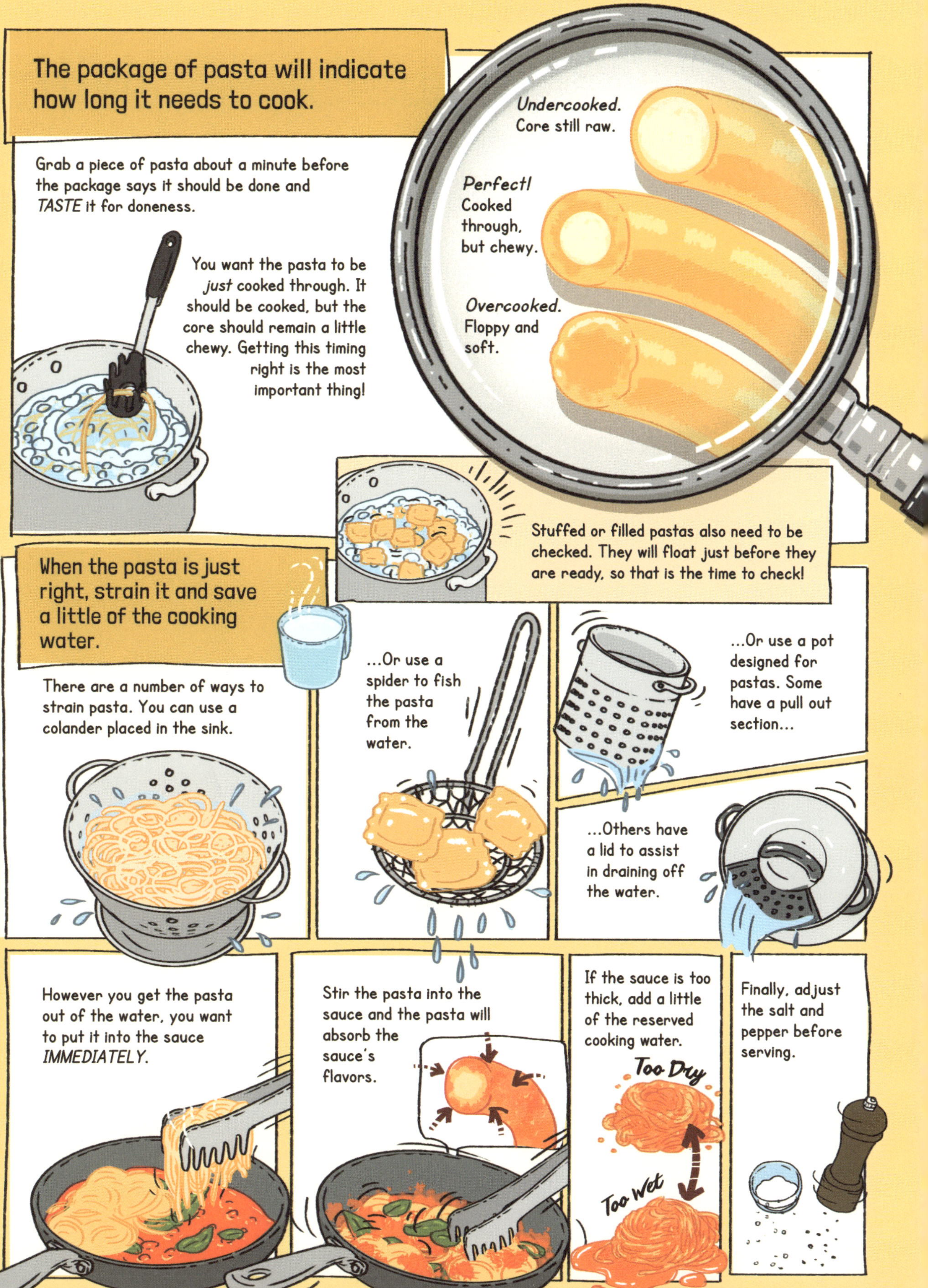
The package of pasta will indicate how long it needs to cook.
Grab a piece of pasta about a minute before the package says it should be done and *TASTE* it for doneness.
You want the pasta to be *just* cooked through. It should be cooked, but the core should remain a little chewy. Getting this timing right is the most important thing!
Undercooked. Core still raw.
Perfect! Cooked through, but chewy.
Overcooked. Floppy and soft.
Stuffed or filled pastas also need to be checked. They will float just before they are ready, so that is the time to check!
When the pasta is just right, strain it and save a little of the cooking water.
There are a number of ways to strain pasta. You can use a colander placed in the sink.
...Or use a spider to fish the pasta from the water.
...Or use a pot designed for pastas. Some have a pull out section...
...Others have a lid to assist in draining off the water.
However you get the pasta out of the water, you want to put it into the sauce *IMMEDIATELY*.
Stir the pasta into the sauce and the pasta will absorb the sauce's flavors.
If the sauce is too thick, add a little of the reserved cooking water.
Too Dry
Too Wet
Finally, adjust the salt and pepper before serving.

Recipe 6

Pasta Carbonara with Chitarra, Pancetta & Thyme

Carbonara is classic, **flavorful**, and calls for ingredients that you probably already have. It's traditionally made with **pancetta**, but you can substitute bacon, which also adds a smoky flavor. Egg yolks are mixed in just before serving, resulting in a rich, **silky** texture.

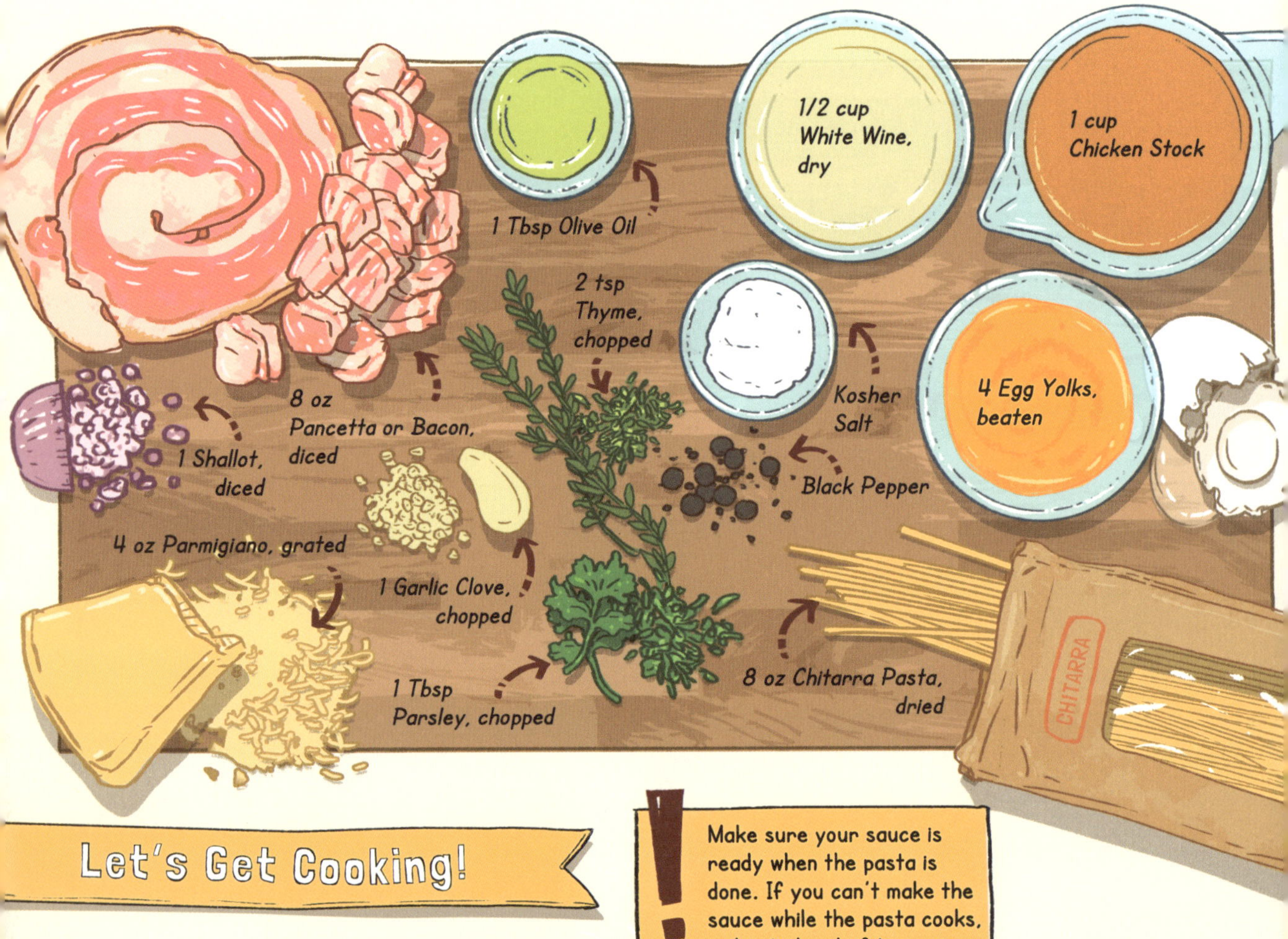

1 Tbsp Olive Oil
1/2 cup White Wine, dry
1 cup Chicken Stock
8 oz Pancetta or Bacon, diced
1 Shallot, diced
2 tsp Thyme, chopped
Kosher Salt
4 Egg Yolks, beaten
Black Pepper
4 oz Parmigiano, grated
1 Garlic Clove, chopped
1 Tbsp Parsley, chopped
8 oz Chitarra Pasta, dried
CHITARRA

Let's Get Cooking!

! Make sure your sauce is ready when the pasta is done. If you can't make the sauce while the pasta cooks, make it ahead of time.

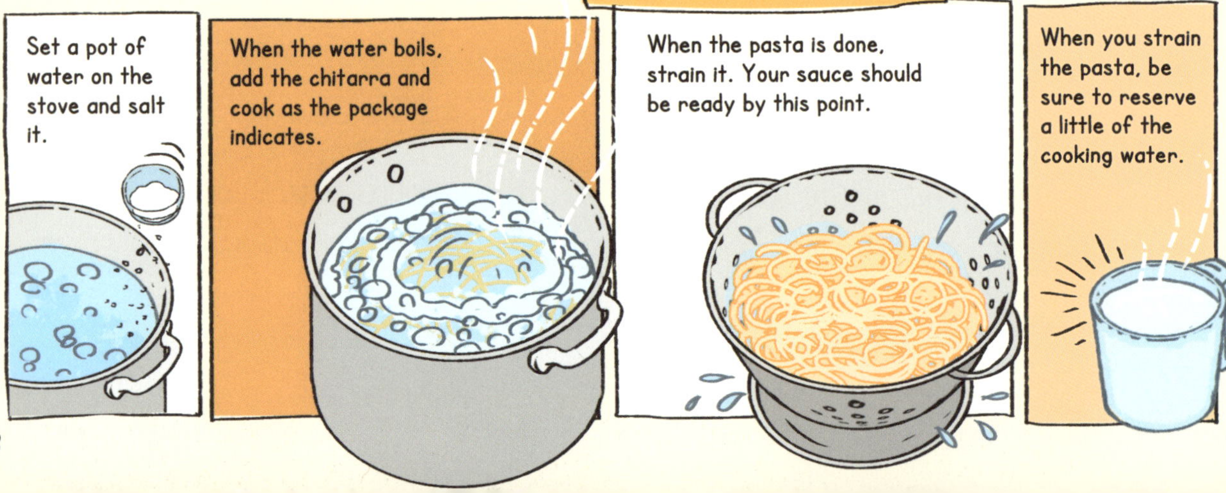

Set a pot of water on the stove and salt it.
When the water boils, add the chitarra and cook as the package indicates.
When the pasta is done, strain it. Your sauce should be ready by this point.
When you strain the pasta, be sure to reserve a little of the cooking water.

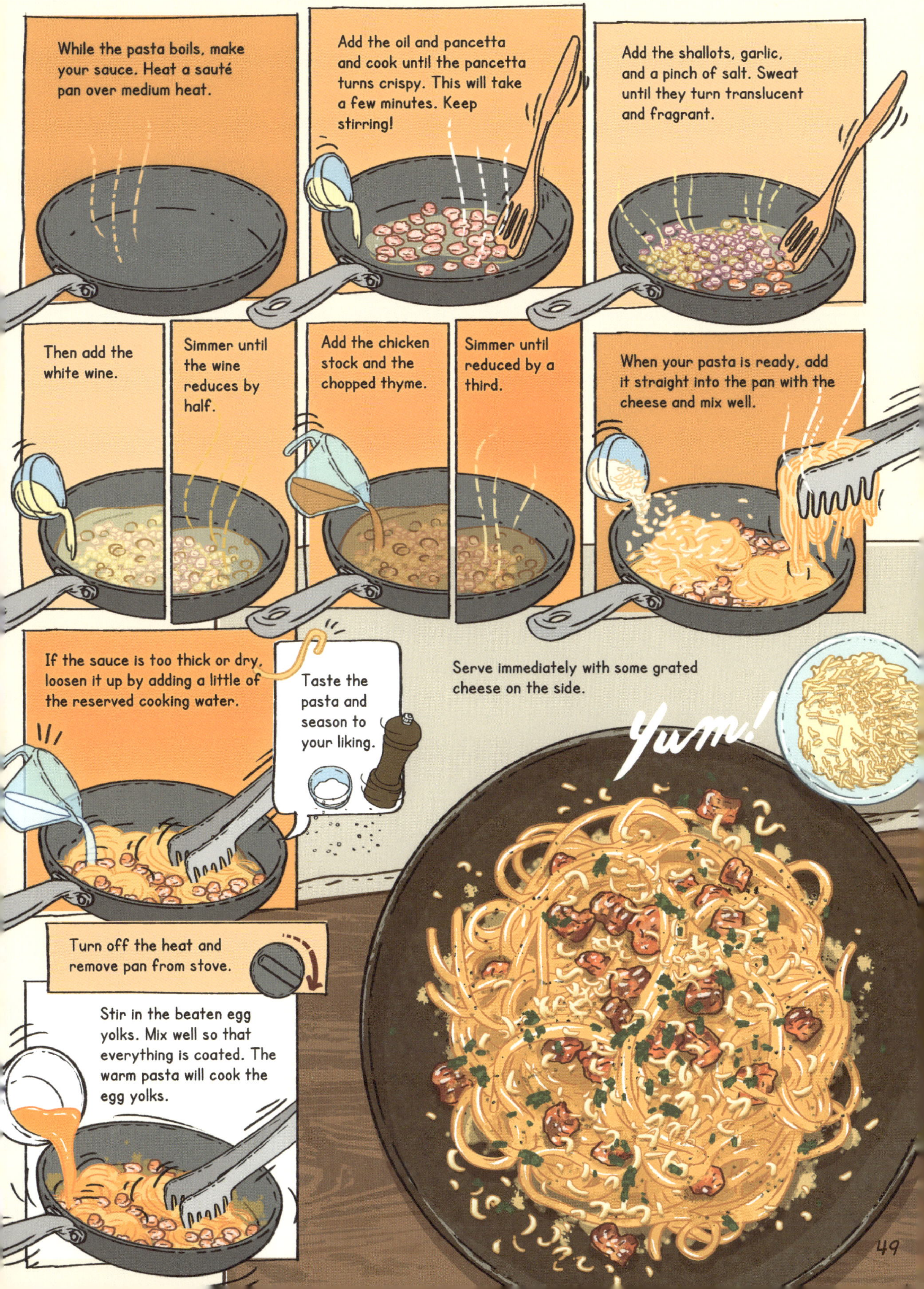
While the pasta boils, make your sauce. Heat a sauté pan over medium heat.
Add the oil and pancetta and cook until the pancetta turns crispy. This will take a few minutes. Keep stirring!
Add the shallots, garlic, and a pinch of salt. Sweat until they turn translucent and fragrant.
Then add the white wine.
Simmer until the wine reduces by half.
Add the chicken stock and the chopped thyme.
Simmer until reduced by a third.
When your pasta is ready, add it straight into the pan with the cheese and mix well.
If the sauce is too thick or dry, loosen it up by adding a little of the reserved cooking water.
Taste the pasta and season to your liking.
Serve immediately with some grated cheese on the side.
Yum!
Turn off the heat and remove pan from stove.
Stir in the beaten egg yolks. Mix well so that everything is coated. The warm pasta will cook the egg yolks.

Recipe 7

Tortellini with Sage Brown Butter

A package of filled pasta in the freezer provides an easy meal in minutes. This sauce is simple, a combination of browned butter and **fragrant sage** that really elevates the pasta. A large handful of arugula at the end adds a peppery note and lends **elegance** to the dish.

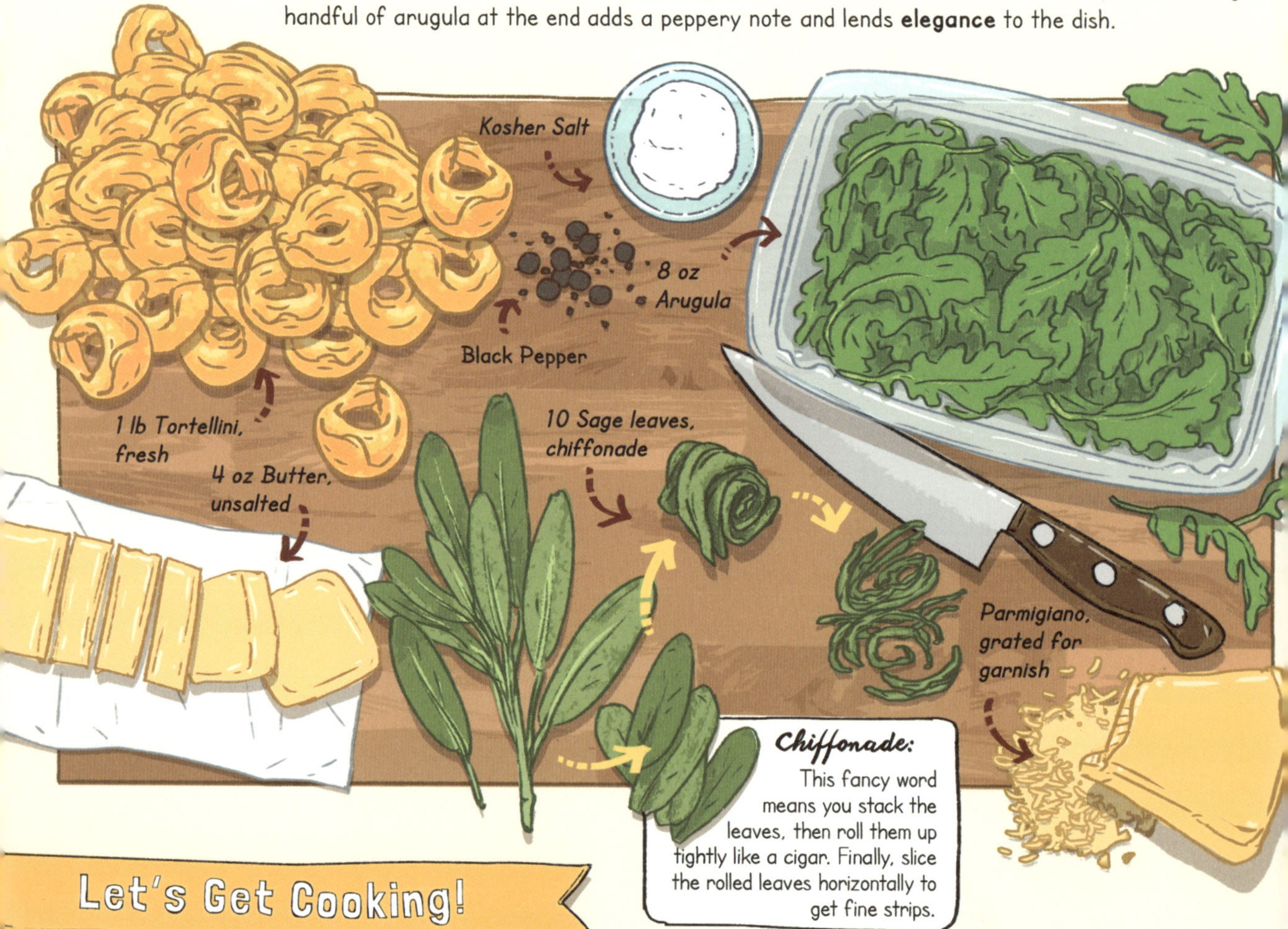
Kosher Salt
8 oz Arugula
Black Pepper
1 lb Tortellini, fresh
10 Sage leaves, chiffonade
4 oz Butter, unsalted
Parmigiano, grated for garnish
Chiffonade:
This fancy word means you stack the leaves, then roll them up tightly like a cigar. Finally, slice the rolled leaves horizontally to get fine strips.

Let's Get Cooking!

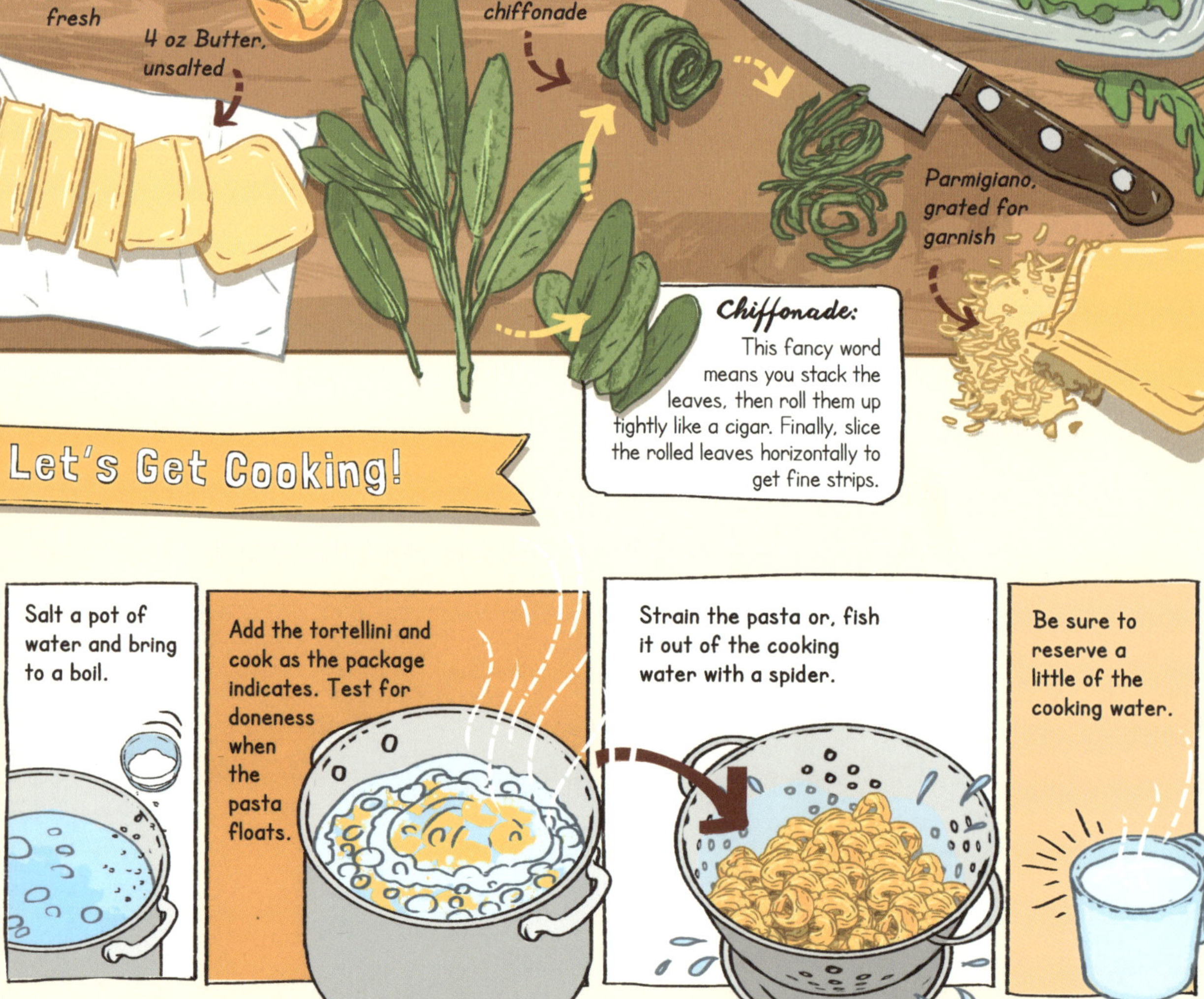
Salt a pot of water and bring to a boil.
Add the tortellini and cook as the package indicates. Test for doneness when the pasta floats.
Strain the pasta or, fish it out of the cooking water with a spider.
Be sure to reserve a little of the cooking water.

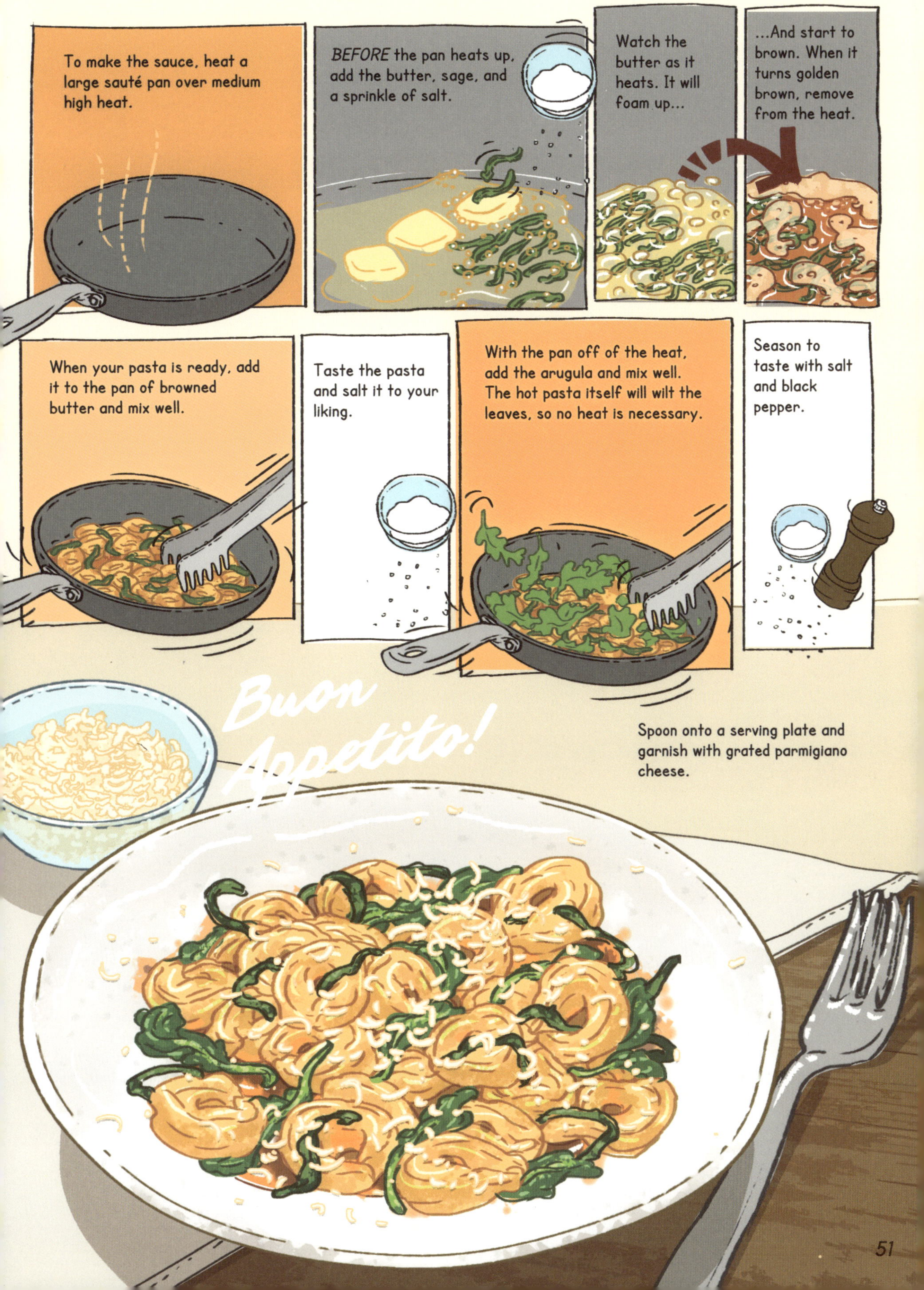
To make the sauce, heat a large sauté pan over medium high heat.
BEFORE the pan heats up, add the butter, sage, and a sprinkle of salt.
Watch the butter as it heats. It will foam up...
...And start to brown. When it turns golden brown, remove from the heat.
When your pasta is ready, add it to the pan of browned butter and mix well.
Taste the pasta and salt it to your liking.
With the pan off of the heat, add the arugula and mix well. The hot pasta itself will wilt the leaves, so no heat is necessary.
Season to taste with salt and black pepper.
Buon Appetito!
Spoon onto a serving plate and garnish with grated parmigiano cheese.

Technique 5

RICE

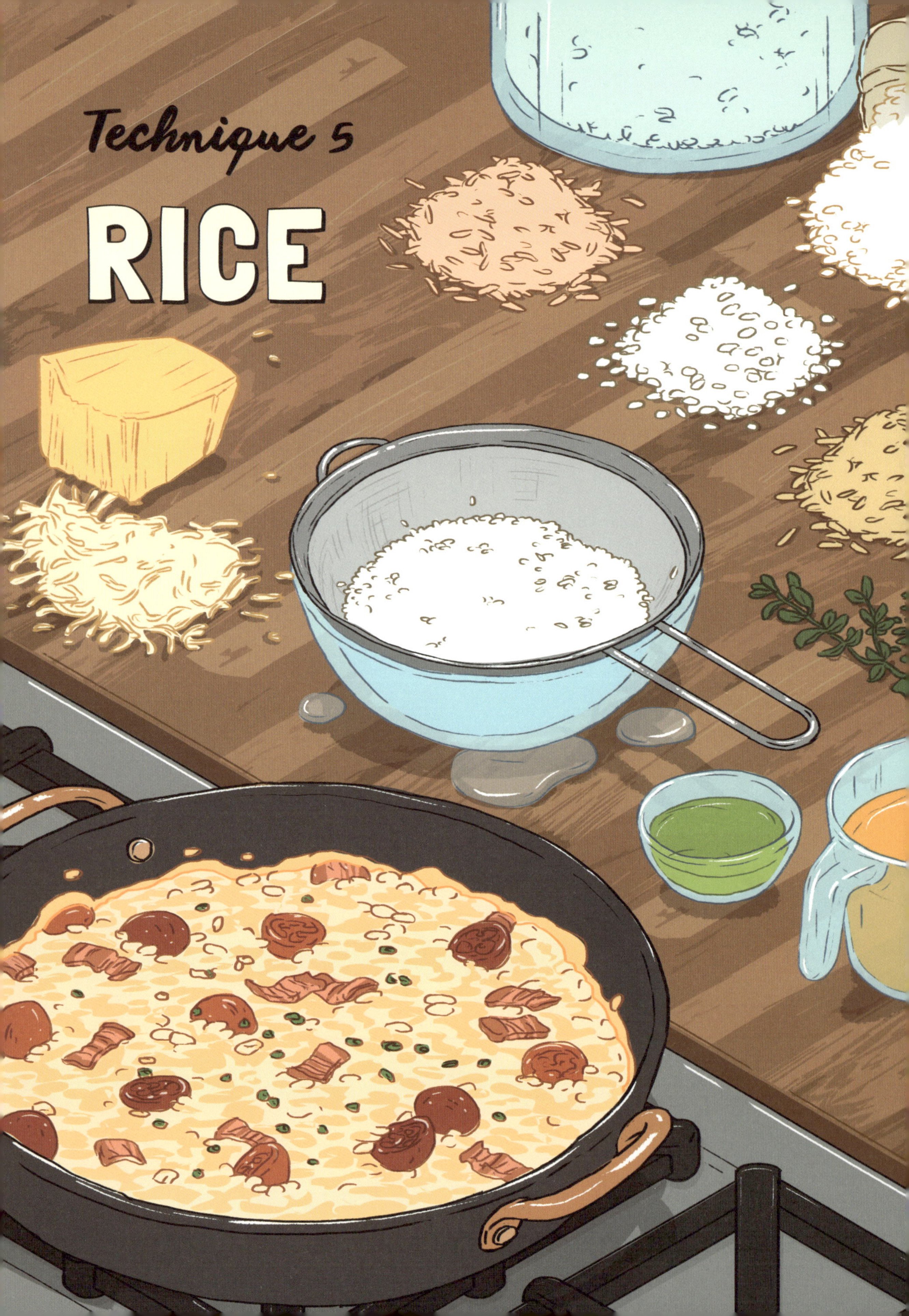

Chef's Note

Rice is one of the most versatile foods in the kitchen, but a lot of people seem to have trouble cooking it, so they shy away from it. What a shame!

When I was a teenager, the only rice I knew how to cook was the instant stuff. It was easy, but it didn't really have any flavor. So I neglected it for years after that, which was a real shame because there's a whole world of different rice varieties that each have a distinct flavor and compliment different foods.

Not only are there different kinds of rice, there are also tons of ways to cook it, each resulting in a different texture. You could write a whole book on rice alone, but this section will introduce you to the main varieties of rice and how to best cook them. Always keep a bag or two in your pantry!

SKILL BADGES

Boiling

Pan Skills

Tasting

Types of Rice

There are **hundreds** of kinds of rice, and an encyclopedic overview of them all is outside the scope of this book. However, most of them tend to fall into a few neat categories, whithin which you can find all the different varietals that make up the world of rice. These **5 types** of rice will cover the vast majority of rice out there, and you should be able to find them all in your local grocery store.

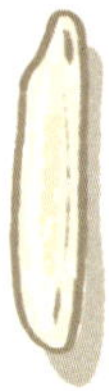

Long Grain:

Long grain rices are longer and thinner than other types. It is the least sticky and most fluffy kind of rice. Plain long grained rice is popular in the U.S., however, Basmati and Jasmine are also long grain varietals. It is most commonly steamed, but it makes a great pilaf as well.

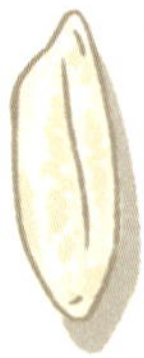

Medium Grain:

Shorter and plumper than long grain, medium grain rice is often used in Mediterranean dishes like risottos and paellas. Its starch lends a lovely creaminess to those dishes. Bomba (Spain), Arborio and Carneroli (Italy), and Calrose (U.S.) are all medium grained, and these rices work best as a pilaf or risotto. Calrose is great steamed, but the excess starch must be washed away first.

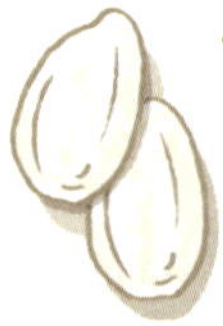

Short Grain:

As its name suggests, this is the shortest and plumpest of the rice grains. It is the stickiest rice, and is often used in Japanese cooking and for sushi rice. It is usually steamed, which keeps its starch and makes the rice sticky. It must be thouroughly rinced before cooking, or it will be mucky after it steams. To prevent that, rinse under water until the rinsing water runs clear.

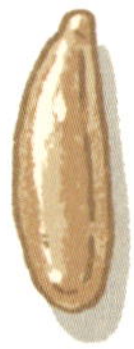

Brown Rice:

Brown rice is the 'whole grain' of the rice world. This means that the germ and the bran are left intact for brown rice, while they are removed to make white rice. It takes longer to cook and it is more perishable than white rice. All types of rice have both a brown and white version. Cook within 6 months of purchase. It is best cooked using the boil method.

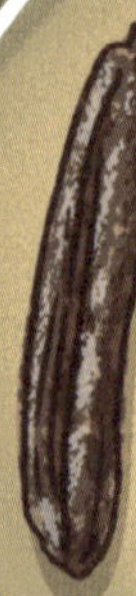

Wild Rice:

Although it is labeled a rice, wild rice is not actually a rice at all. Wild rices are the seeds of grasses. Although you can cook wild rice with success using any method, my favorite is to boil it like pasta. Regardless, it does take longer to cook.

Cooking Rice

Cooking rice requires few ingredients and little equipment. Rice cookers are a great tool that turn out perfect rice every time, but you don't need one to cook rice successfully. There are 2 basic methods to cook plain rice on your stovetop, **steaming** and **boiling**, and a 3rd method for cooking risottos and pilafs.

1. Steamed

This is probably the most popular method, but I think is actually one of the more difficult ways to cook rice.

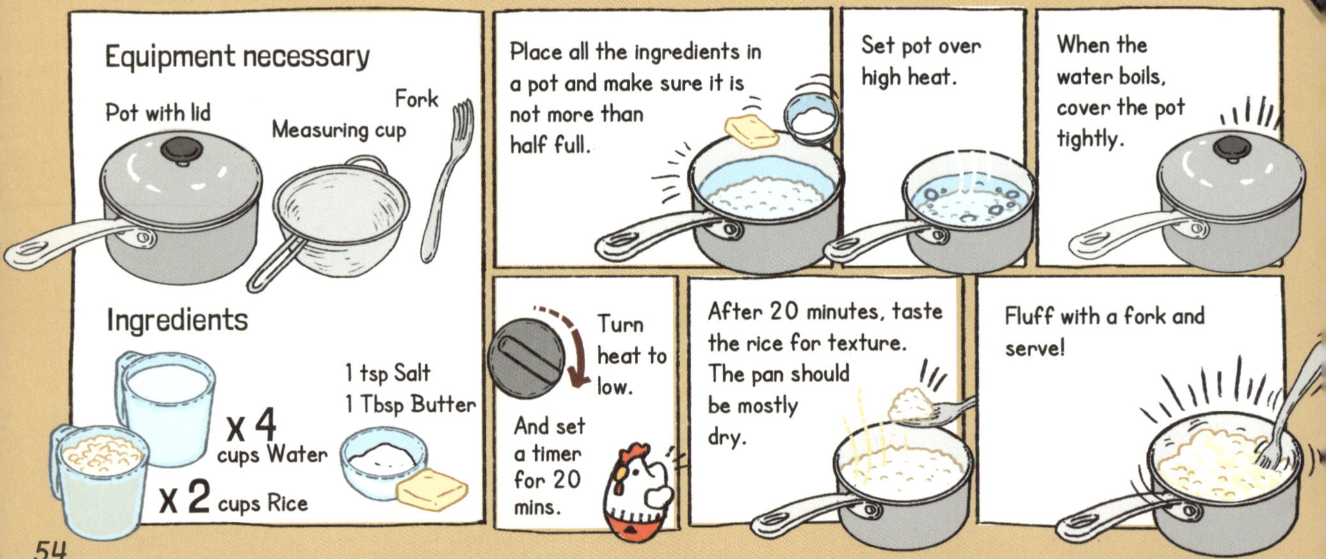
Equipment necessary
Pot with lid
Measuring cup
Fork
Ingredients
x 4 cups Water
x 2 cups Rice
1 tsp Salt
1 Tbsp Butter
Place all the ingredients in a pot and make sure it is not more than half full.
Set pot over high heat.
When the water boils, cover the pot tightly.
Turn heat to low.
And set a timer for 20 mins.
After 20 minutes, taste the rice for texture. The pan should be mostly dry.
Fluff with a fork and serve!

2. Boiled

I discovered this method relatively recently, and I've been cooking for a long time. Why this method is so uncommon is a mystery, because it's essentially a **foolproof** way to make a pot of plain rice.

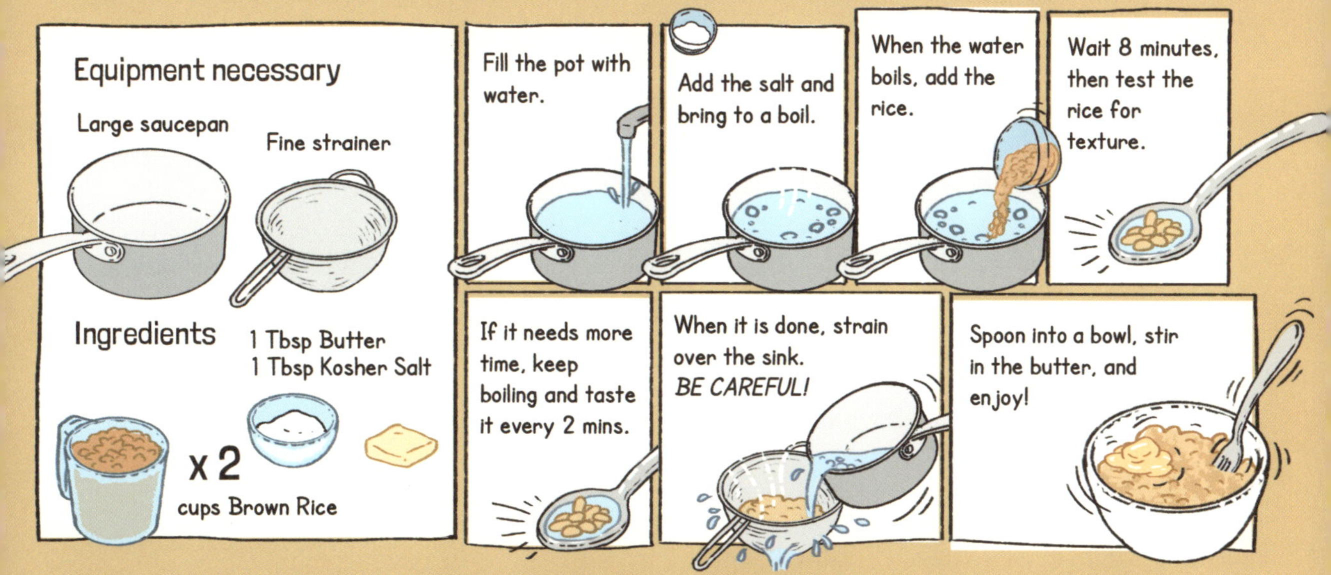

Equipment necessary
Large saucepan
Fine strainer
Ingredients
1 Tbsp Butter
1 Tbsp Kosher Salt
x 2
cups Brown Rice
Fill the pot with water.
Add the salt and bring to a boil.
When the water boils, add the rice.
Wait 8 minutes, then test the rice for texture.
If it needs more time, keep boiling and taste it every 2 mins.
When it is done, strain over the sink.
BE CAREFUL!
Spoon into a bowl, stir in the butter, and enjoy!

3. Risotto or Pilaf

The last way to cook rice is by making it into a risotto or pilaf. This is my favorite way to cook rice, but it does take a bit more attention than the previous two methods. The best part is that you can add additional ingredients and flavors during the cooking process, so that when the rice is done you have a whole finished dish!

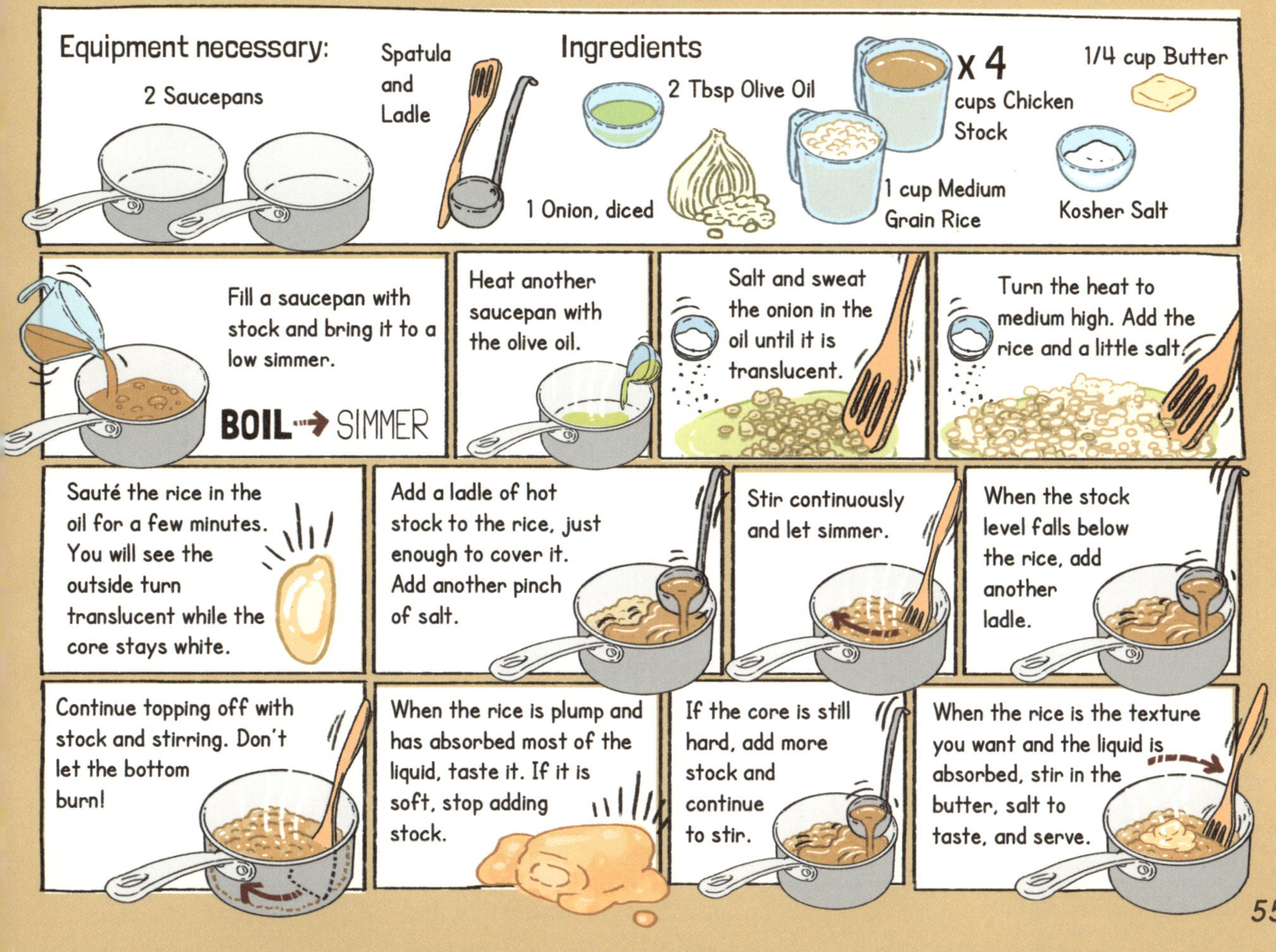

Equipment necessary:
2 Saucepans
Spatula and Ladle
Ingredients
2 Tbsp Olive Oil
1 Onion, diced
x 4
cups Chicken Stock
1 cup Medium Grain Rice
1/4 cup Butter
Kosher Salt
Fill a saucepan with stock and bring it to a low simmer.
BOIL → SIMMER
Heat another saucepan with the olive oil.
Salt and sweat the onion in the oil until it is translucent.
Turn the heat to medium high. Add the rice and a little salt.
Sauté the rice in the oil for a few minutes. You will see the outside turn translucent while the core stays white.
Add a ladle of hot stock to the rice, just enough to cover it. Add another pinch of salt.
Stir continuously and let simmer.
When the stock level falls below the rice, add another ladle.
Continue topping off with stock and stirring. Don't let the bottom burn!
When the rice is plump and has absorbed most of the liquid, taste it. If it is soft, stop adding stock.
If the core is still hard, add more stock and continue to stir.
When the rice is the texture you want and the liquid is absorbed, stir in the butter, salt to taste, and serve.

Recipe 8

Chicken & Kimchee Fried Rice with Fried Egg

Fried rice is a very **flexible** dish that can work with almost anything. This recipe includes kimchee and a fried egg. If you don't like kimchee, leave it out. If you prefer your egg fully-cooked and mixed in with the rice, do that. If you have a favorite vegetable that you want to add, add it! **Use your imagination**!

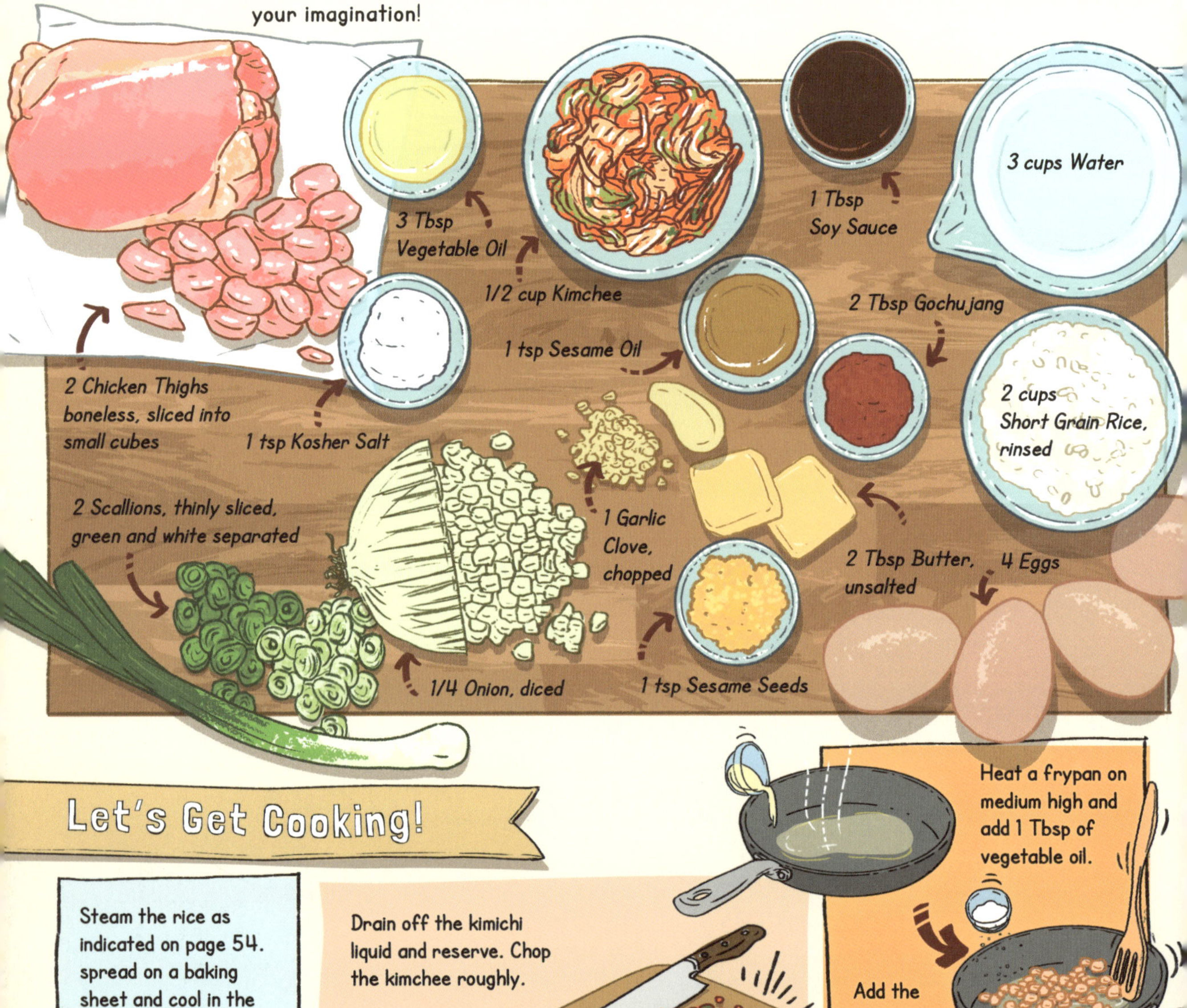

3 Tbsp Vegetable Oil
1/2 cup Kimchee
1 Tbsp Soy Sauce
3 cups Water
2 Tbsp Gochujang
1 tsp Sesame Oil
2 Chicken Thighs boneless, sliced into small cubes
1 tsp Kosher Salt
2 cups Short Grain Rice, rinsed
2 Scallions, thinly sliced, green and white separated
1 Garlic Clove, chopped
2 Tbsp Butter, unsalted
4 Eggs
1/4 Onion, diced
1 tsp Sesame Seeds

Let's Get Cooking!

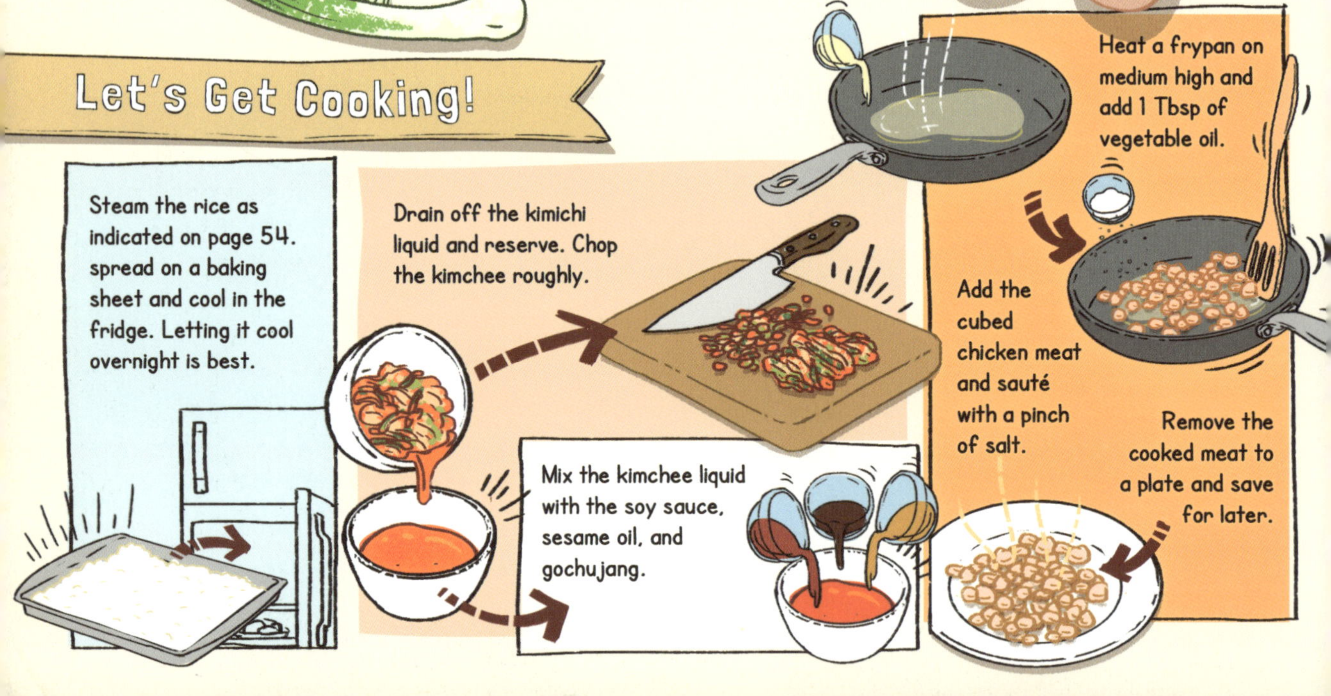

Steam the rice as indicated on page 54. spread on a baking sheet and cool in the fridge. Letting it cool overnight is best.
Drain off the kimichi liquid and reserve. Chop the kimchee roughly.
Mix the kimchee liquid with the soy sauce, sesame oil, and gochujang.
Heat a frypan on medium high and add 1 Tbsp of vegetable oil.
Add the cubed chicken meat and sauté with a pinch of salt.
Remove the cooked meat to a plate and save for later.

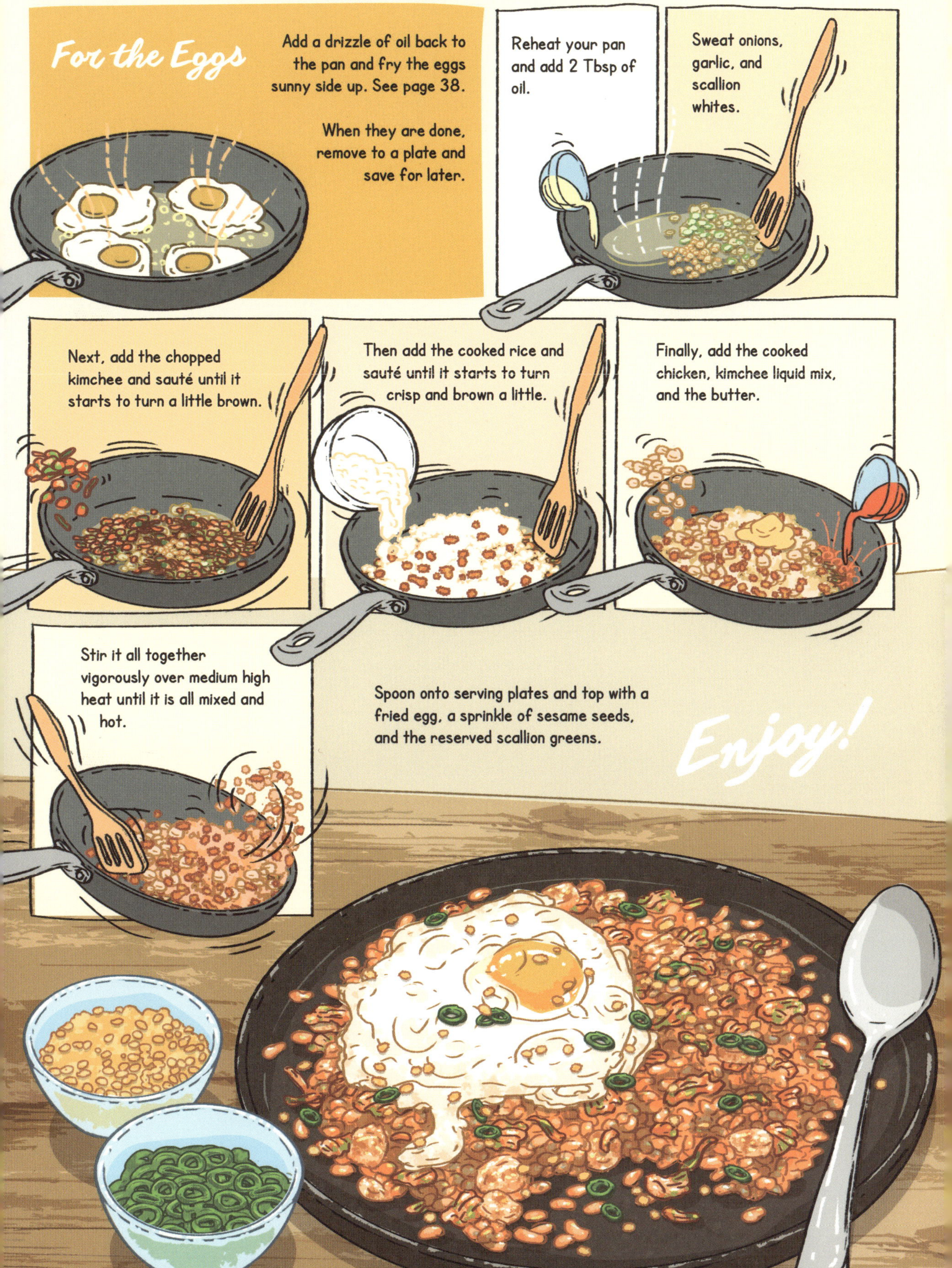
For the Eggs
Add a drizzle of oil back to the pan and fry the eggs sunny side up. See page 38.
When they are done, remove to a plate and save for later.
Reheat your pan and add 2 Tbsp of oil.
Sweat onions, garlic, and scallion whites.
Next, add the chopped kimchee and sauté until it starts to turn a little brown.
Then add the cooked rice and sauté until it starts to turn crisp and brown a little.
Finally, add the cooked chicken, kimchee liquid mix, and the butter.
Stir it all together vigorously over medium high heat until it is all mixed and hot.
Spoon onto serving plates and top with a fried egg, a sprinkle of sesame seeds, and the reserved scallion greens.
Enjoy!

Recipe 9

Tomato Risotto with Parmigiano Reggiano

Risotto is warm, **creamy**, and full of cheese and butter. There are few things more **soul-warming** on a cold night than a plate full of hot risotto, and it works with anything. In this recipe, the rich risotto is filled with **fruity** tomatoes—delicious!

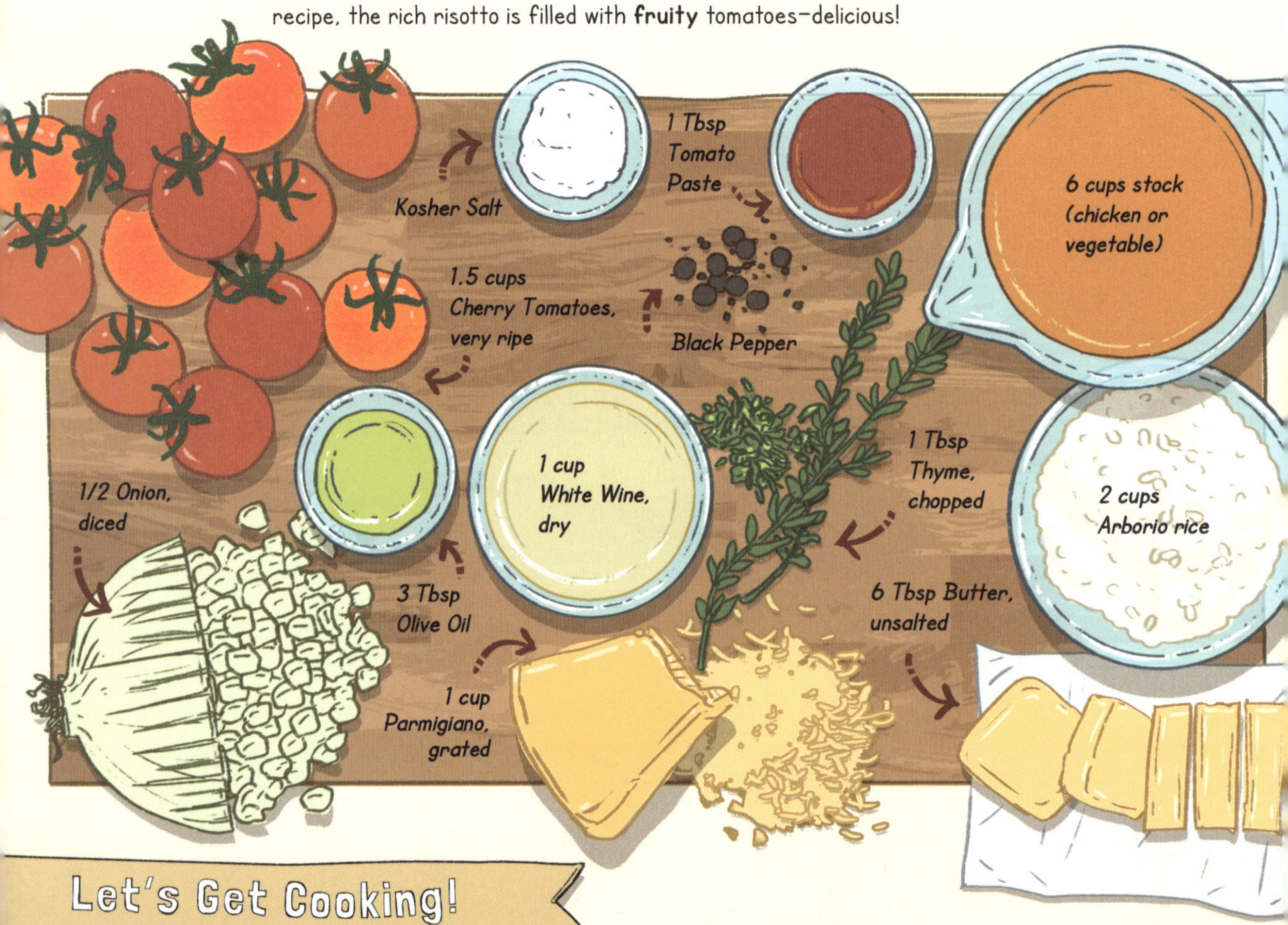
Kosher Salt
1 Tbsp Tomato Paste
6 cups stock (chicken or vegetable)
1.5 cups Cherry Tomatoes, very ripe
Black Pepper
1 Tbsp Thyme, chopped
2 cups Arborio rice
1/2 Onion, diced
1 cup White Wine, dry
3 Tbsp Olive Oil
6 Tbsp Butter, unsalted
1 cup Parmigiano, grated

Let's Get Cooking!

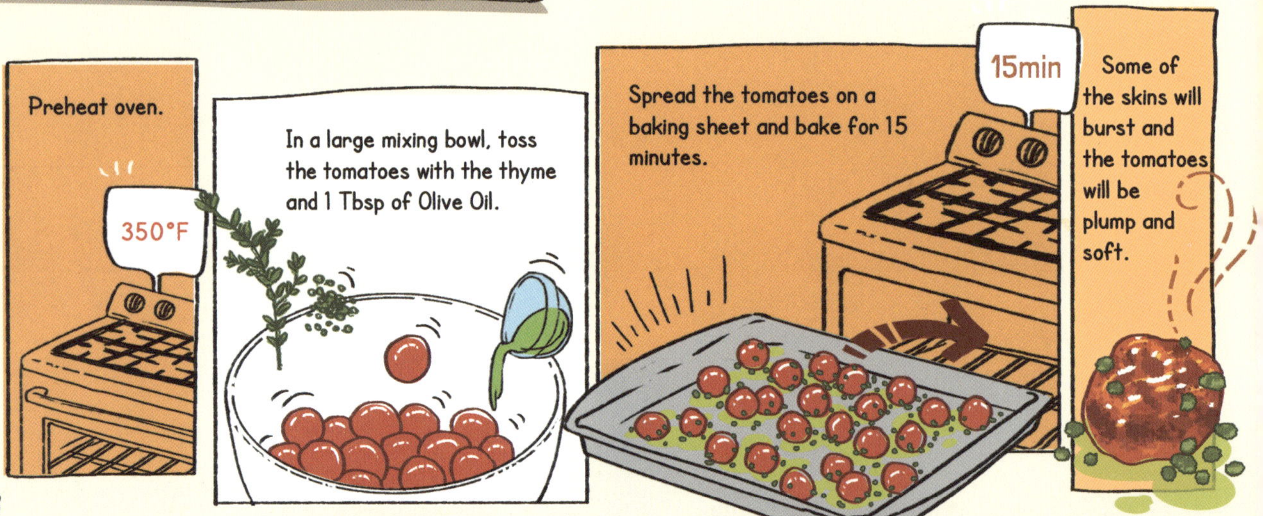
Preheat oven.
350°F
In a large mixing bowl, toss the tomatoes with the thyme and 1 Tbsp of Olive Oil.
Spread the tomatoes on a baking sheet and bake for 15 minutes.
15min
Some of the skins will burst and the tomatoes will be plump and soft.

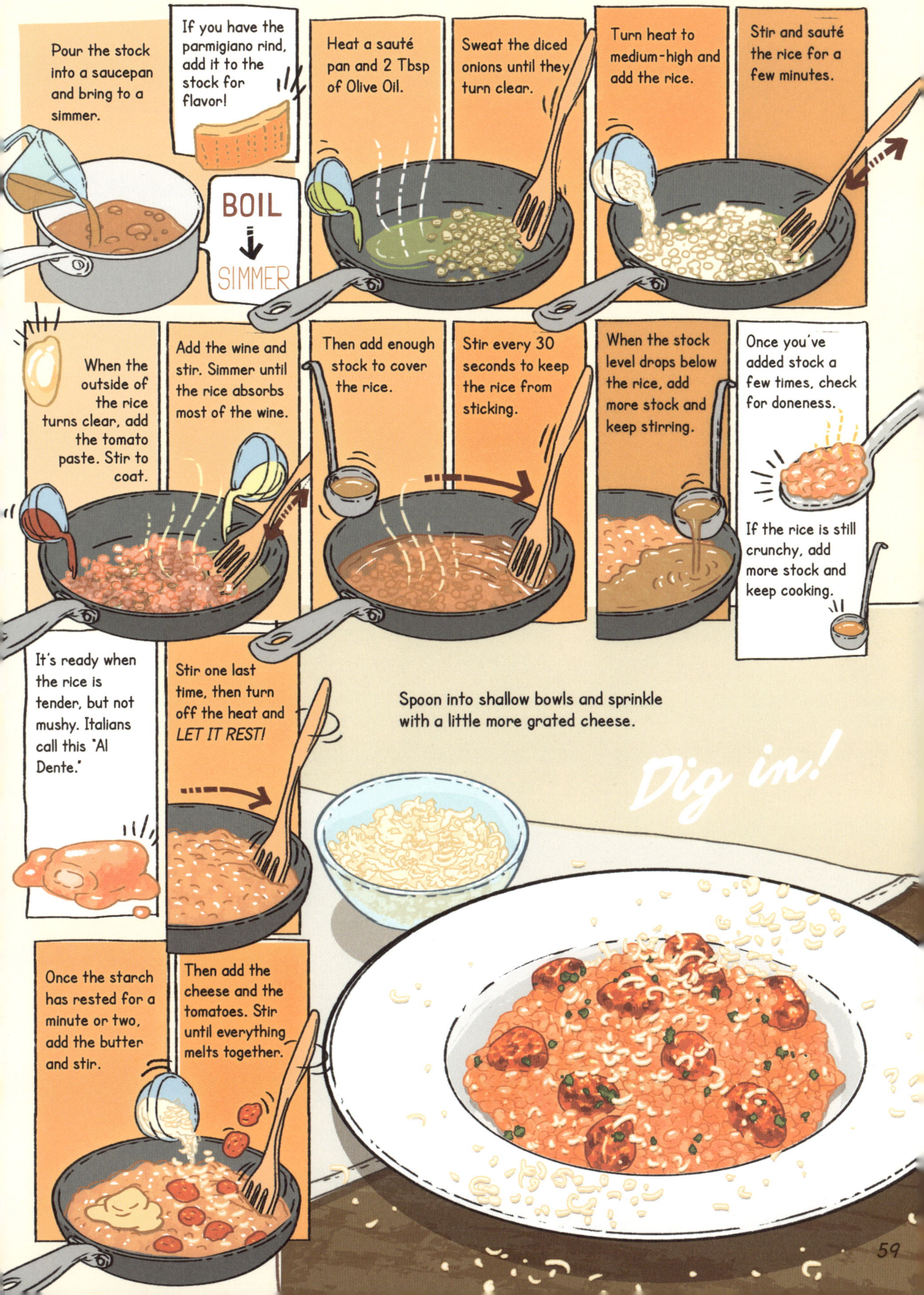

Pour the stock into a saucepan and bring to a simmer.
If you have the parmigiano rind, add it to the stock for flavor!
BOIL
SIMMER
Heat a sauté pan and 2 Tbsp of Olive Oil.
Sweat the diced onions until they turn clear.
Turn heat to medium-high and add the rice.
Stir and sauté the rice for a few minutes.
When the outside of the rice turns clear, add the tomato paste. Stir to coat.
Add the wine and stir. Simmer until the rice absorbs most of the wine.
Then add enough stock to cover the rice.
Stir every 30 seconds to keep the rice from sticking.
When the stock level drops below the rice, add more stock and keep stirring.
Once you've added stock a few times, check for doneness.
If the rice is still crunchy, add more stock and keep cooking.
It's ready when the rice is tender, but not mushy. Italians call this "Al Dente."
Stir one last time, then turn off the heat and *LET IT REST!*
Spoon into shallow bowls and sprinkle with a little more grated cheese.
Dig in!
Once the starch has rested for a minute or two, add the butter and stir.
Then add the cheese and the tomatoes. Stir until everything melts together.

Technique 6

SAUTÉING

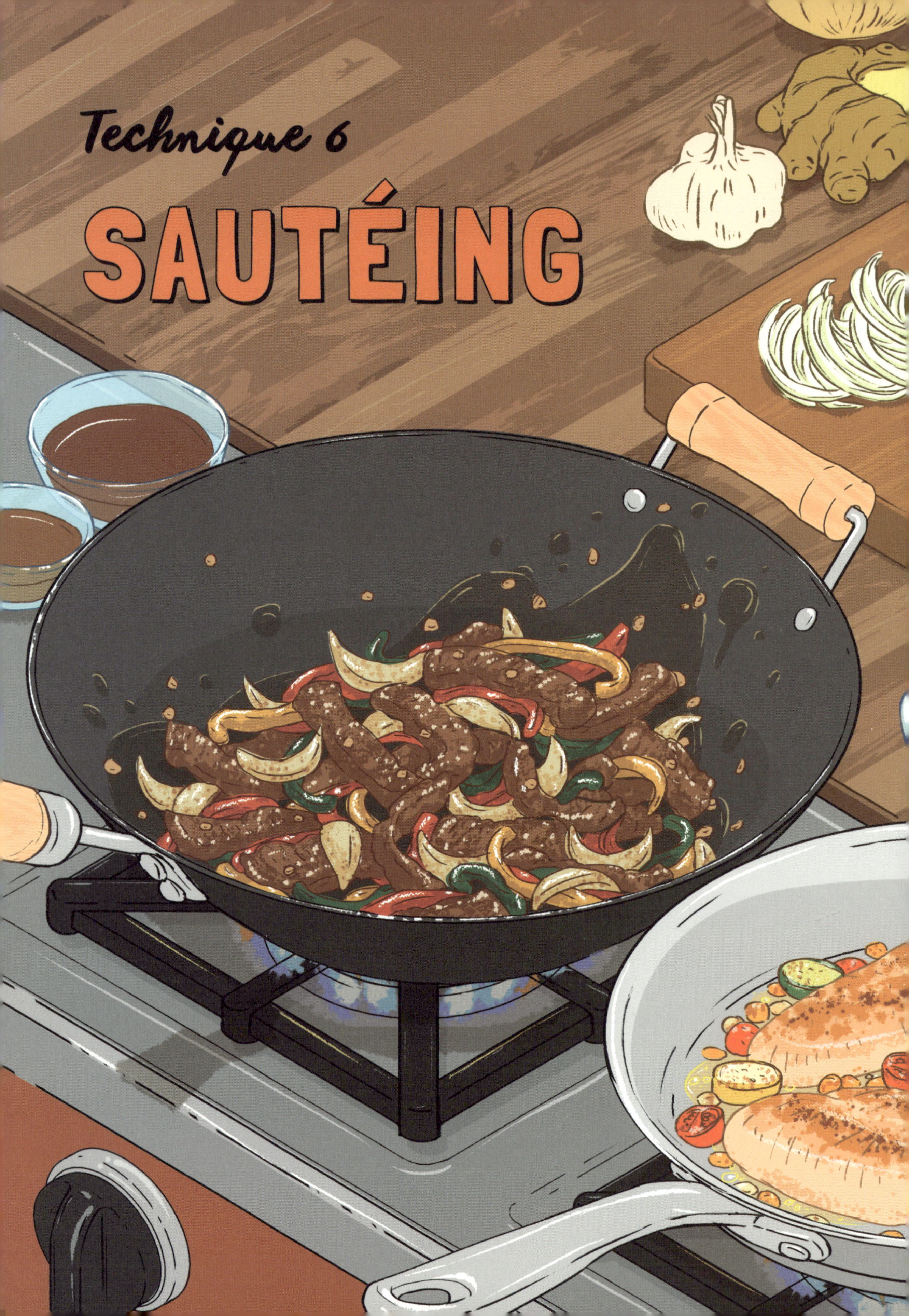

Chef's Note

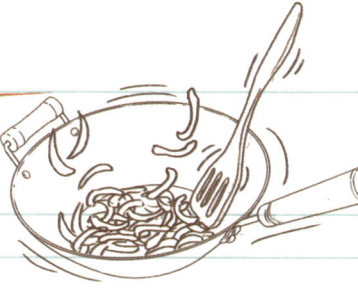

Sautéing is probably the most logical, most useful technique in this book. In culinary school, everyone learns that "sauté" means "to jump." Poetic-sounding terms are rarely so accurate! Generally, a sauté is something cooked quickly over high heat.

Chances are, if you've ever cooked anything in a kitchen, you know how to sauté. If you've ever fried an egg, then you have sautéed. When you put a frying pan (also known as a sauté pan) on the stove and cook just about anything in it, you can say you are sautéing. It's a very popular technique because it is quick, uses one pan and most people have some level of experience with it. Still, depending on the dish and the level of technique involved, it can be intimidating. Let's fix that: armed with a little kitchen know-how, sautéing is both easy and delicious.

SKILL BADGES

Knife Skills

Marinading

Reduction

SAUTÉING TECHNIQUE

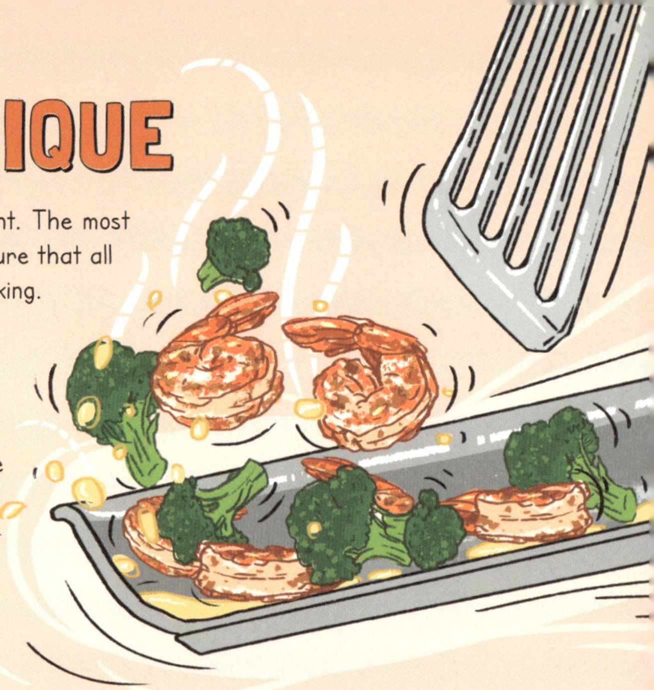

Sautéing is a quick cooking method, so timing is paramount. The most important thing you can do to ensure success is to make sure that all of your ingredients are ready to go **before** you start cooking. If you try to prepare some ingredients when others are already cooking you are going to be rushed, stressed out, and will probably burn something.

There two major things to consider when sautéing: the size of the items you are cooking, and whether or not you want to **caramelize** your food. Caramelization is that wonderful **golden brown color** that adds depth of flavor to your food. It is delicious, but you don't always want it. Control it using heat and timing.

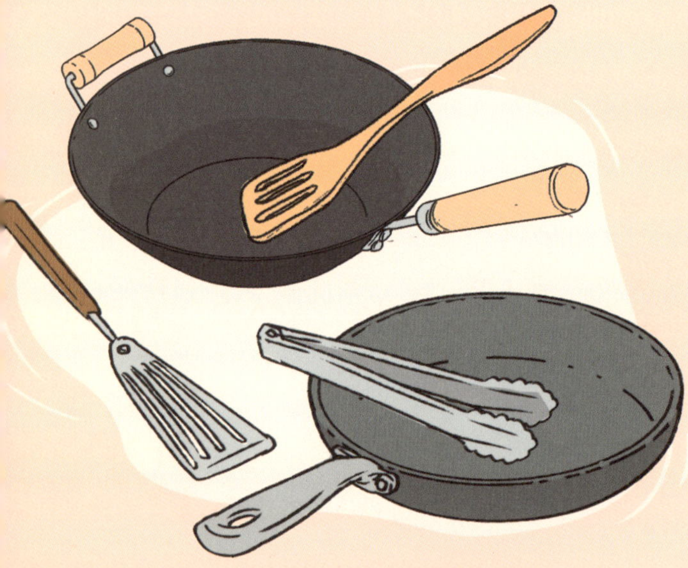

Equipment Necessary

- **Sauté pan** Also called a fry pan, a good sauté pan is probably the most important investment you can make in your kitchen. When looking for a pan, there are a few things you should consider:

  1) It should have a thick bottom, sometimes called a 'heavy bottomed' pan.

  2) It should be large enough to cook whatever it is that you are cooking, but not so large that it is hard for you to manage.

  3) It should be oven safe. Make sure it has a handle that can go in the oven. Plastic will melt, but silicon is generally safe.

- **Tongs**
- **Metal fish spatula**
- **Heat proof spatula (wood or silicon)**

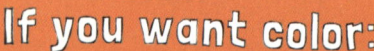

If you want color:

Heat your sauté pan on high heat.

You want to make sure the pan itself is hot before you add anything to it.

Add oil to the pan and wait for it to get hot. You will know it is hot enough because it will start to shimmer.

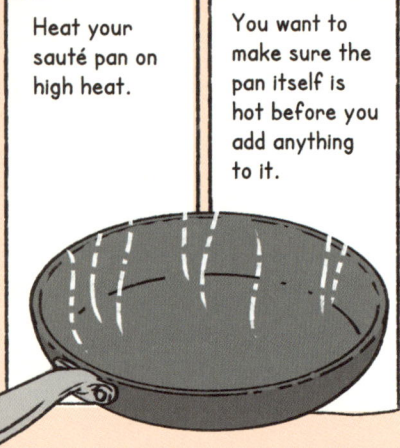

Tips:

When cooking on high heat, use oil and not butter to cook in. Butter contains protiens that will burn if it gets too hot!

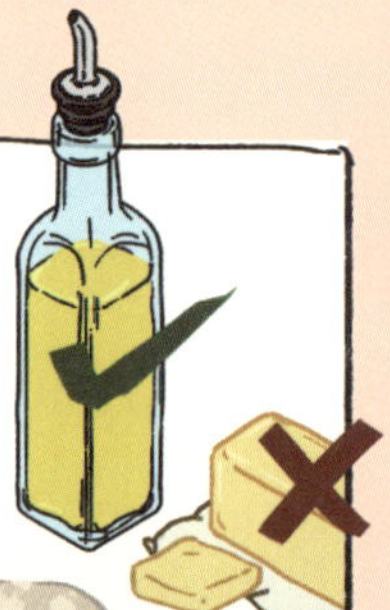

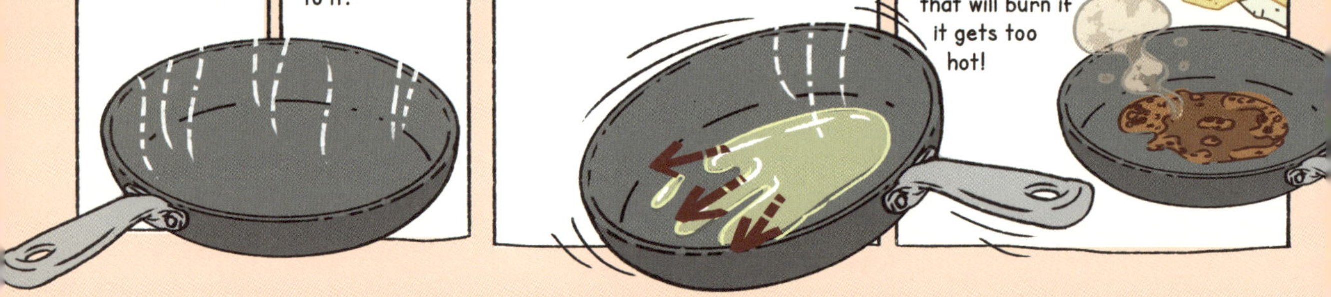

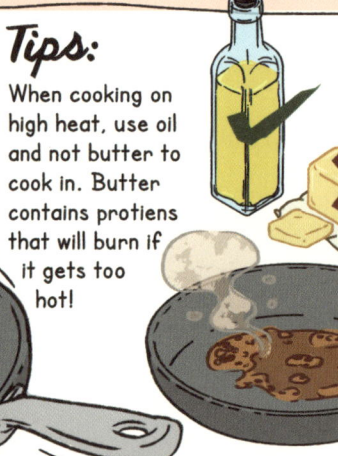

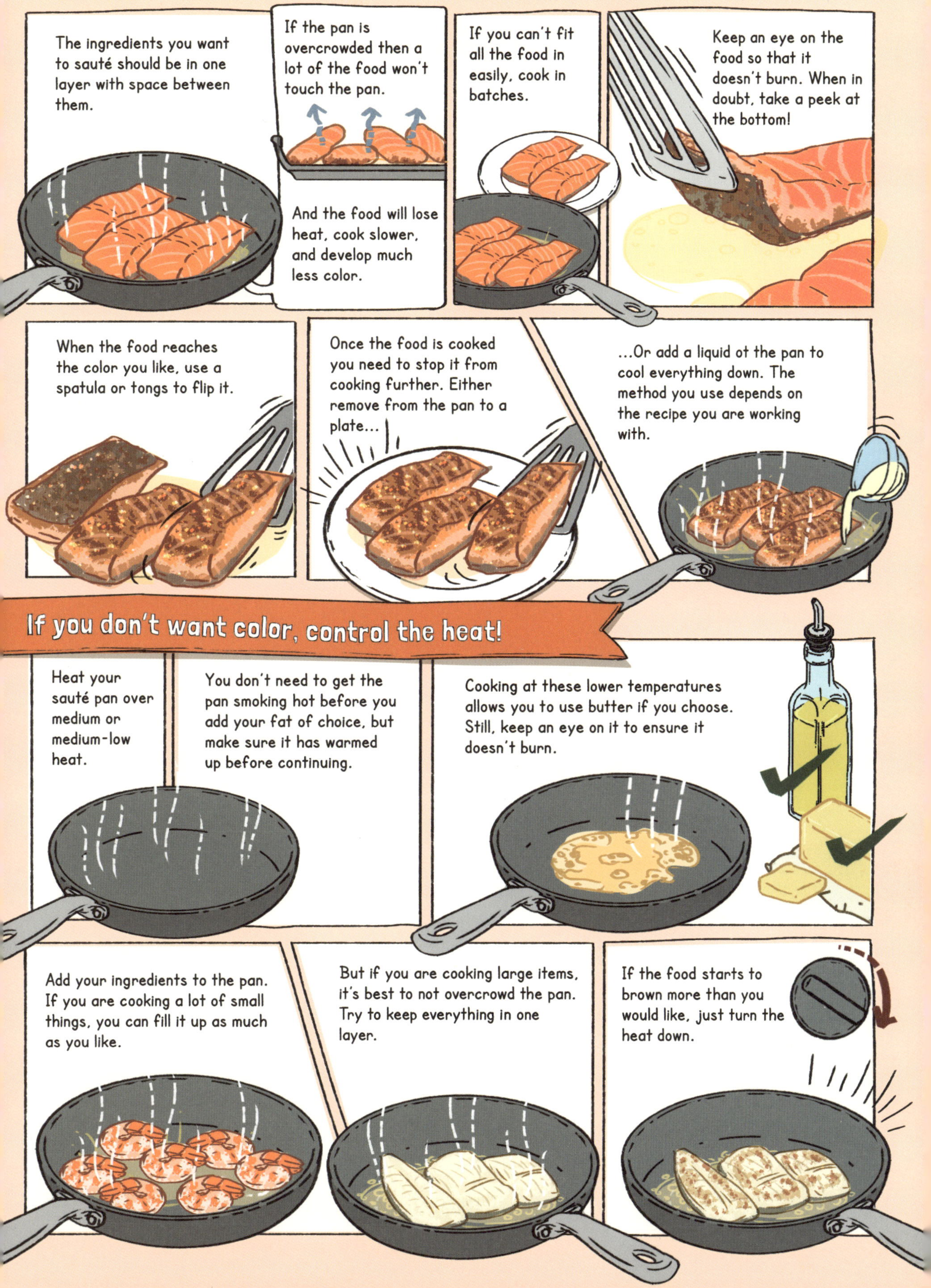

The ingredients you want to sauté should be in one layer with space between them.
If the pan is overcrowded then a lot of the food won't touch the pan.
And the food will lose heat, cook slower, and develop much less color.
If you can't fit all the food in easily, cook in batches.
Keep an eye on the food so that it doesn't burn. When in doubt, take a peek at the bottom!
When the food reaches the color you like, use a spatula or tongs to flip it.
Once the food is cooked you need to stop it from cooking further. Either remove from the pan to a plate...
...Or add a liquid ot the pan to cool everything down. The method you use depends on the recipe you are working with.
If you don't want color, control the heat!
Heat your sauté pan over medium or medium-low heat.
You don't need to get the pan smoking hot before you add your fat of choice, but make sure it has warmed up before continuing.
Cooking at these lower temperatures allows you to use butter if you choose. Still, keep an eye on it to ensure it doesn't burn.
Add your ingredients to the pan. If you are cooking a lot of small things, you can fill it up as much as you like.
But if you are cooking large items, it's best to not overcrowd the pan. Try to keep everything in one layer.
If the food starts to brown more than you would like, just turn the heat down.

Recipe 10

Chicken Breasts with Summer Vegetable Medley

This dish that works well both as a **quick** weeknight meal or **relaxed** dinner party in the summer. You can switch this recipe up easily by swapping out different vegetables or meats—the salsa verde works well with so many different things, and it's **healthy** too!

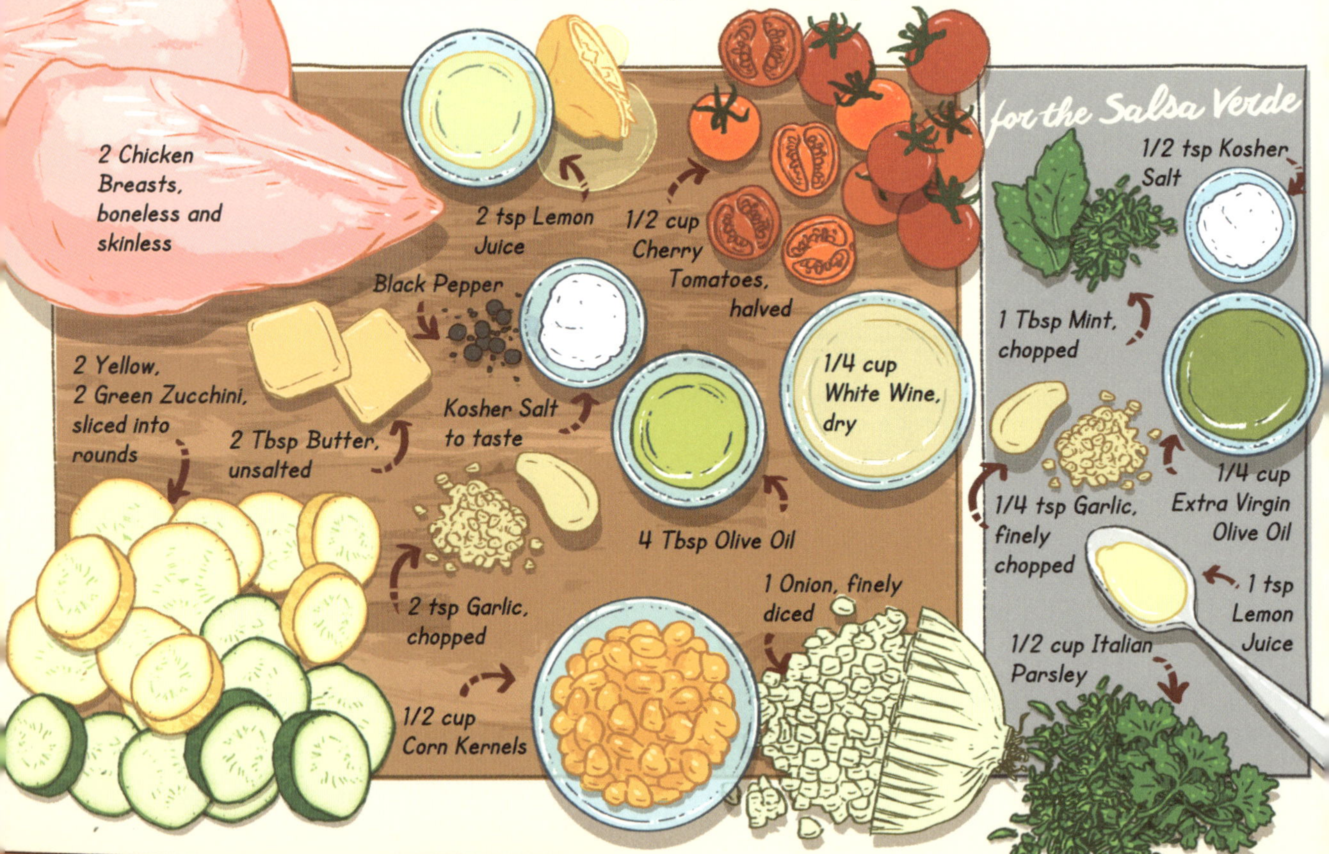
2 Chicken Breasts, boneless and skinless
2 tsp Lemon Juice
1/2 cup Cherry Tomatoes, halved
Black Pepper
2 Yellow, 2 Green Zucchini, sliced into rounds
2 Tbsp Butter, unsalted
Kosher Salt to taste
1/4 cup White Wine, dry
4 Tbsp Olive Oil
2 tsp Garlic, chopped
1 Onion, finely diced
1/2 cup Corn Kernels
for the Salsa Verde
1/2 tsp Kosher Salt
1 Tbsp Mint, chopped
1/4 tsp Garlic, finely chopped
1/4 cup Extra Virgin Olive Oil
1 tsp Lemon Juice
1/2 cup Italian Parsley

Let's Get Cooking!

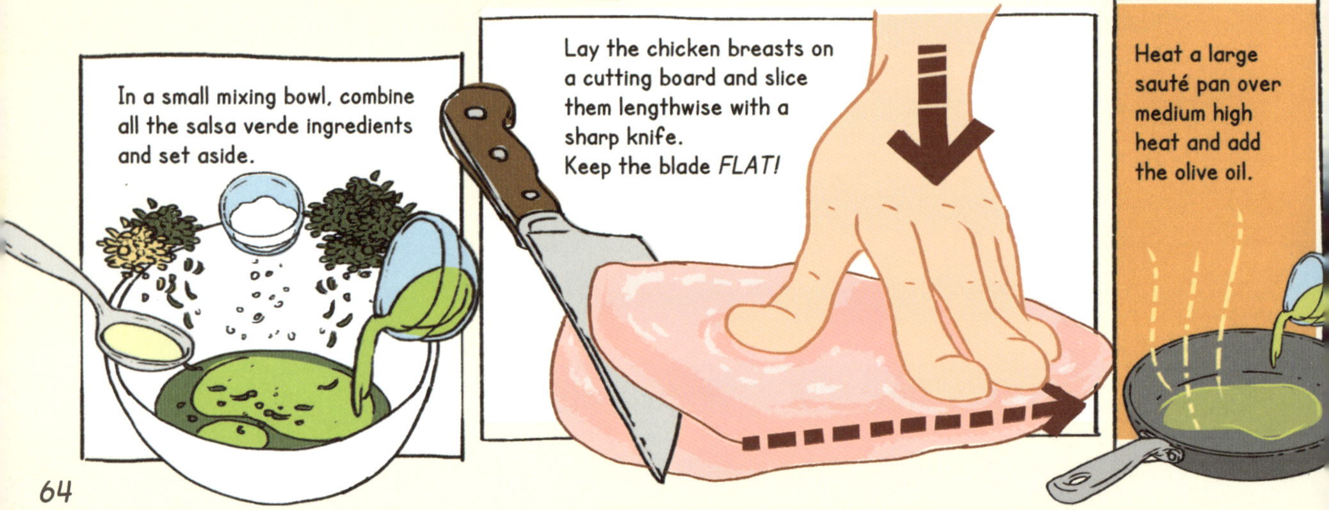
In a small mixing bowl, combine all the salsa verde ingredients and set aside.
Lay the chicken breasts on a cutting board and slice them lengthwise with a sharp knife.
Keep the blade *FLAT!*
Heat a large sauté pan over medium high heat and add the olive oil.

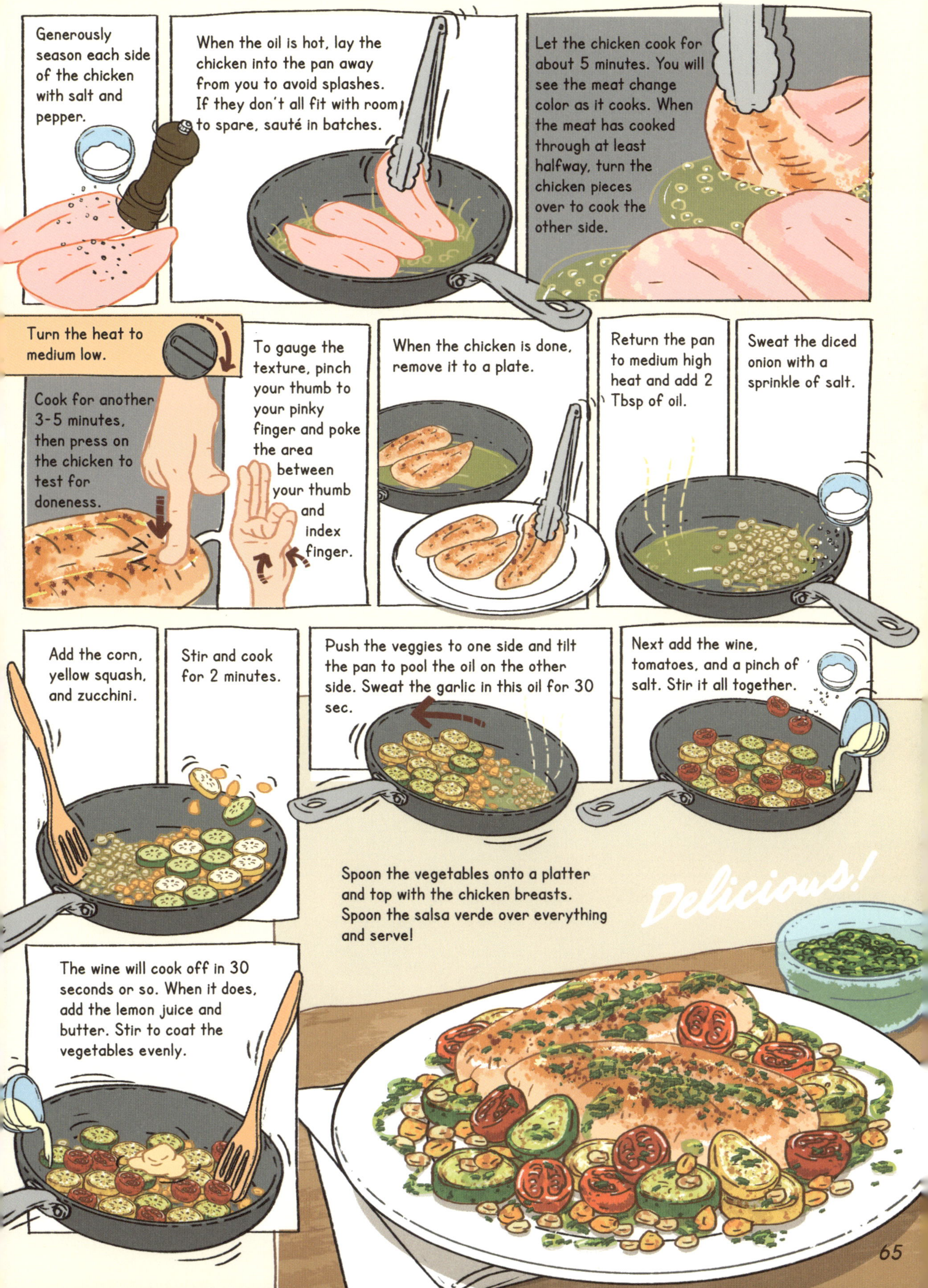
Generously season each side of the chicken with salt and pepper.
When the oil is hot, lay the chicken into the pan away from you to avoid splashes. If they don't all fit with room to spare, sauté in batches.
Let the chicken cook for about 5 minutes. You will see the meat change color as it cooks. When the meat has cooked through at least halfway, turn the chicken pieces over to cook the other side.
Turn the heat to medium low.
Cook for another 3-5 minutes, then press on the chicken to test for doneness.
To gauge the texture, pinch your thumb to your pinky finger and poke the area between your thumb and index finger.
When the chicken is done, remove it to a plate.
Return the pan to medium high heat and add 2 Tbsp of oil.
Sweat the diced onion with a sprinkle of salt.
Add the corn, yellow squash, and zucchini.
Stir and cook for 2 minutes.
Push the veggies to one side and tilt the pan to pool the oil on the other side. Sweat the garlic in this oil for 30 sec.
Next add the wine, tomatoes, and a pinch of salt. Stir it all together.
The wine will cook off in 30 seconds or so. When it does, add the lemon juice and butter. Stir to coat the vegetables evenly.
Spoon the vegetables onto a platter and top with the chicken breasts. Spoon the salsa verde over everything and serve!
Delicious!

Recipe 11

Skirt Steak and Yakisoba Noodle Stir Fry

Stir frying is essentially sautéing, except that it is traditionally done in a wok. If you have a wok, go ahead and put it to use here, but if you don't, just use a large sauté pan. You should be able to find the Yakisoba noodles in your local grocery, but ramen noodles work just as well!

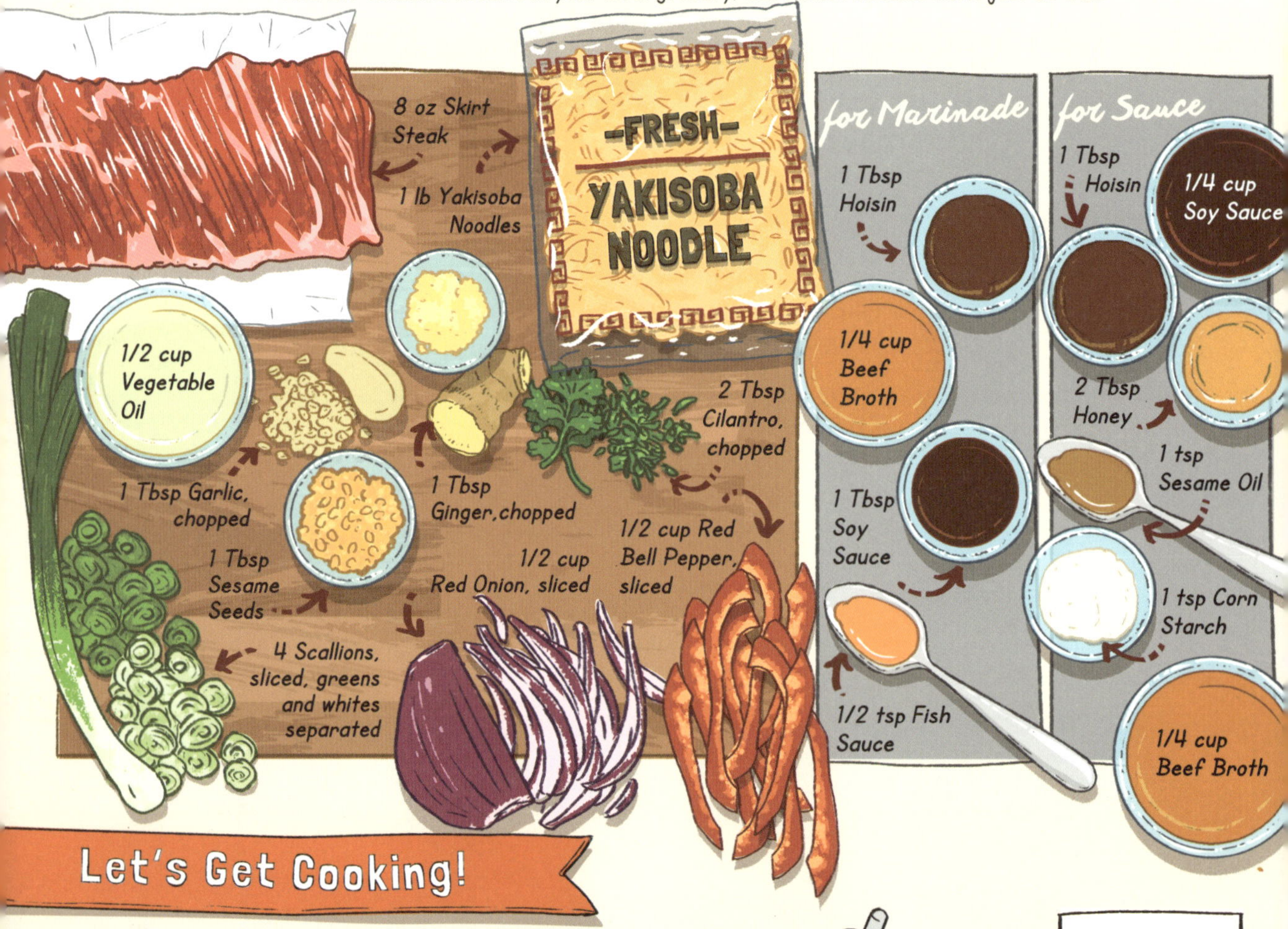
8 oz Skirt Steak
1 lb Yakisoba Noodles
-FRESH-
YAKISOBA NOODLE
1/2 cup Vegetable Oil
1 Tbsp Garlic, chopped
1 Tbsp Ginger, chopped
2 Tbsp Cilantro, chopped
1 Tbsp Sesame Seeds
1/2 cup Red Onion, sliced
1/2 cup Red Bell Pepper, sliced
4 Scallions, sliced, greens and whites separated
for Marinade
1 Tbsp Hoisin
1/4 cup Beef Broth
1 Tbsp Soy Sauce
1/2 tsp Fish Sauce
for Sauce
1 Tbsp Hoisin
1/4 cup Soy Sauce
2 Tbsp Honey
1 tsp Sesame Oil
1 tsp Corn Starch
1/4 cup Beef Broth

Let's Get Cooking!

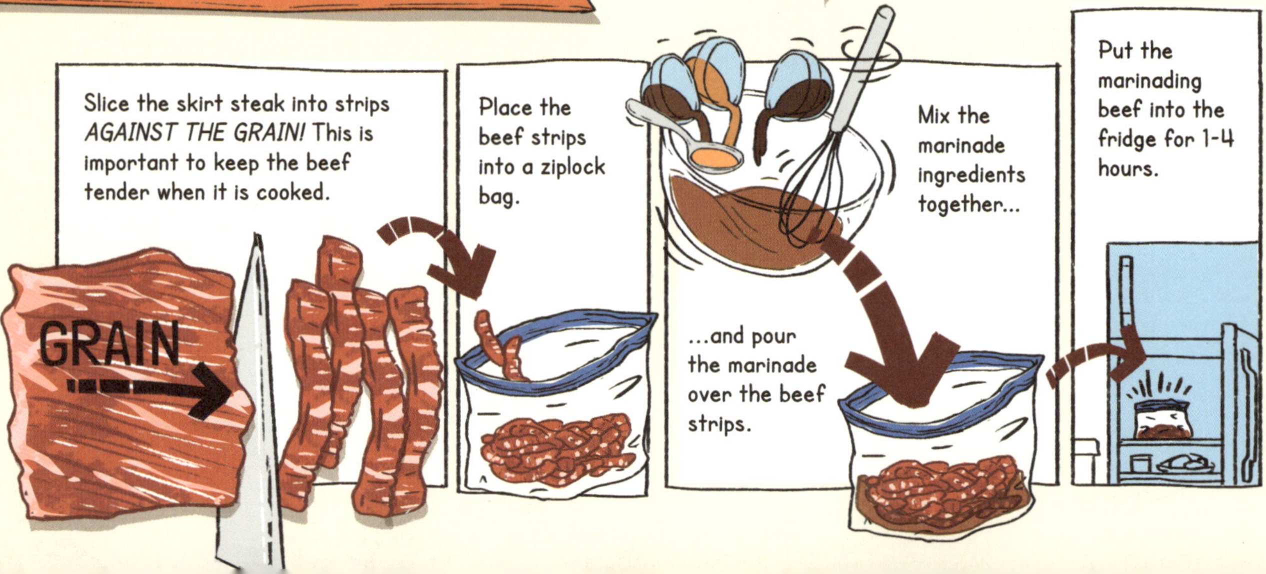
Slice the skirt steak into strips AGAINST THE GRAIN! This is important to keep the beef tender when it is cooked.
GRAIN
Place the beef strips into a ziplock bag.
Mix the marinade ingredients together...
...and pour the marinade over the beef strips.
Put the marinading beef into the fridge for 1-4 hours.

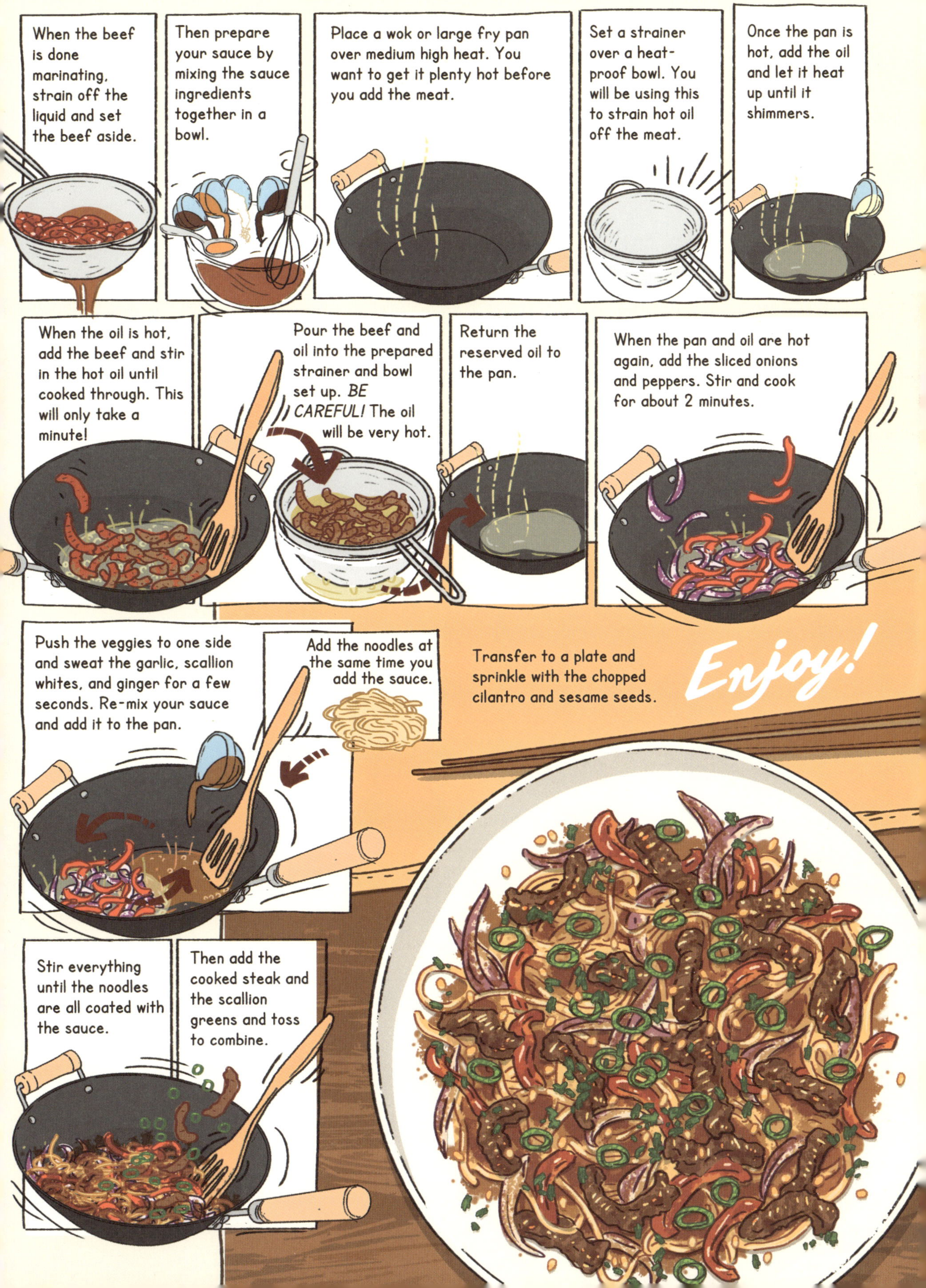
When the beef is done marinating, strain off the liquid and set the beef aside.
Then prepare your sauce by mixing the sauce ingredients together in a bowl.
Place a wok or large fry pan over medium high heat. You want to get it plenty hot before you add the meat.
Set a strainer over a heat-proof bowl. You will be using this to strain hot oil off the meat.
Once the pan is hot, add the oil and let it heat up until it shimmers.
When the oil is hot, add the beef and stir in the hot oil until cooked through. This will only take a minute!
Pour the beef and oil into the prepared strainer and bowl set up. *BE CAREFUL!* The oil will be very hot.
Return the reserved oil to the pan.
When the pan and oil are hot again, add the sliced onions and peppers. Stir and cook for about 2 minutes.
Push the veggies to one side and sweat the garlic, scallion whites, and ginger for a few seconds. Re-mix your sauce and add it to the pan.
Add the noodles at the same time you add the sauce.
Stir everything until the noodles are all coated with the sauce.
Then add the cooked steak and the scallion greens and toss to combine.
Transfer to a plate and sprinkle with the chopped cilantro and sesame seeds.
Enjoy!

Technique 7

GRILLING

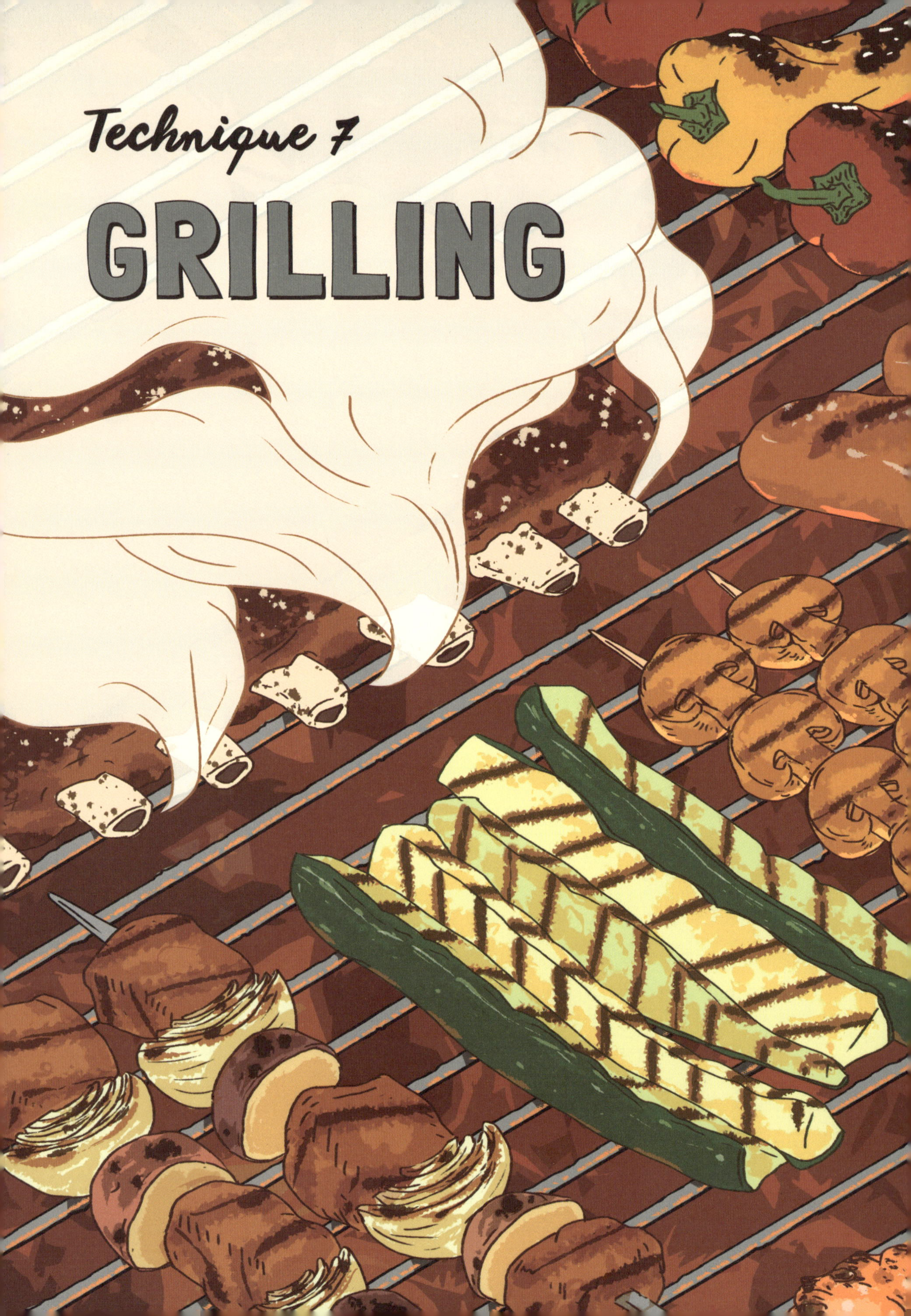

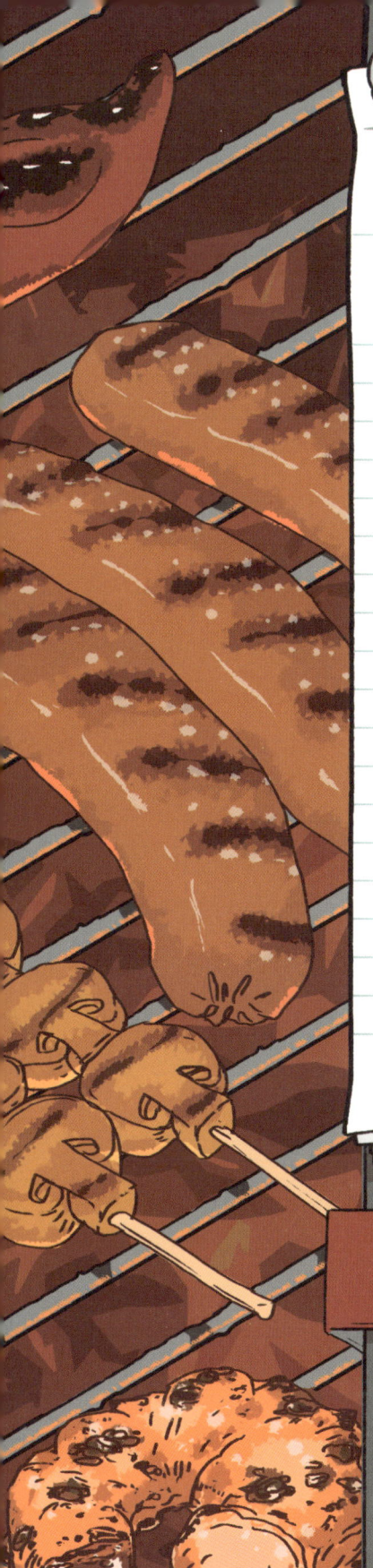

Chef's Note

There is a certain flavor that you can only achieve on the grill. It's that combination of char and smoke and caramelized sugars that you only get from the intense contact heat that a grill provides. Grilling is fast, hot, and normally done on weekends in the summer with a drink in one hand. It's a great way to cook any savory food (not just burgers and hot dogs), but even some sweet foods benefit from a little time on the grill.

Grills get so hot that the grill bars can sear your food in just a few minutes, producing that wonderful charred flavor. Those little burned areas on the food, or "grill marks," are what grilling is all about! While the grill bars sear the food, juices drip down between the bars and splatter on the intense heat source below, instantly turning into a puff of smoke that rises right back up to flavor the food. This combination of char and smoke is what makes the flavor of grilled foods immediately recognizable.

SKILL BADGES

Searing

Marinading

Knife Skills

GRILLING TECHNIQUE

Grilling is **not** the most complicated thing in the world, and you'll do well if you just memorize this short list of do's and don'ts. The recipes in this book assume that you are grilling on a gas or charcoal grill, but don't lose hope if you don't have one! The flavor won't be the exact same, but you can duplicate much of the grilling experience with a stovetop grill pan.

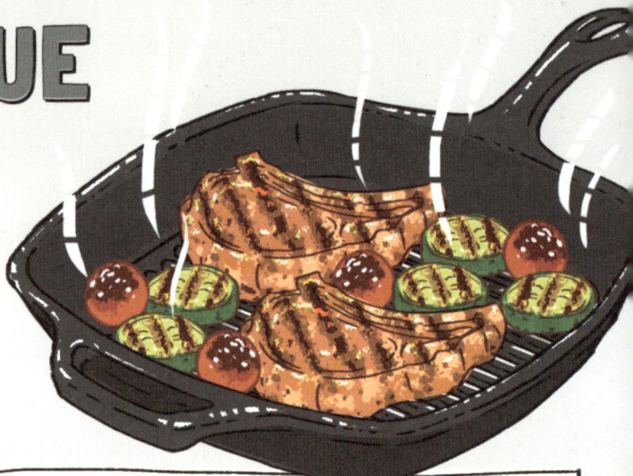

Do's

DO clean the grill bars with a brush or an old food safe towel.

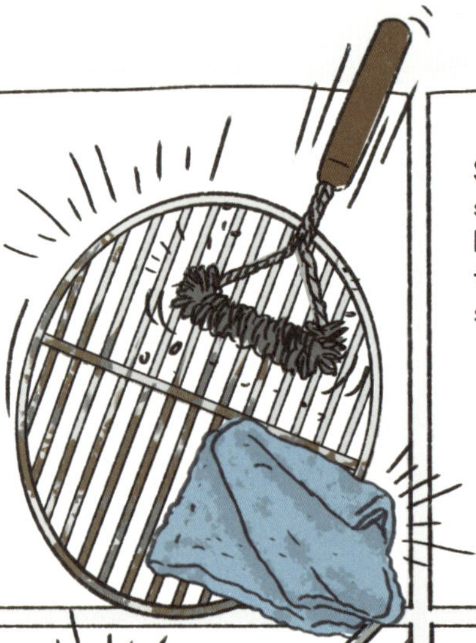

Some foods don't sit well on the grill bars. If the food is too small to grill, skewer it!

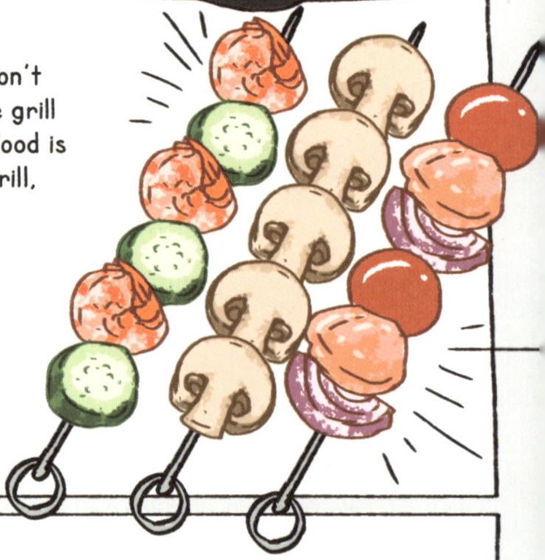

DO use oil! The food will grill best with a thin layer of oil between the bars and the food, so either oil the food, or oil the grill bars.

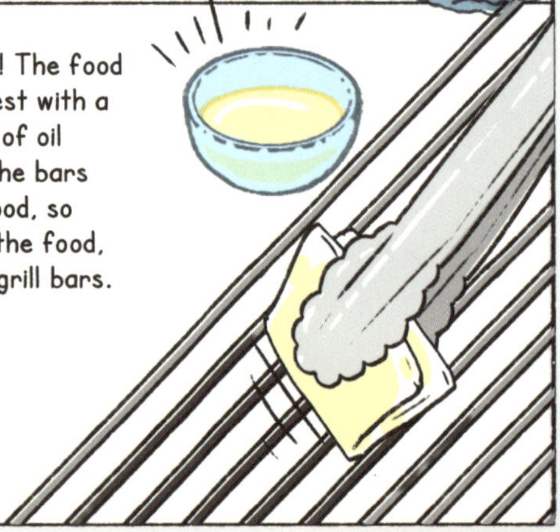

DO get to know your grill. Hold your hand over it to learn where its hot and cold spots are.

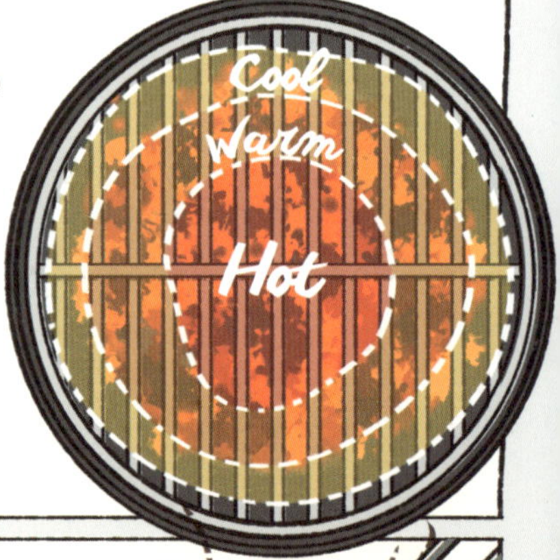
Cool
Warm
Hot

DO let the food get hot and caramelize a little before you start moving it around and checking it. Don't let it burn, but don't move it if you don't have to.

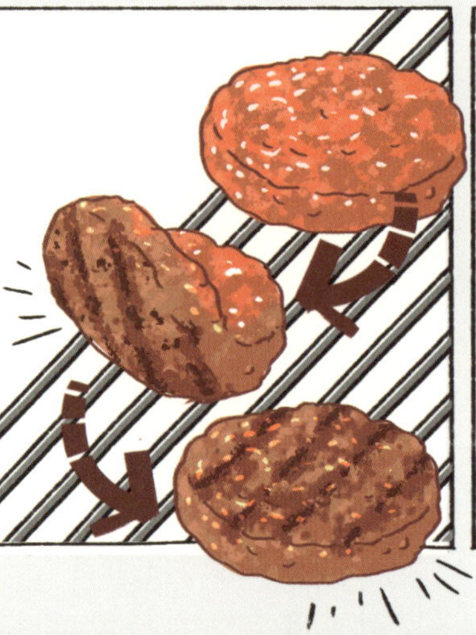

If the flames flare up, *DO* move the food away from them. They are caused by the fat dripping off the food and setting on fire.

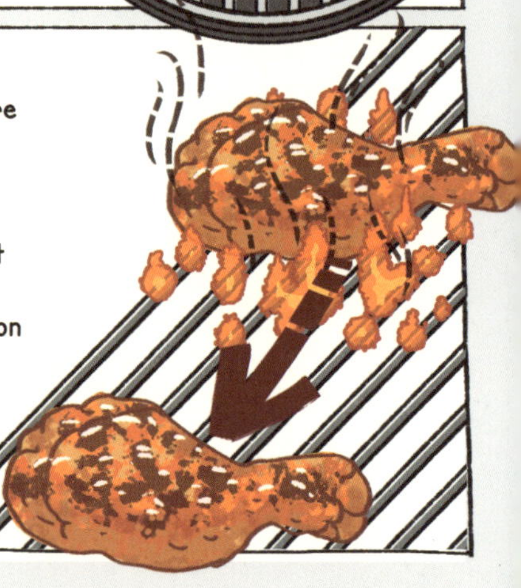

If the food chars too quickly, move it to a cooler area of the grill.

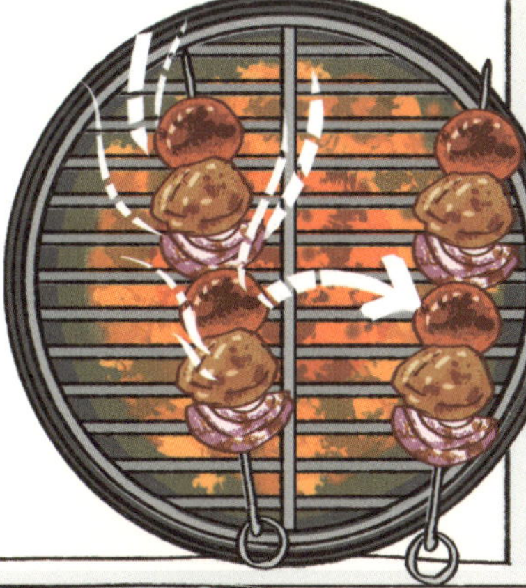

DO make sure you understand the average cooking times that the food will need before you get started.

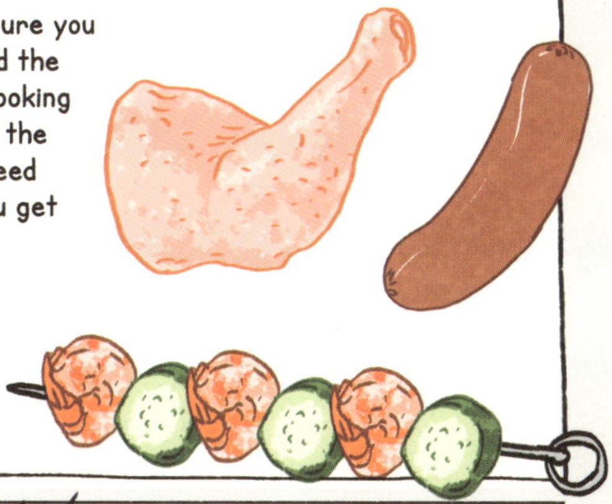

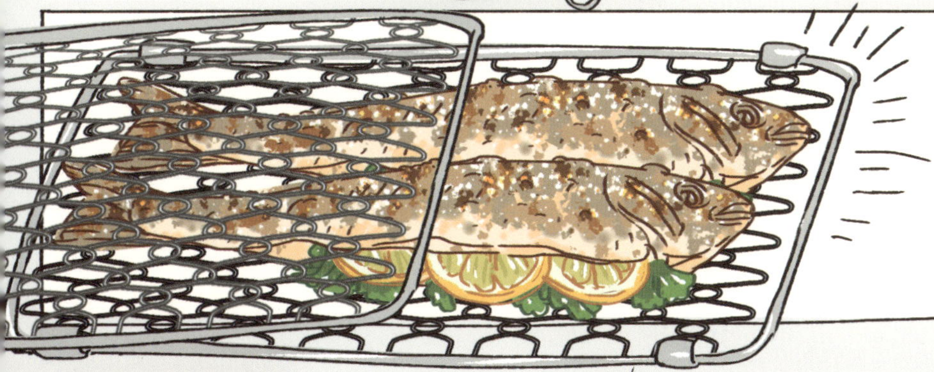

Fish is very delicate. If you want to grill fish, *DO* use a specially-designed grilling basket.

Don'ts

Don't cook on a dirty grill. The old bits of burnt food and oil will stick to your food and make it taste burnt.

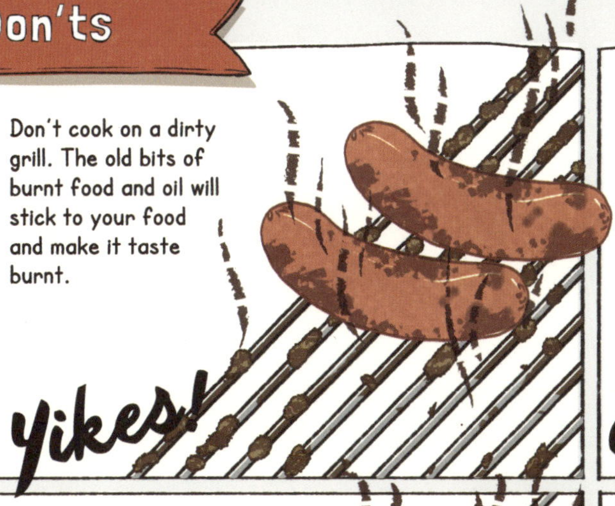
Yikes!

DON'T keep flipping and fiddling your food. Try to only turn the items once.

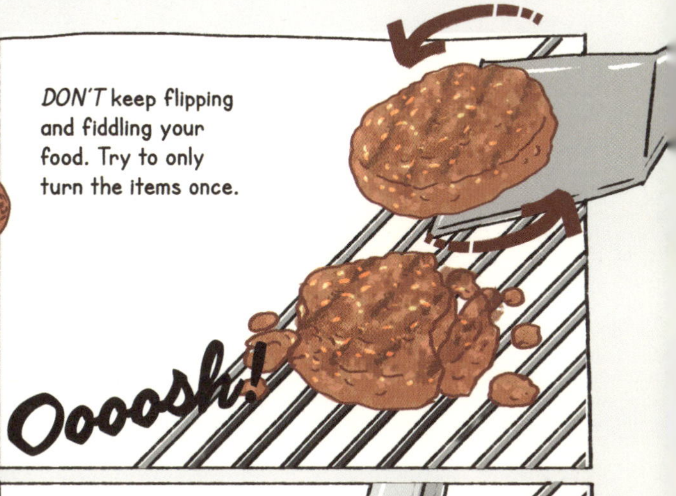
Oooosh!

DON'T let flare ups turn your food into charcoal. Move the food out of direct flames.

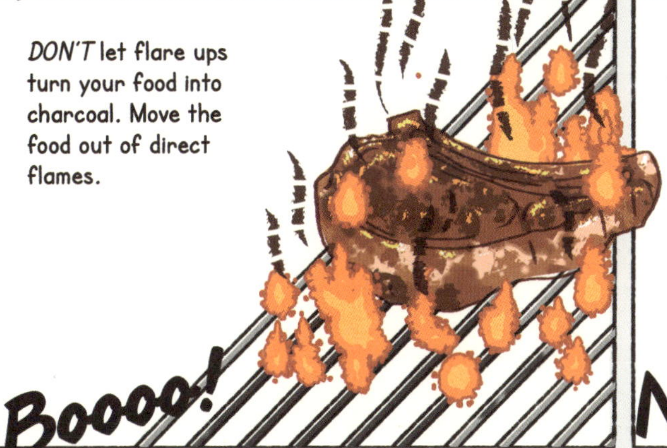
Boooo!

DON'T pull on food that is sticking to the bars. If the food was oiled, then it will release from the bars when it has cooked enough.

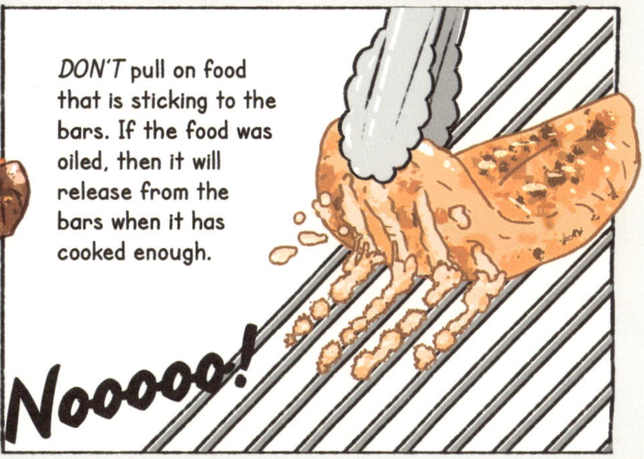
Nooooo!

Recipe 12

Jerk Chicken Thighs with Rice & Cucumber Salad

Jamaican Jerk Chicken is one of the best kinds of **BBQ** there is. **Aromatic** with a solid backbone of **heat**, it turns ordinary chicken thighs into something incredible. You can make it as hot or as mild you want. The cool cucumber salad and rice help cut the heat if the spice is too much.

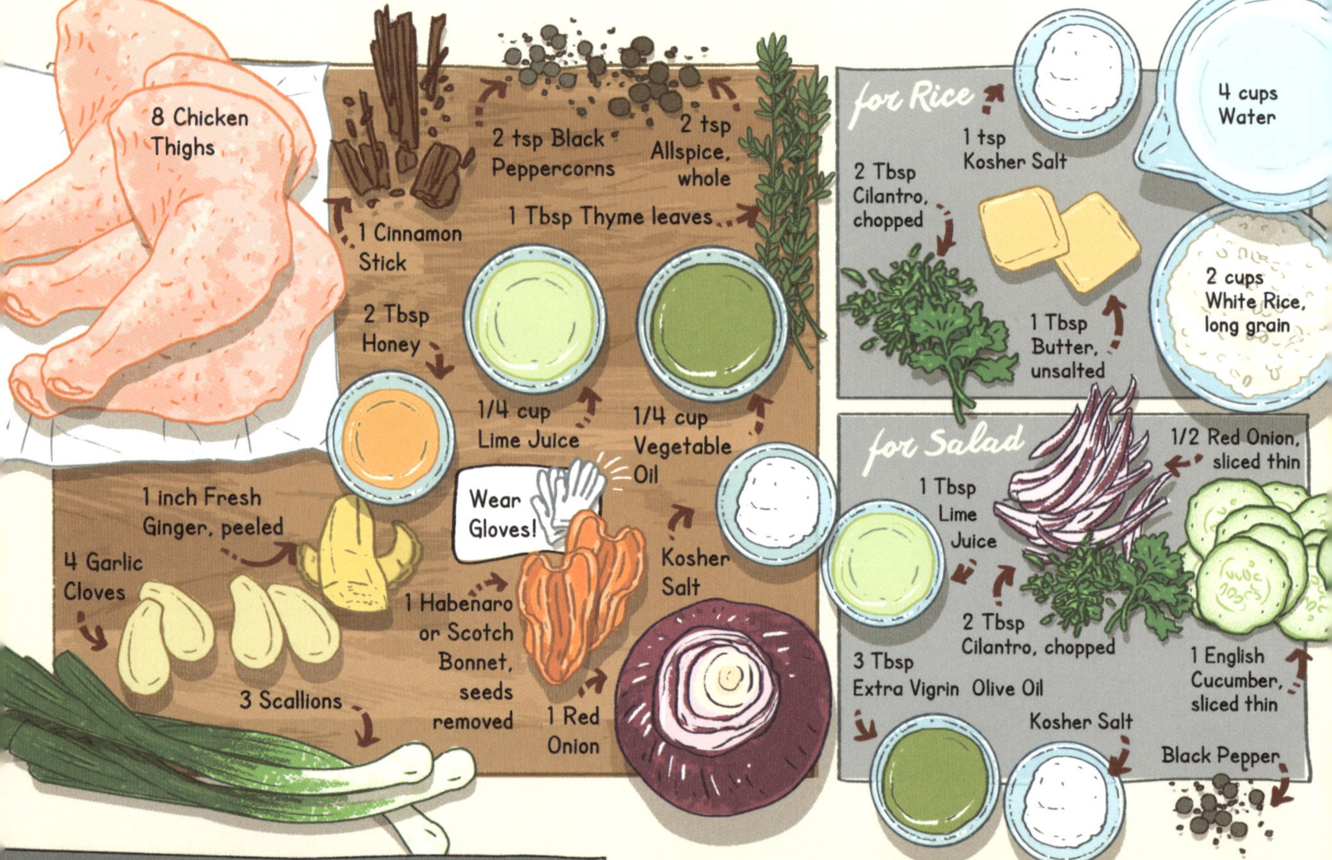

8 Chicken Thighs
1 Cinnamon Stick
2 tsp Black Peppercorns
2 tsp Allspice, whole
1 Tbsp Thyme leaves
2 Tbsp Honey
1/4 cup Lime Juice
1/4 cup Vegetable Oil
Kosher Salt
Wear Gloves!
1 inch Fresh Ginger, peeled
4 Garlic Cloves
1 Habenaro or Scotch Bonnet, seeds removed
3 Scallions
1 Red Onion
for Rice
1 tsp Kosher Salt
4 cups Water
2 Tbsp Cilantro, chopped
1 Tbsp Butter, unsalted
2 cups White Rice, long grain
for Salad
1 Tbsp Lime Juice
1/2 Red Onion, sliced thin
2 Tbsp Cilantro, chopped
3 Tbsp Extra Vigrin Olive Oil
Kosher Salt
1 English Cucumber, sliced thin
Black Pepper

Let's Get Cooking!

for the Rice

Cook the rice. See page 54 for instructions. When the rice is done, fluff with a forkand stir in the cilantro.

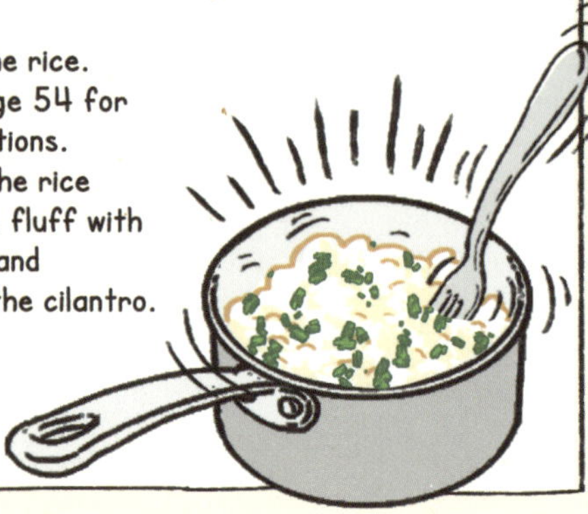

for the Salad

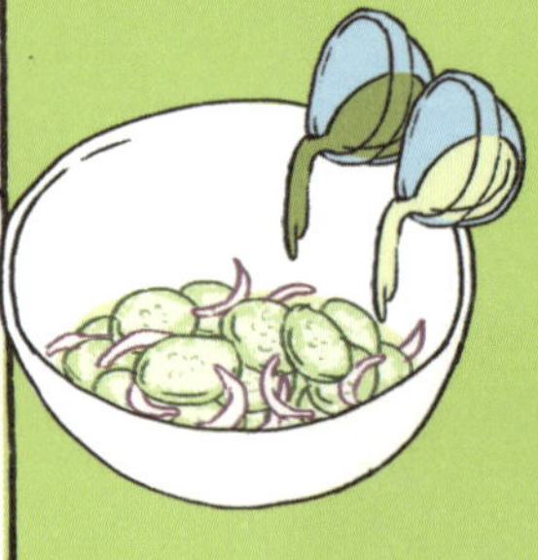

Combine all of the ingredients except for the cilantro in a bowl and mix well.

Season to taste with kosher salt and freshly ground black pepper.

Mix in the cilnatro just before you serve the salad.

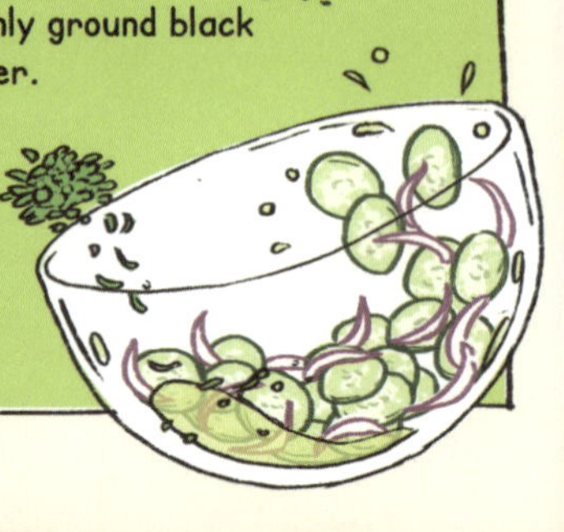

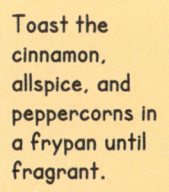
Toast the cinnamon, allspice, and peppercorns in a frypan until fragrant.

Add the spices, onion, garlic, ginger, and habenaro to a food processor and purée until smooth.

Put the chicken thighs in a bag and pour the marinade over it.

Massage the marinade all over the chicken.

Refridgerate for at least 4 hours.

Preheat your grill on *LOW* heat. Aim for 275°F

Remove chicken from marinade and shake off excess.

Season with salt and pepper.

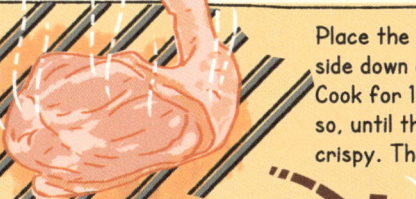
Place the chicken skin side down on the grill. Cook for 10 minutes or so, until the skin is crispy. Then flip.

Move the chicken out of any flames that flare up.

As the chicken cooks, keep an eye on the grill marks. If they are getting too dark, move the chicken to a cooler spot.

Serve with the cilantro rice and cucumber salad.

When the chicken is done, remove to a plate and cover loosely with foil. Let rest for 5 minutes.

More please!

Recipe 13

Sausages with Grilled Vegetables & Peaches

Nothing says **summer** like grilled sausages. Make them more festive and **fresh** with grilled peaches and fennel, a **sweet** and **aromatic** compliment to the rich sausage. If you've never hard grilled fruit it might sound strange, but it's delicious!

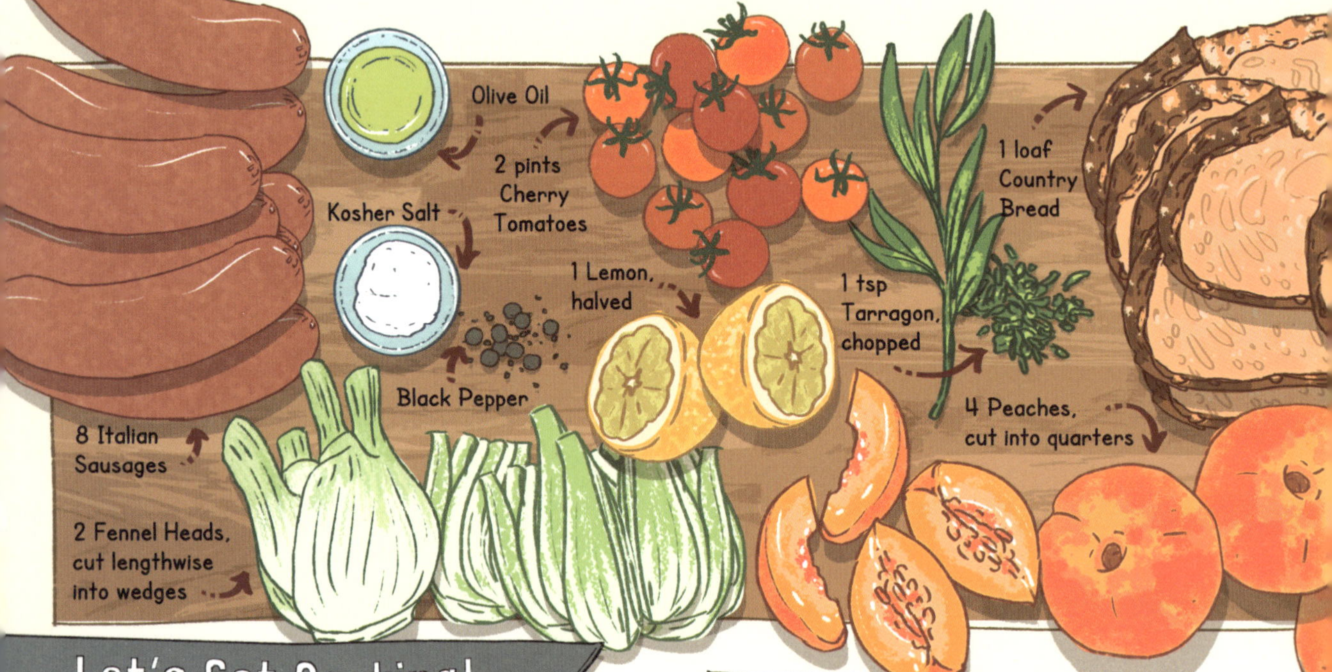
Olive Oil
2 pints Cherry Tomatoes
Kosher Salt
1 Lemon, halved
1 loaf Country Bread
1 tsp Tarragon, chopped
Black Pepper
8 Italian Sausages
4 Peaches, cut into quarters
2 Fennel Heads, cut lengthwise into wedges

Let's Get Cooking!

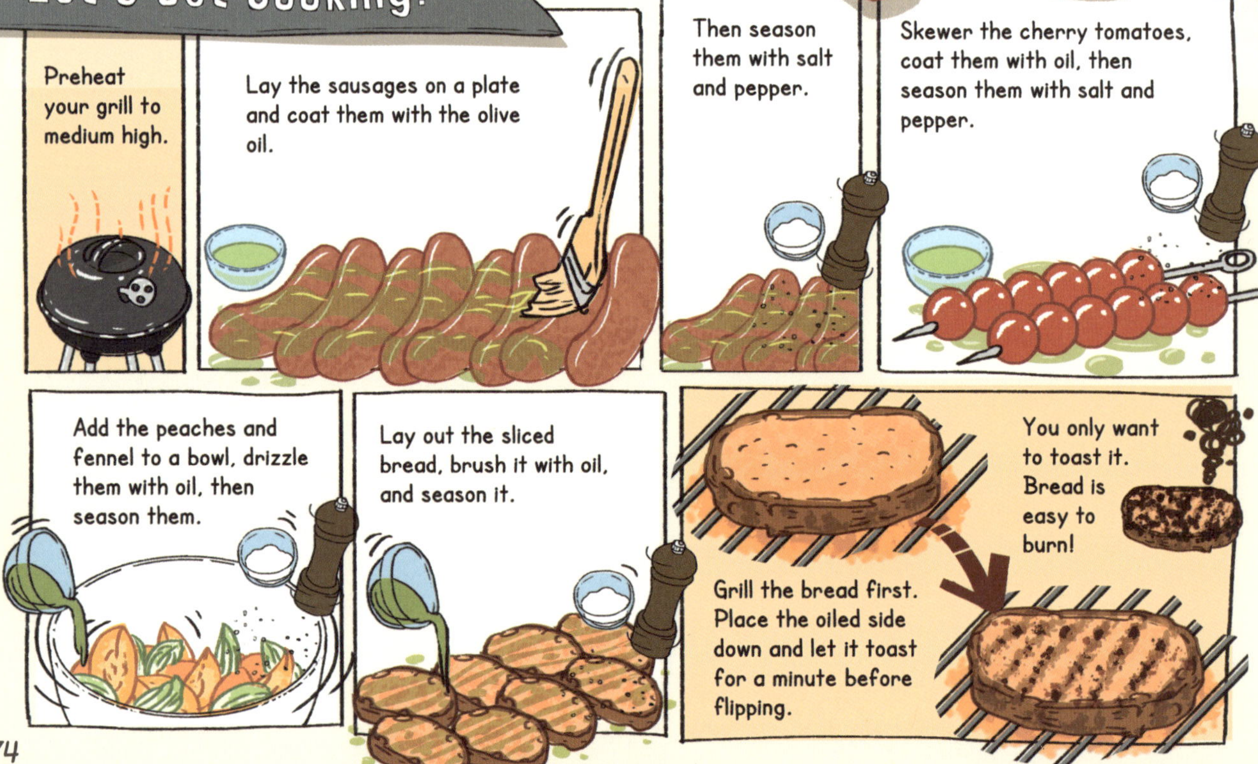
Preheat your grill to medium high.
Lay the sausages on a plate and coat them with the olive oil.
Then season them with salt and pepper.
Skewer the cherry tomatoes, coat them with oil, then season them with salt and pepper.
Add the peaches and fennel to a bowl, drizzle them with oil, then season them.
Lay out the sliced bread, brush it with oil, and season it.
Grill the bread first. Place the oiled side down and let it toast for a minute before flipping.
You only want to toast it. Bread is easy to burn!

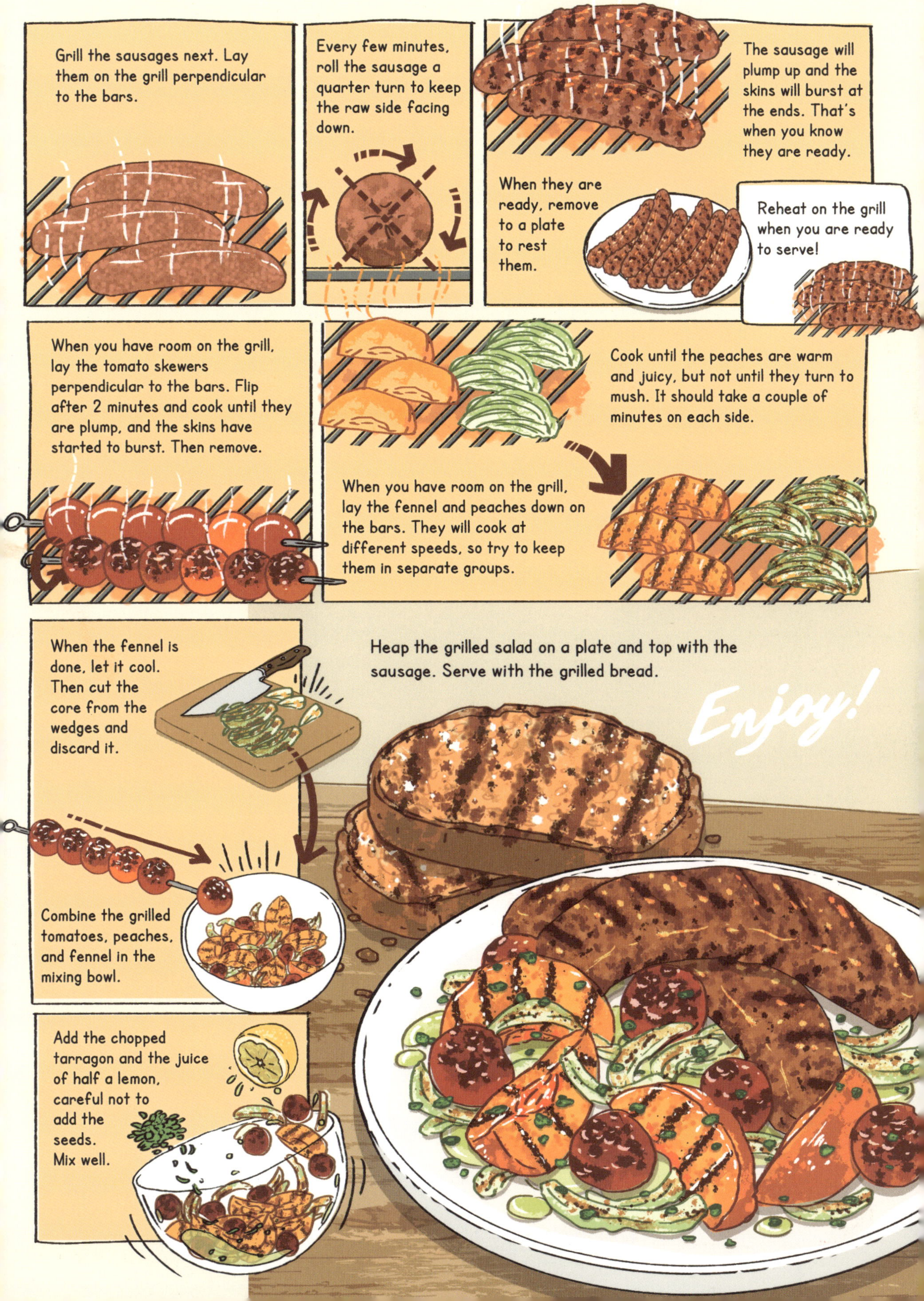
Grill the sausages next. Lay them on the grill perpendicular to the bars.
Every few minutes, roll the sausage a quarter turn to keep the raw side facing down.
The sausage will plump up and the skins will burst at the ends. That's when you know they are ready.
When they are ready, remove to a plate to rest them.
Reheat on the grill when you are ready to serve!
When you have room on the grill, lay the tomato skewers perpendicular to the bars. Flip after 2 minutes and cook until they are plump, and the skins have started to burst. Then remove.
When you have room on the grill, lay the fennel and peaches down on the bars. They will cook at different speeds, so try to keep them in separate groups.
Cook until the peaches are warm and juicy, but not until they turn to mush. It should take a couple of minutes on each side.
When the fennel is done, let it cool. Then cut the core from the wedges and discard it.
Combine the grilled tomatoes, peaches, and fennel in the mixing bowl.
Add the chopped tarragon and the juice of half a lemon, careful not to add the seeds. Mix well.
Heap the grilled salad on a plate and top with the sausage. Serve with the grilled bread.
Enjoy!

Technique 8

ROASTING

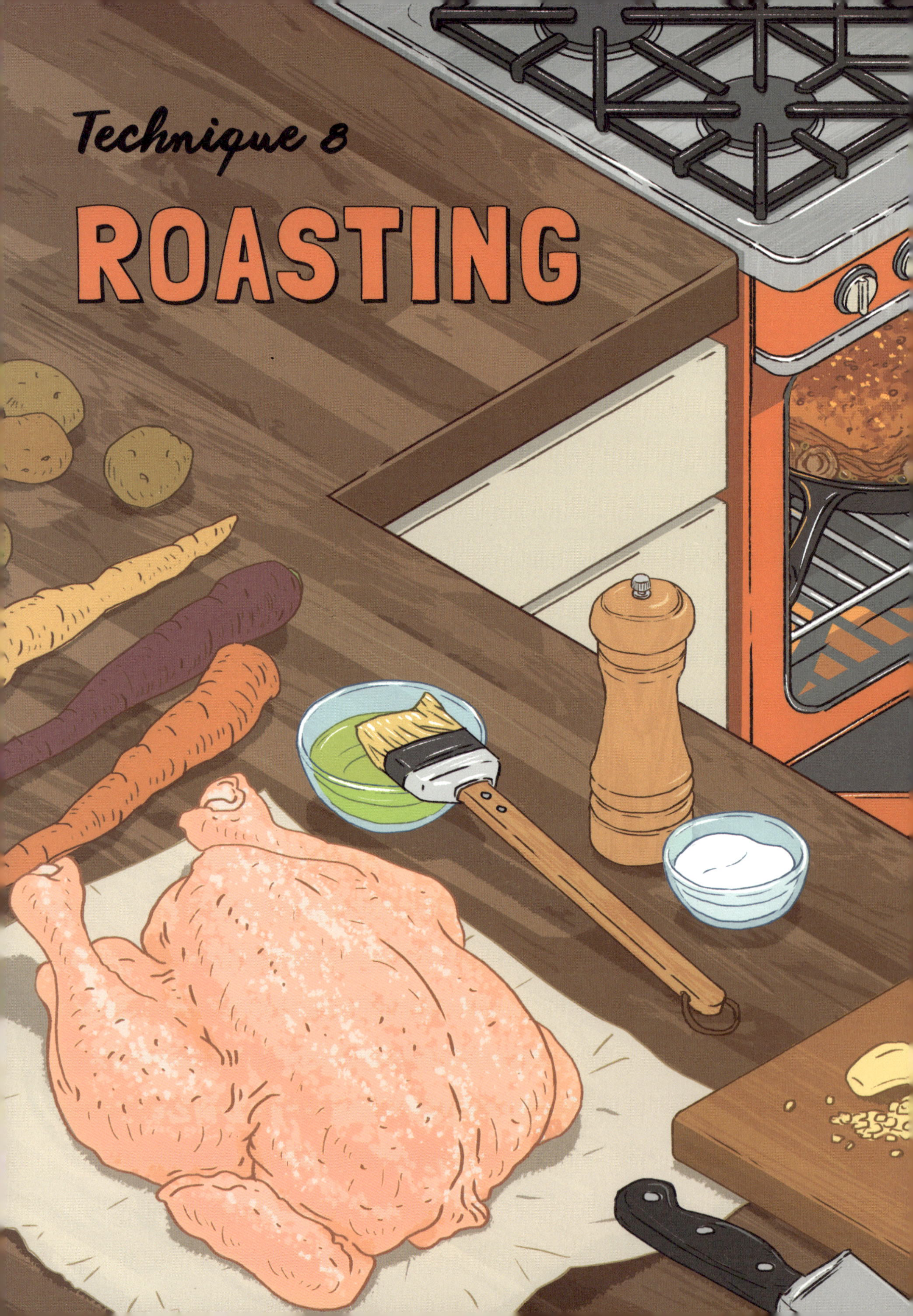

Chef's Note

Roasting uses your oven to cook food with "dry heat", which basically just means the food is surrounded by hot air and no liquid is involved. Roasting is great because once the food is in the oven, there isn't very much that the cook has to do!

Granted, making a good roast requires a little forethought, planning, and a solid understanding your oven (they all have quirks). Considering how delicious a good roast can be, those are pretty minor investments! There's another great thing about roasting—often your sides can be cooked right in the same pan as the main dish, and all at the same time. Once again, roasting minimizes your active time in the kitchen. Furthermore, if you have a lot of people over for dinner, the roasting can be done ahead of time. When everyone arrives, just reheat in a hot oven and you are ready to go.

SKILL BADGES

Knife Skills

Oven Skills

Reduction

ROASTING TECHNIQUE

When roasting, the food in the oven is surrounded on all sides by **very hot, very dry** air. This quickly cooks the outside of the meat, and as the hot air continues to surround the meat, the carbohydrates in the meat start to turn brown and take on a deep, roasted sweetness. This is called **caramelization**. Throughout this process, the dry heat slowly moves into the interior othe meat, pulling out excess water as the food cooks. This process concentrates the flavors already in your food. Timing is key here! You want to pull the food from the oven when its flavors are concentrated, but **NOT** dried out. Because of this process, a roast chicken will taste more "chickeny" than a boiled or braised chicken. How far you carry this process depends on the type of meat being cooked. Roast beef, for example, is best when the interior is still pink (medium rare or rare). On the other hand, you should never eat a pink chicken. When in doubt, use a thermometer to check!

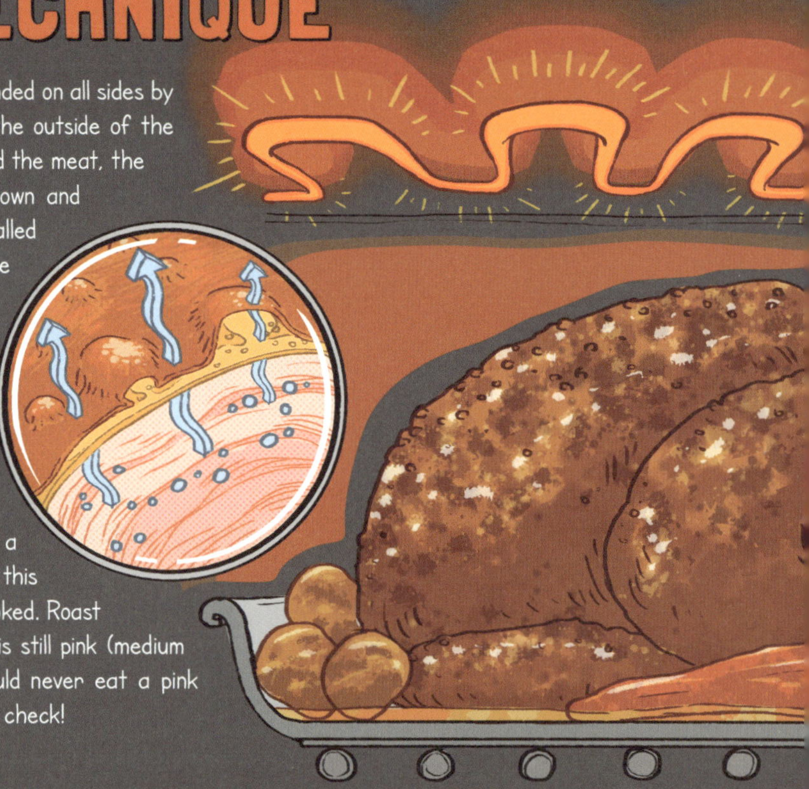

Getting the oven temperature right is important!

Getting a perfectly cooked **crust** and a moist interior depends on the temperature of your oven. If the oven is set too **low**, then the crust will never form, and by the time the interior is cooked the outside will be dry. You need to watch out for the other extreme too. If the oven is too **hot**, then the outside will burn and your interior will be raw! The ideal temperature depends on what you are trying to cook, but the basics are pretty easy to grasp. Some foods really benefit from roasting at a higher temperature than you might normally think. For example, when I roast a chicken, I crank my oven to at least 450, which yields a crispy-skinned, moist chicken in about an hour.

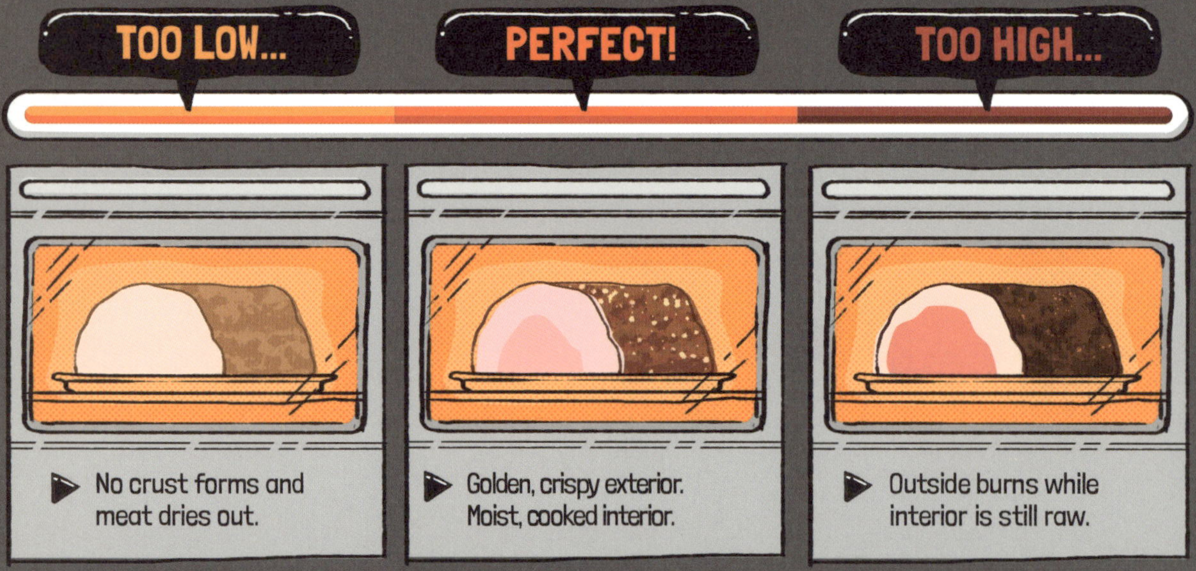
TOO LOW...
PERFECT!
TOO HIGH...
No crust forms and meat dries out.
Golden, crispy exterior. Moist, cooked interior.
Outside burns while interior is still raw.

Basic Technique

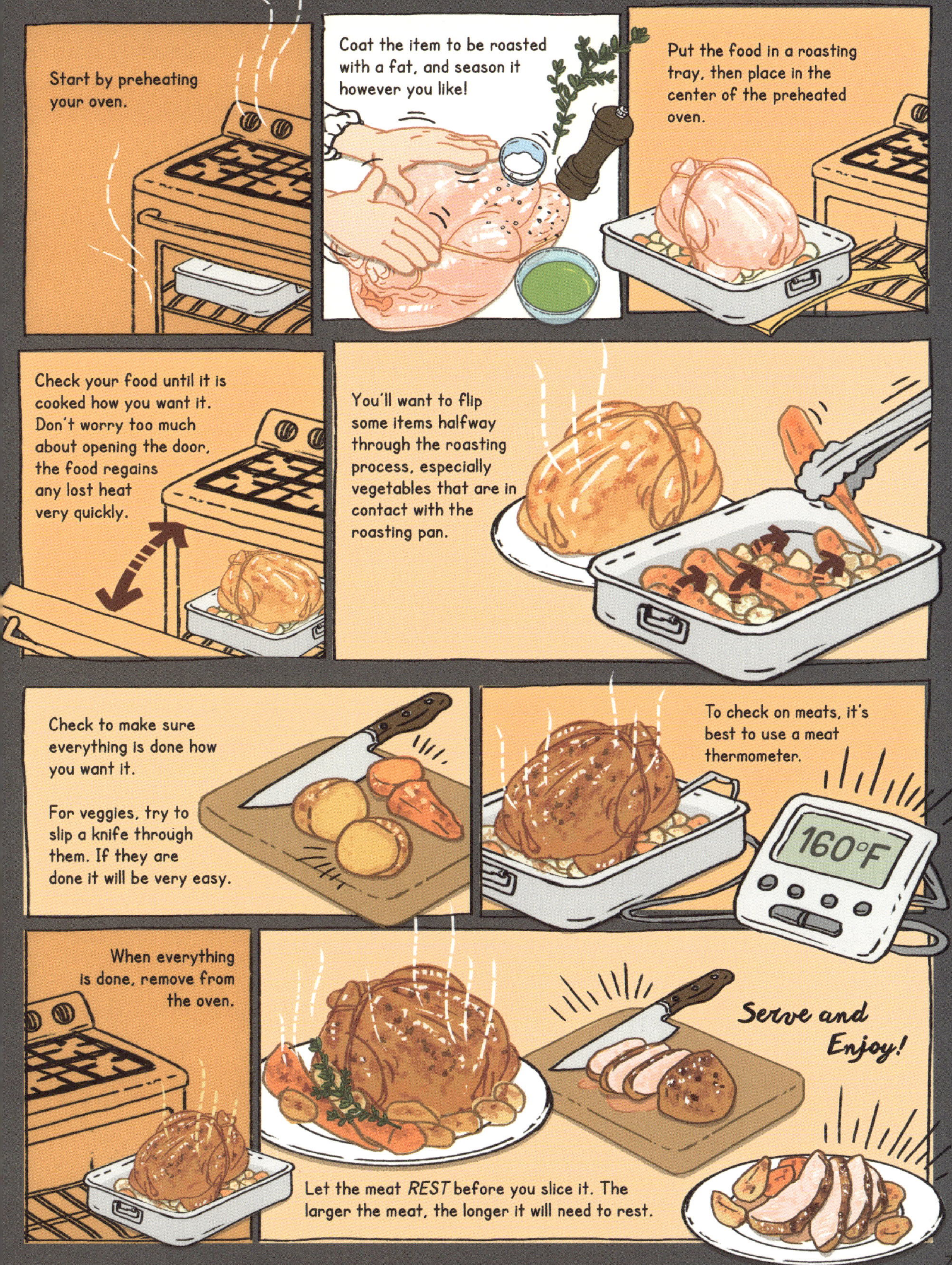

Start by preheating your oven.
Coat the item to be roasted with a fat, and season it however you like!
Put the food in a roasting tray, then place in the center of the preheated oven.
Check your food until it is cooked how you want it. Don't worry too much about opening the door, the food regains any lost heat very quickly.
You'll want to flip some items halfway through the roasting process, especially vegetables that are in contact with the roasting pan.
Check to make sure everything is done how you want it.
For veggies, try to slip a knife through them. If they are done it will be very easy.
To check on meats, it's best to use a meat thermometer.
160°F
When everything is done, remove from the oven.
Let the meat *REST* before you slice it. The larger the meat, the longer it will need to rest.
Serve and Enjoy!

Recipe 14

Roasted pork belly with Cabbage & whole grain mustard jus and pickled vegetables

Few cuts of meat can match the venerable pork belly when it comes to texture and flavor. In this recipe, we glaze the belly with brown sugar, which turns into **crispy caramel** through the roasting process. The pickles help cut through the **richness** of the belly, which balances the dish.

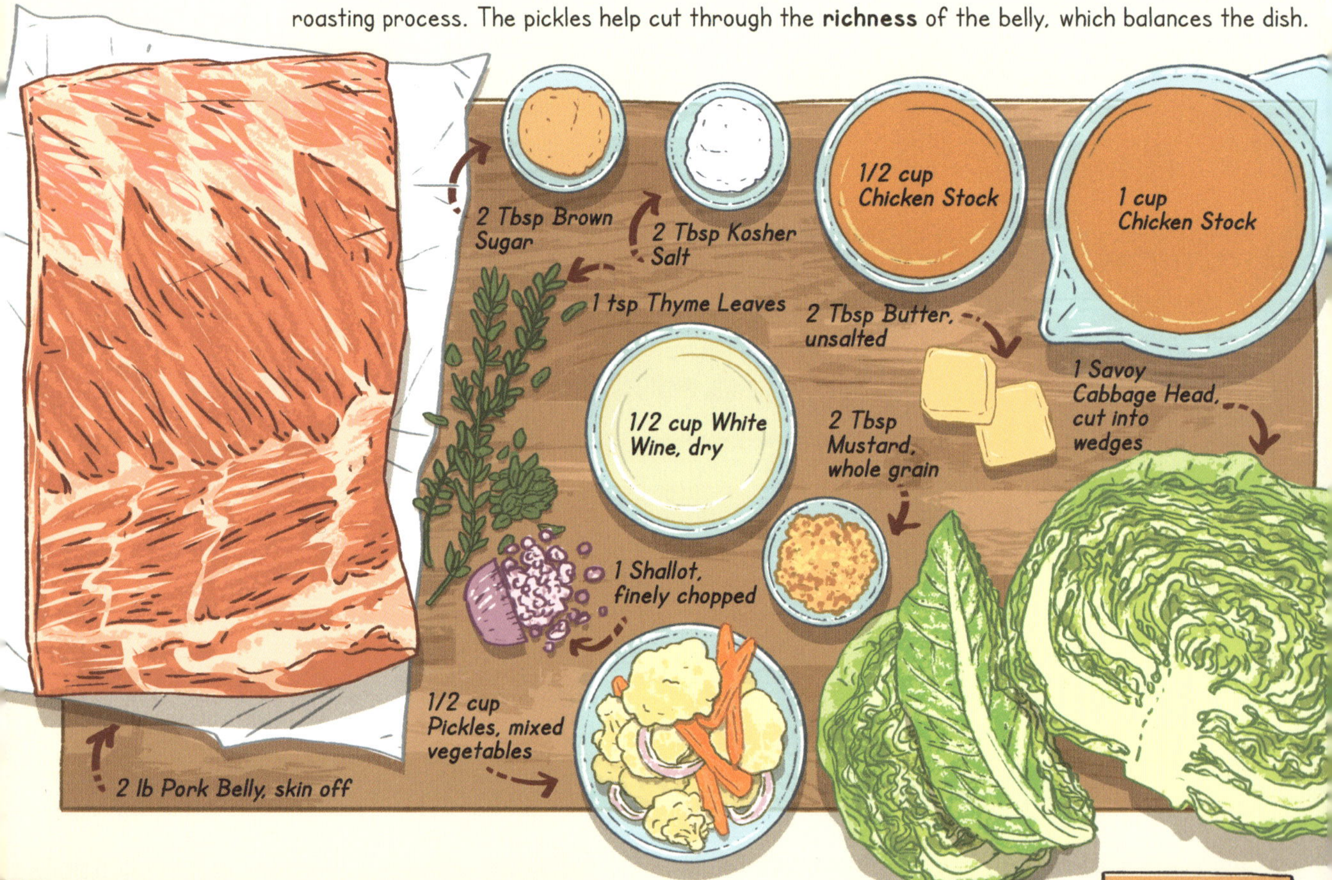

2 Tbsp Brown Sugar
2 Tbsp Kosher Salt
1/2 cup Chicken Stock
1 cup Chicken Stock
1 tsp Thyme Leaves
2 Tbsp Butter, unsalted
1/2 cup White Wine, dry
2 Tbsp Mustard, whole grain
1 Savoy Cabbage Head, cut into wedges
1 Shallot, finely chopped
1/2 cup Pickles, mixed vegetables
2 lb Pork Belly, skin off

Let's Get Cooking!

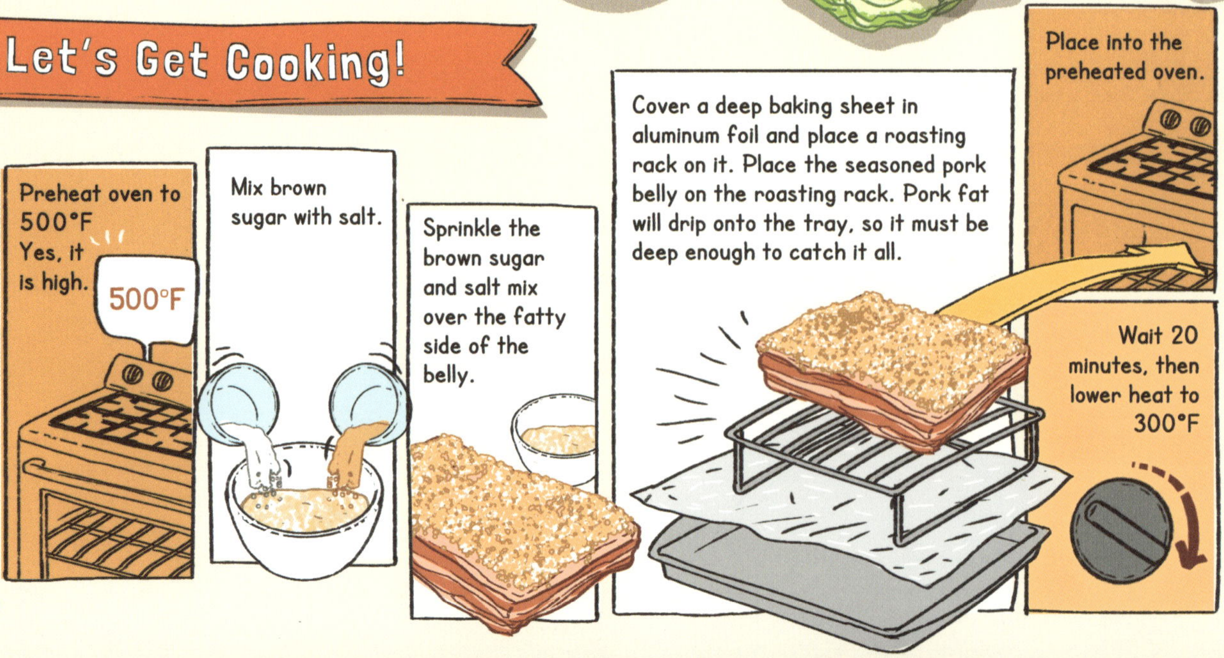

Preheat oven to 500°F Yes, it is high.
500°F
Mix brown sugar with salt.
Sprinkle the brown sugar and salt mix over the fatty side of the belly.
Cover a deep baking sheet in aluminum foil and place a roasting rack on it. Place the seasoned pork belly on the roasting rack. Pork fat will drip onto the tray, so it must be deep enough to catch it all.
Place into the preheated oven.
Wait 20 minutes, then lower heat to 300°F

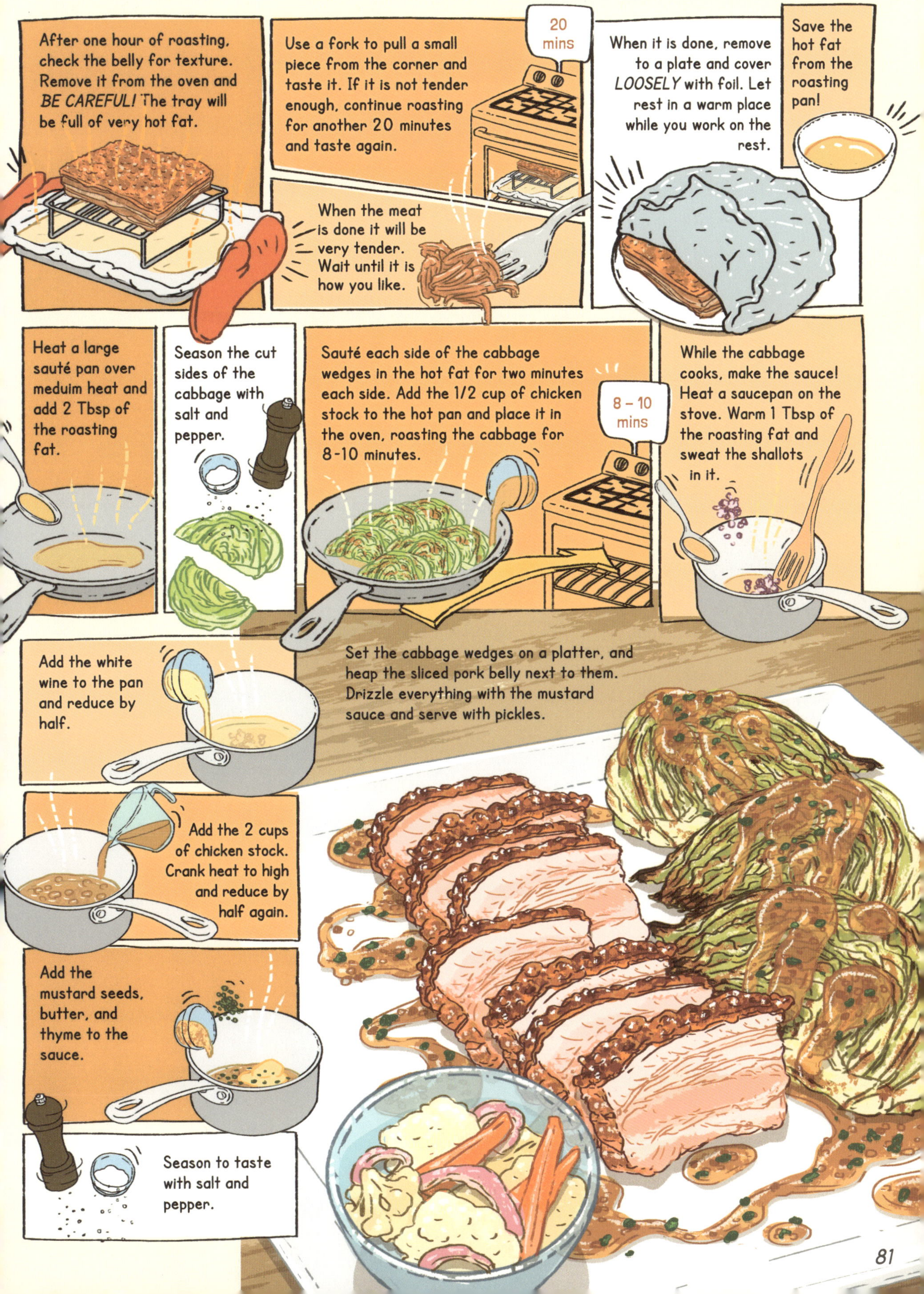
After one hour of roasting, check the belly for texture. Remove it from the oven and *BE CAREFUL!* The tray will be full of very hot fat.
Use a fork to pull a small piece from the corner and taste it. If it is not tender enough, continue roasting for another 20 minutes and taste again.
20 mins
When the meat is done it will be very tender. Wait until it is how you like.
When it is done, remove to a plate and cover *LOOSELY* with foil. Let rest in a warm place while you work on the rest.
Save the hot fat from the roasting pan!
Heat a large sauté pan over meduim heat and add 2 Tbsp of the roasting fat.
Season the cut sides of the cabbage with salt and pepper.
Sauté each side of the cabbage wedges in the hot fat for two minutes each side. Add the 1/2 cup of chicken stock to the hot pan and place it in the oven, roasting the cabbage for 8-10 minutes.
8 – 10 mins
While the cabbage cooks, make the sauce! Heat a saucepan on the stove. Warm 1 Tbsp of the roasting fat and sweat the shallots in it.
Add the white wine to the pan and reduce by half.
Add the 2 cups of chicken stock. Crank heat to high and reduce by half again.
Add the mustard seeds, butter, and thyme to the sauce.
Season to taste with salt and pepper.
Set the cabbage wedges on a platter, and heap the sliced pork belly next to them. Drizzle everything with the mustard sauce and serve with pickles.

Recipe 15

Roasted chicken with root vegetables & Pan Gravy

Roast chicken is as **traditional** and declicious as it gets. Few meals are so **simple**, delicious, and easy. The cipollini onions and parsnips add a **roasted sweetness**, and the simple pan gravy ties it all together.

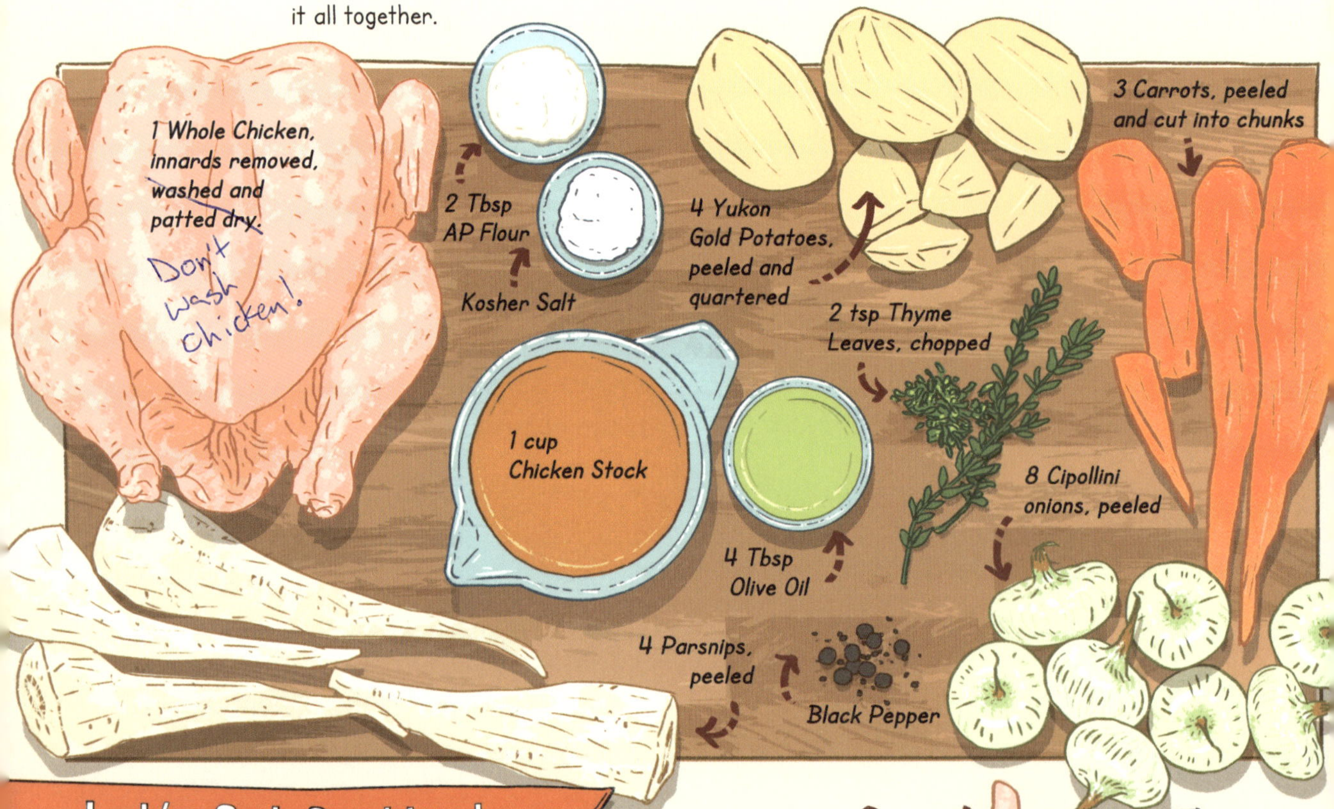
1 Whole Chicken, innards removed, ~~washed and patted dry.~~
Don't wash chicken!
2 Tbsp AP Flour
Kosher Salt
4 Yukon Gold Potatoes, peeled and quartered
3 Carrots, peeled and cut into chunks
2 tsp Thyme Leaves, chopped
1 cup Chicken Stock
4 Tbsp Olive Oil
8 Cipollini onions, peeled
4 Parsnips, peeled
Black Pepper

Let's Get Cooking!

Extra Equipment Needed	Roasting pan, Baking sheet, or Dutch Oven Butcher's twine Digital Meat Thermometer

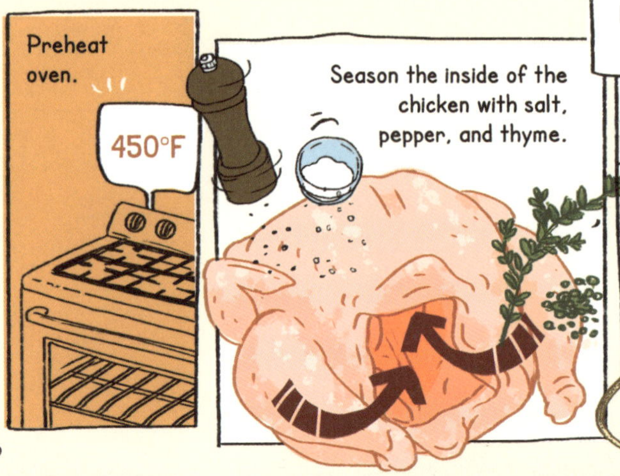
Preheat oven.
450°F
Season the inside of the chicken with salt, pepper, and thyme.

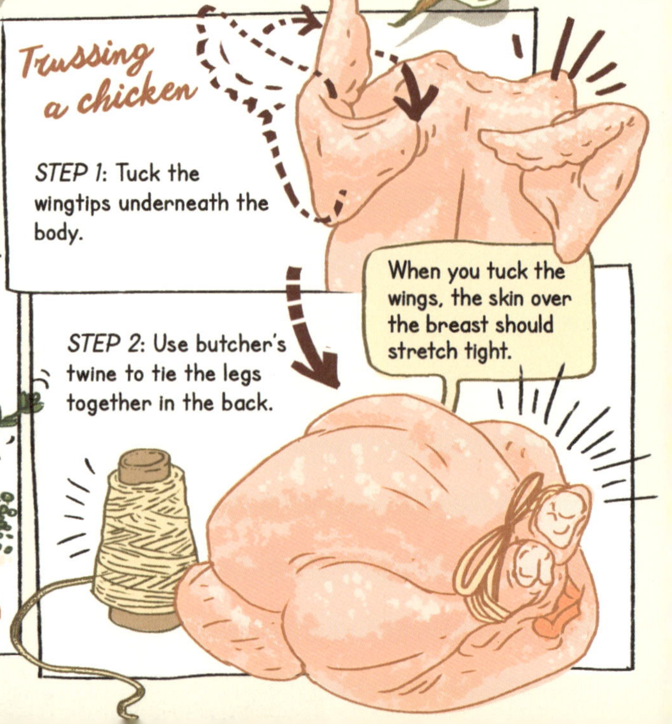
Trussing a chicken
STEP 1: Tuck the wingtips underneath the body.
STEP 2: Use butcher's twine to tie the legs together in the back.
When you tuck the wings, the skin over the breast should stretch tight.

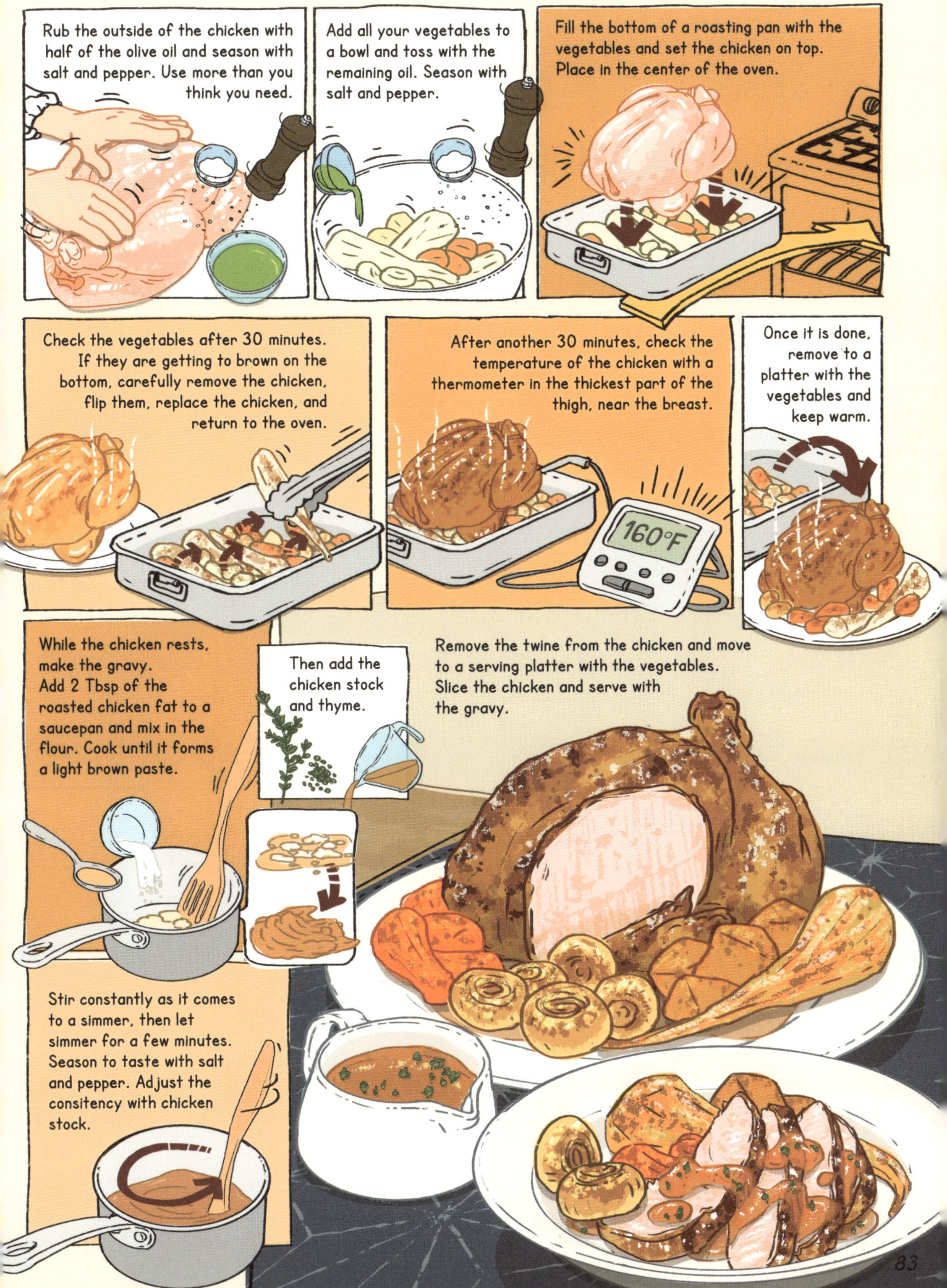
Rub the outside of the chicken with half of the olive oil and season with salt and pepper. Use more than you think you need.
Add all your vegetables to a bowl and toss with the remaining oil. Season with salt and pepper.
Fill the bottom of a roasting pan with the vegetables and set the chicken on top. Place in the center of the oven.
Check the vegetables after 30 minutes. If they are getting to brown on the bottom, carefully remove the chicken, flip them, replace the chicken, and return to the oven.
After another 30 minutes, check the temperature of the chicken with a thermometer in the thickest part of the thigh, near the breast.
160°F
Once it is done, remove to a platter with the vegetables and keep warm.
While the chicken rests, make the gravy. Add 2 Tbsp of the roasted chicken fat to a saucepan and mix in the flour. Cook until it forms a light brown paste.
Then add the chicken stock and thyme.
Remove the twine from the chicken and move to a serving platter with the vegetables. Slice the chicken and serve with the gravy.
Stir constantly as it comes to a simmer, then let simmer for a few minutes. Season to taste with salt and pepper. Adjust the consitency with chicken stock.

Technique 9

FRYING

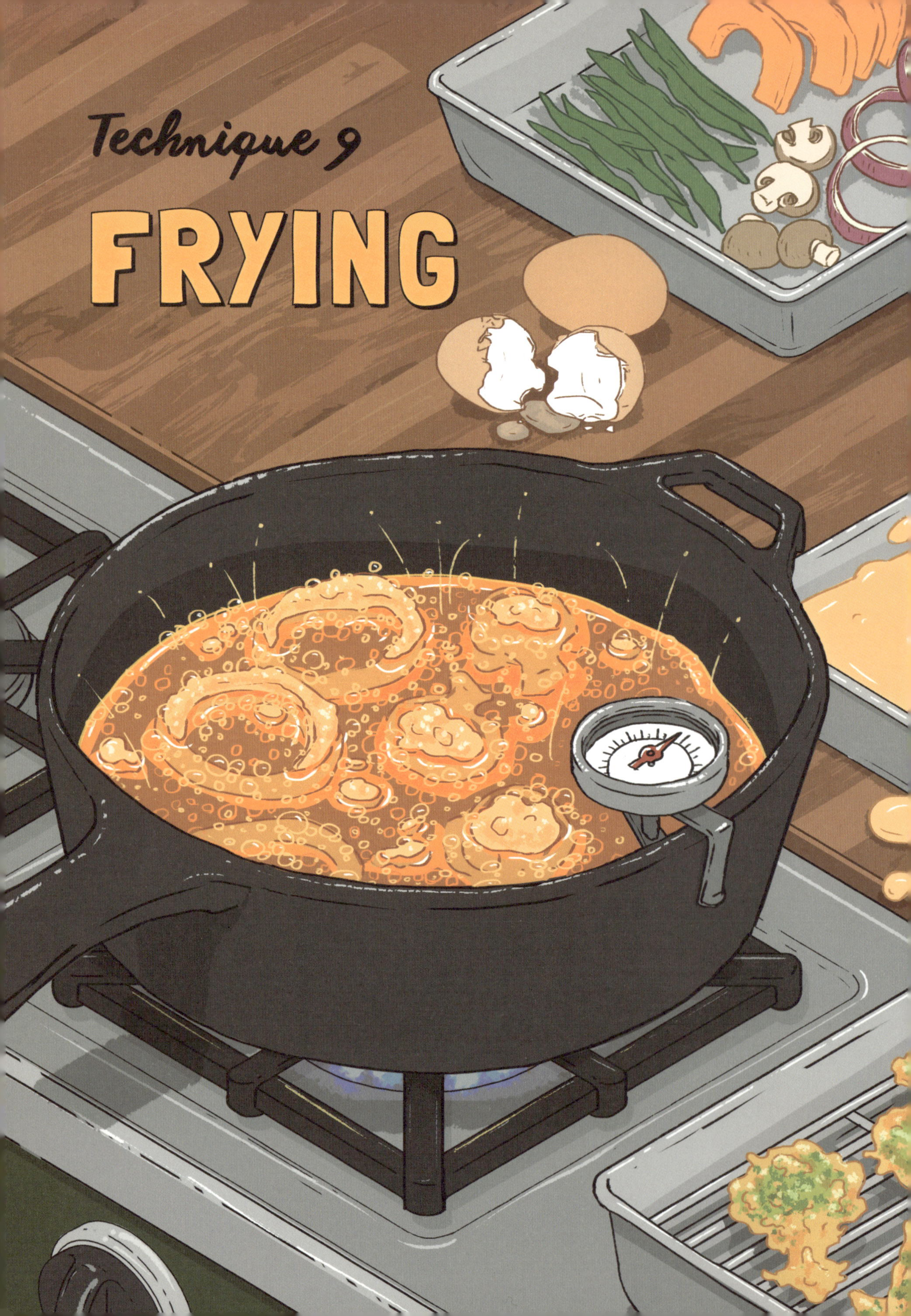

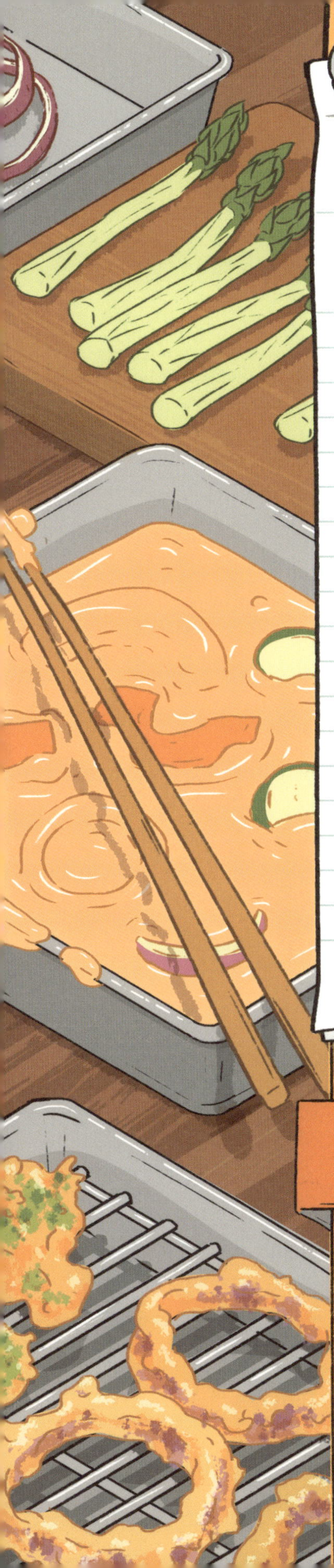

Chef's Note

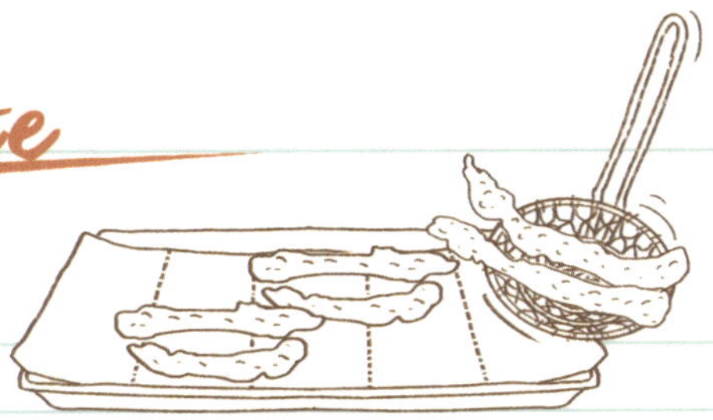

EVERYONE loves fried food. Pretty much every culture in the world incorporates some kind of fried food in their cuisine. It's the unique, wonderful, crunchy texture of fried foods that we love. Plus, cooking the food in fat insures that it packs a ton of flavor into every bite.

The first thing that comes to mind might be french fries, or fried chicken. But there is so much more to frying than that! Donuts are fried. Croutons are fried. And what about hush puppies? Or even rice crispies? Fancy restraunts even garnish dishes with fried herbs, which lend a little crunch along with their aromas.

Frying doesn't have to be a pain. If you stay organized and have a plan, your fried foods will come out great!

SKILL BADGES

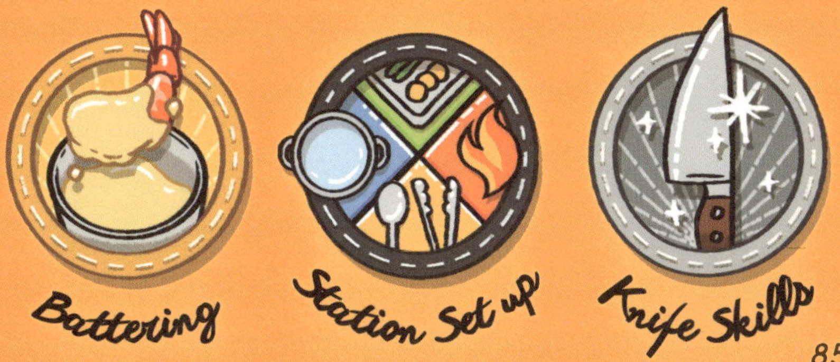
Battering
Station Set up
Knife Skills

Equipment Necessary

- Heavy bottomed pot with high sides
- Spider
- Counter top fryer
- Paper towels
- Thermometer

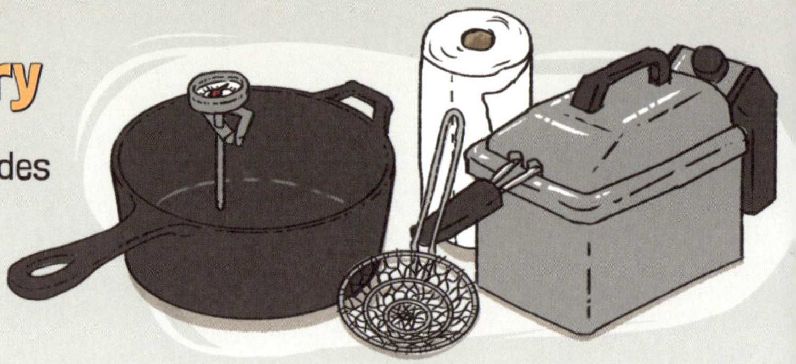

Fats to Fry in

The best fats to use for frying are those with a high smoke point. That means that they can be heated to very high temperatures without burning.

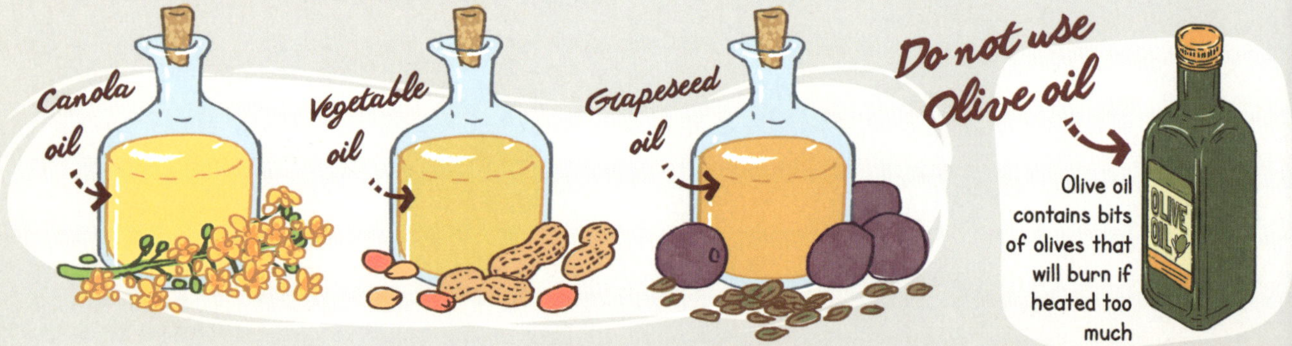

Canola oil
Vegetable oil
Grapeseed oil
Do not use Olive oil
Olive oil contains bits of olives that will burn if heated too much
OLIVE OIL

Basic Method

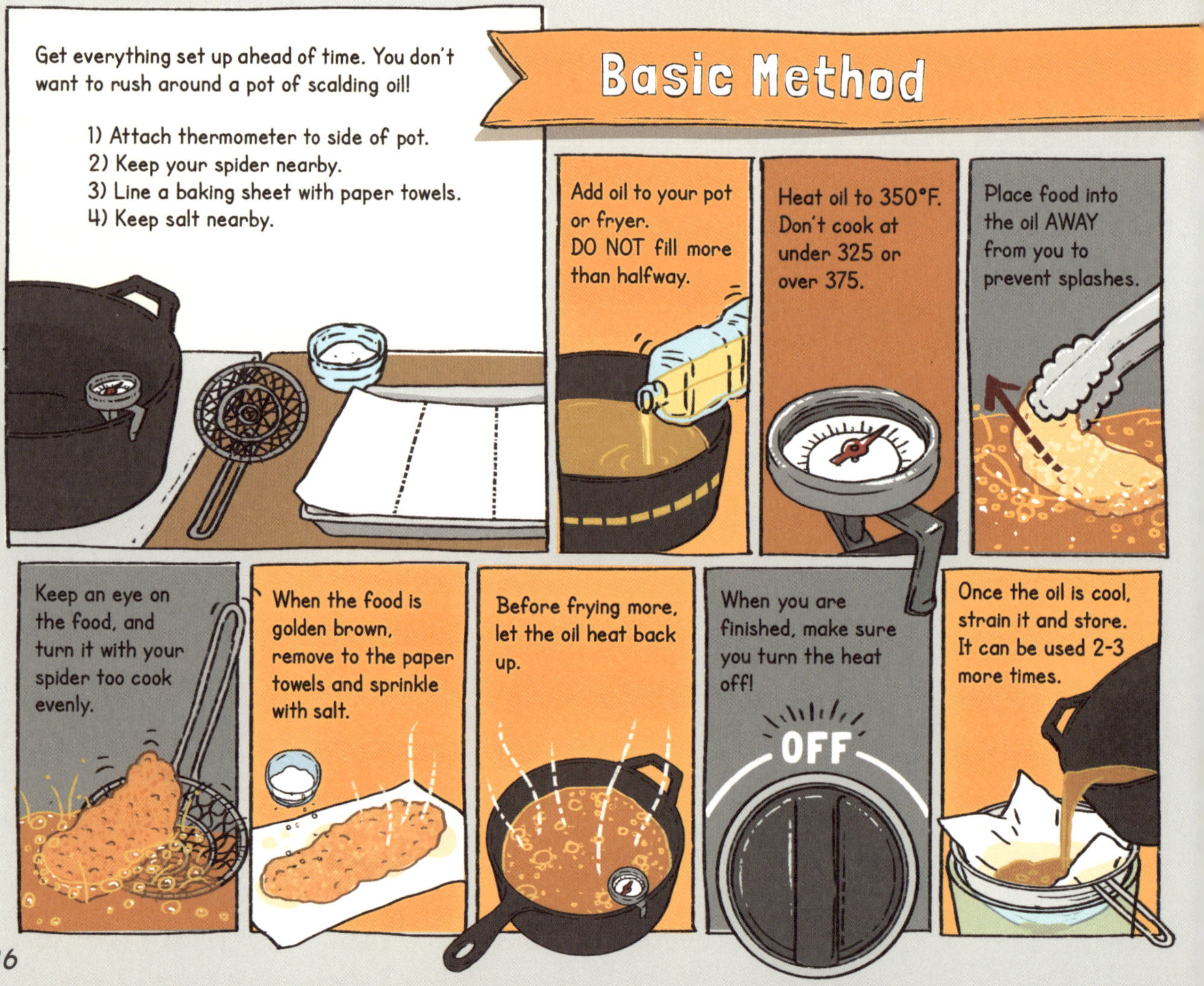

Get everything set up ahead of time. You don't want to rush around a pot of scalding oil!
1) Attach thermometer to side of pot.
2) Keep your spider nearby.
3) Line a baking sheet with paper towels.
4) Keep salt nearby.
Add oil to your pot or fryer.
DO NOT fill more than halfway.
Heat oil to 350°F. Don't cook at under 325 or over 375.
Place food into the oil AWAY from you to prevent splashes.
Keep an eye on the food, and turn it with your spider too cook evenly.
When the food is golden brown, remove to the paper towels and sprinkle with salt.
Before frying more, let the oil heat back up.
When you are finished, make sure you turn the heat off!
OFF
Once the oil is cool, strain it and store. It can be used 2-3 more times.

Battering and Frying

Many fried foods are battered or breaded before they are fried, which means they are dipped in a liquid before they are cooked. Keeping everything organized can be tricky, but is key to success.

Battering ingredients:

- Flour
- Eggs
- Something for the crust, like panko, bread crumbs, corn meal, semolina flour, etc.
- Kosher salt
- Black Pepper

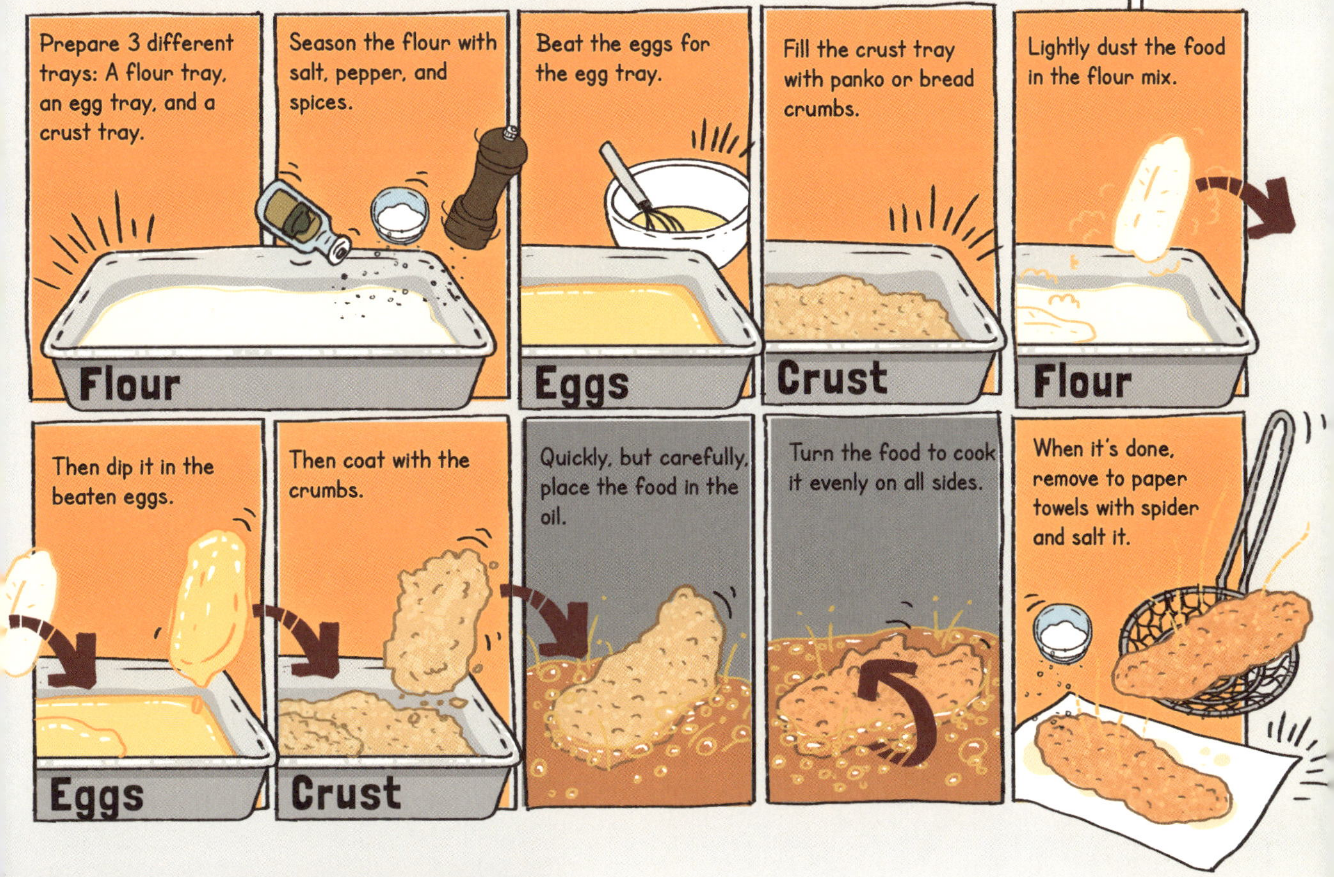

Prepare 3 different trays: A flour tray, an egg tray, and a crust tray.
Flour
Season the flour with salt, pepper, and spices.
Beat the eggs for the egg tray.
Eggs
Fill the crust tray with panko or bread crumbs.
Crust
Lightly dust the food in the flour mix.
Flour
Then dip it in the beaten eggs.
Eggs
Then coat with the crumbs.
Crust
Quickly, but carefully, place the food in the oil.
Turn the food to cook it evenly on all sides.
When it's done, remove to paper towels with spider and salt it.

What NOT to do

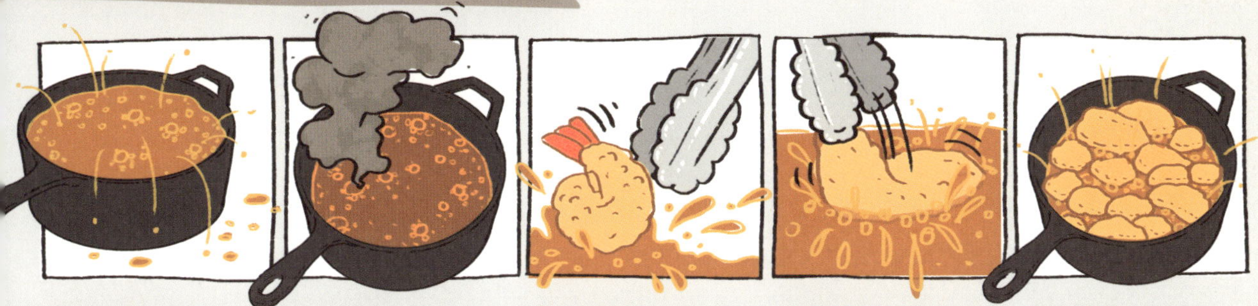

DO NOT fill the pot more than halfway up with oil. You do not want the oil bubbling over the side of the pot.

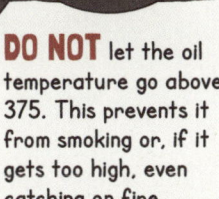

DO NOT let the oil temperature go above 375. This prevents it from smoking or, if it gets too high, even catching on fire.

DO NOT use tongs to take things out of the oil. If they slip out of your hand they can send hot oil flying.

DO NOT drop items in the oil. Instead, lay them in the oil gently, away from you.

DO NOT overload the fryer. All the items in the fryer should fit in a single layer. If you need to fry more than that, fry in batches.

Recipe 16

Vegetable Tempura with Ginger Sauce

The key to awesome tempura is to keep the batter **light** and **crispy**, so the rice flour and sparkling water are important. Still, if you don't have those things the recipe works with cold water and all purpose flour. These veggies are just a suggestion, so experiment! You can tempura anything!

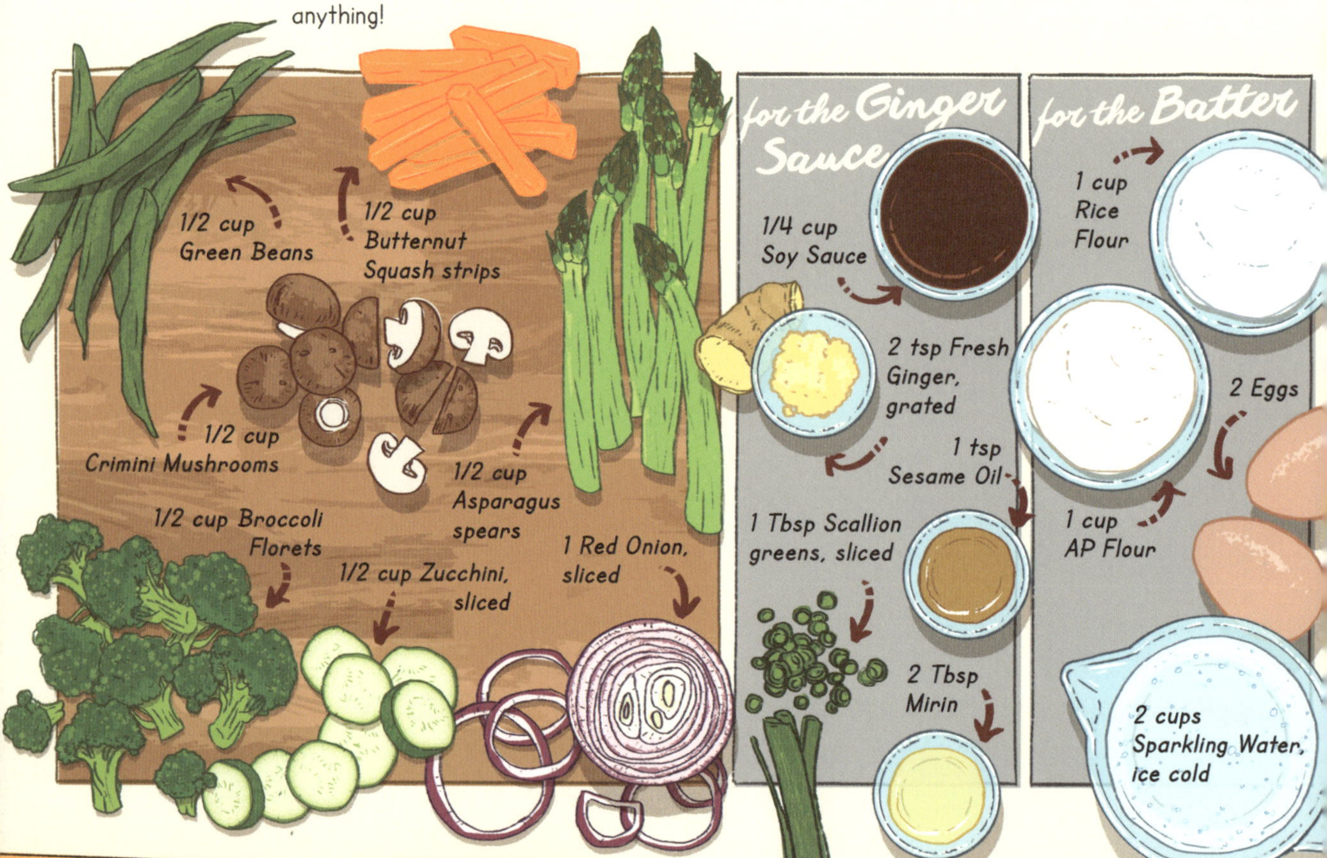
1/2 cup Green Beans
1/2 cup Butternut Squash strips
1/2 cup Crimini Mushrooms
1/2 cup Asparagus spears
1/2 cup Broccoli Florets
1/2 cup Zucchini, sliced
1 Red Onion, sliced
for the Ginger Sauce
1/4 cup Soy Sauce
2 tsp Fresh Ginger, grated
1 tsp Sesame Oil
1 Tbsp Scallion greens, sliced
2 Tbsp Mirin
for the Batter
1 cup Rice Flour
2 Eggs
1 cup AP Flour
2 cups Sparkling Water, ice cold

Let's Get Cooking!

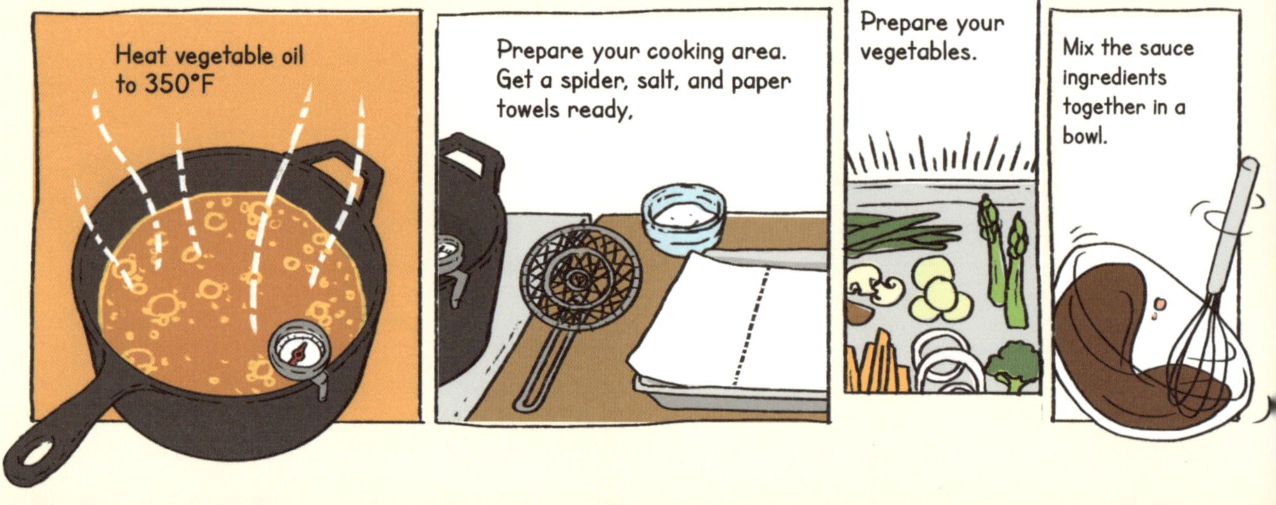
Heat vegetable oil to 350°F
Prepare your cooking area. Get a spider, salt, and paper towels ready.
Prepare your vegetables.
Mix the sauce ingredients together in a bowl.

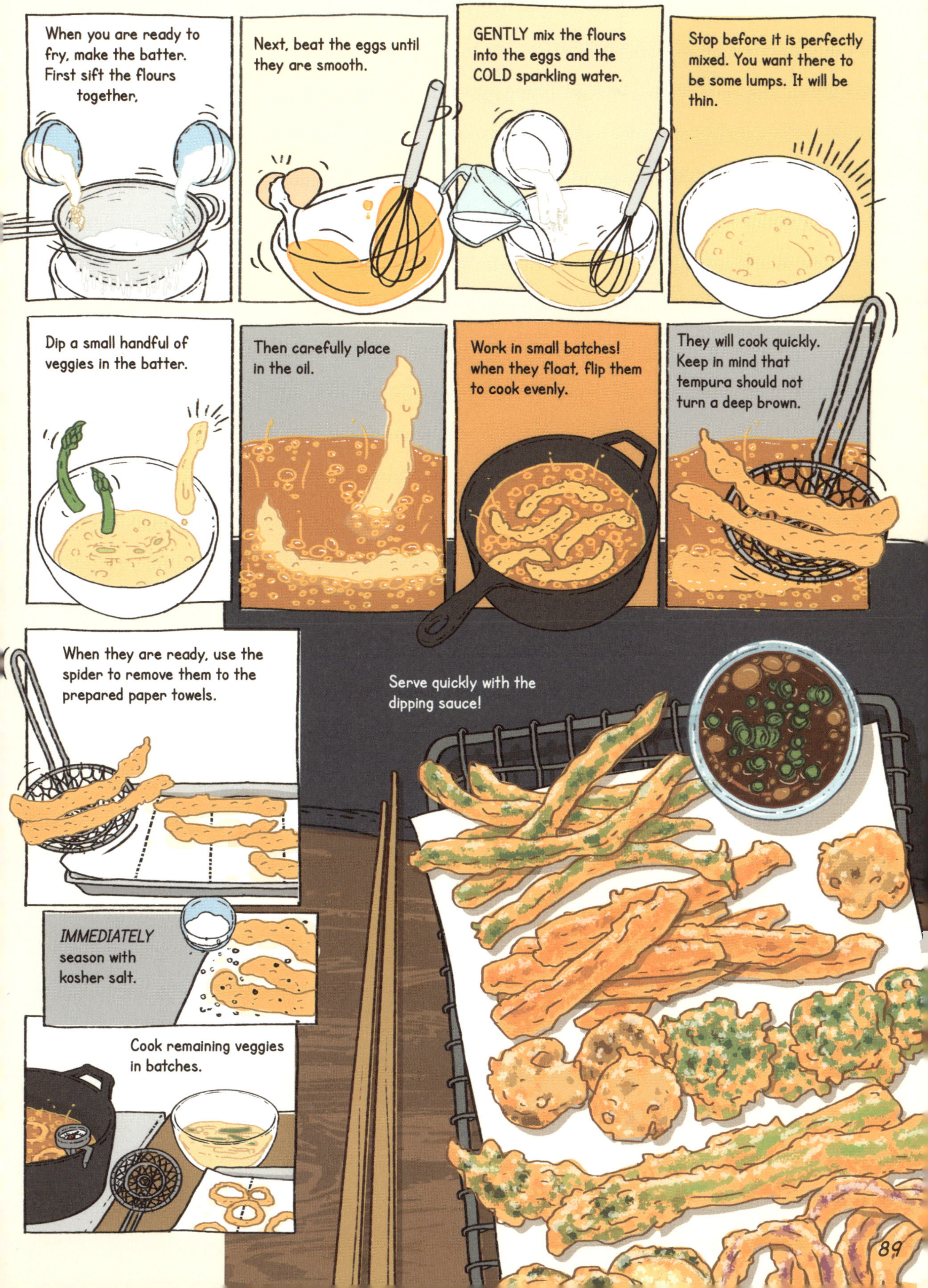

When you are ready to fry, make the batter. First sift the flours together.
Next, beat the eggs until they are smooth.
GENTLY mix the flours into the eggs and the COLD sparkling water.
Stop before it is perfectly mixed. You want there to be some lumps. It will be thin.
Dip a small handful of veggies in the batter.
Then carefully place in the oil.
Work in small batches! when they float, flip them to cook evenly.
They will cook quickly. Keep in mind that tempura should not turn a deep brown.
When they are ready, use the spider to remove them to the prepared paper towels.
IMMEDIATELY season with kosher salt.
Cook remaining veggies in batches.
Serve quickly with the dipping sauce!

Recipe 17

Fried Clam Po' boy with Tartar Sauce

Frying seafood is one of the best ways to treat it, whether it is oysters, clams, shrimp, or fish. Frying works so well for these foods because it create a **crunchy** exterior to balance the **delicate** meat. Po' Boys are a great way to make a meal out of fried seafood, but this technique is the same if you want to just enjoy a plate of fried clams with tartar sauce and lemon.

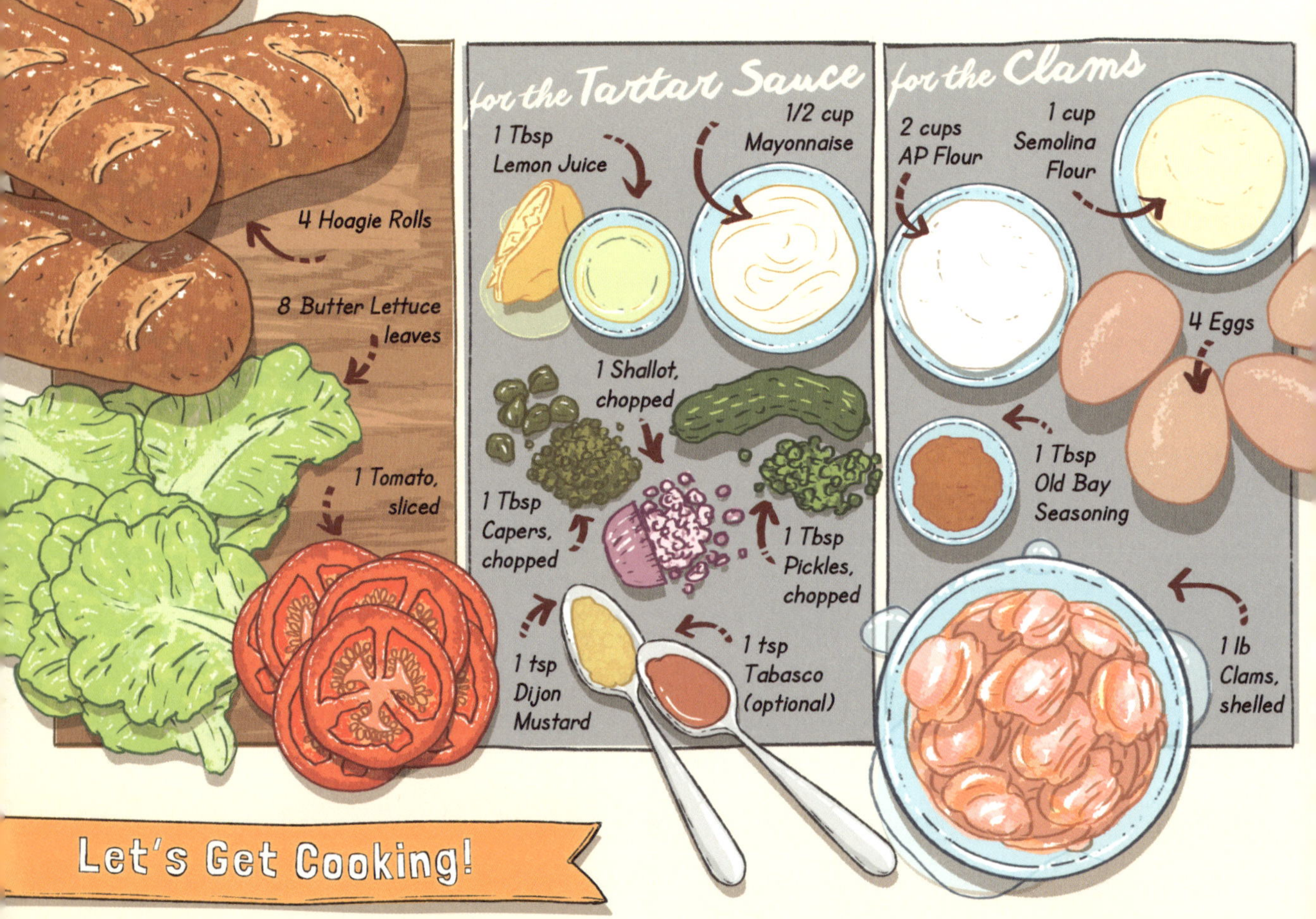

4 Hoagie Rolls
8 Butter Lettuce leaves
1 Tomato, sliced
for the Tartar Sauce
1 Tbsp Lemon Juice
1/2 cup Mayonnaise
1 Shallot, chopped
1 Tbsp Capers, chopped
1 Tbsp Pickles, chopped
1 tsp Dijon Mustard
1 tsp Tabasco (optional)
for the Clams
2 cups AP Flour
1 cup Semolina Flour
4 Eggs
1 Tbsp Old Bay Seasoning
1 lb Clams, shelled

Let's Get Cooking!

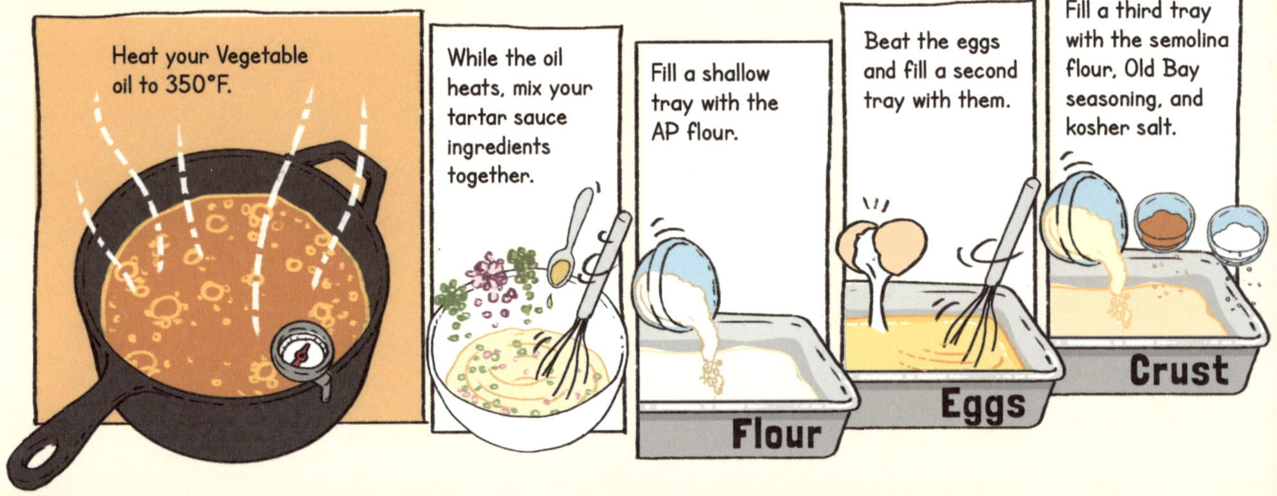

Heat your Vegetable oil to 350°F.
While the oil heats, mix your tartar sauce ingredients together.
Fill a shallow tray with the AP flour.
Flour
Beat the eggs and fill a second tray with them.
Eggs
Fill a third tray with the semolina flour, Old Bay seasoning, and kosher salt.
Crust

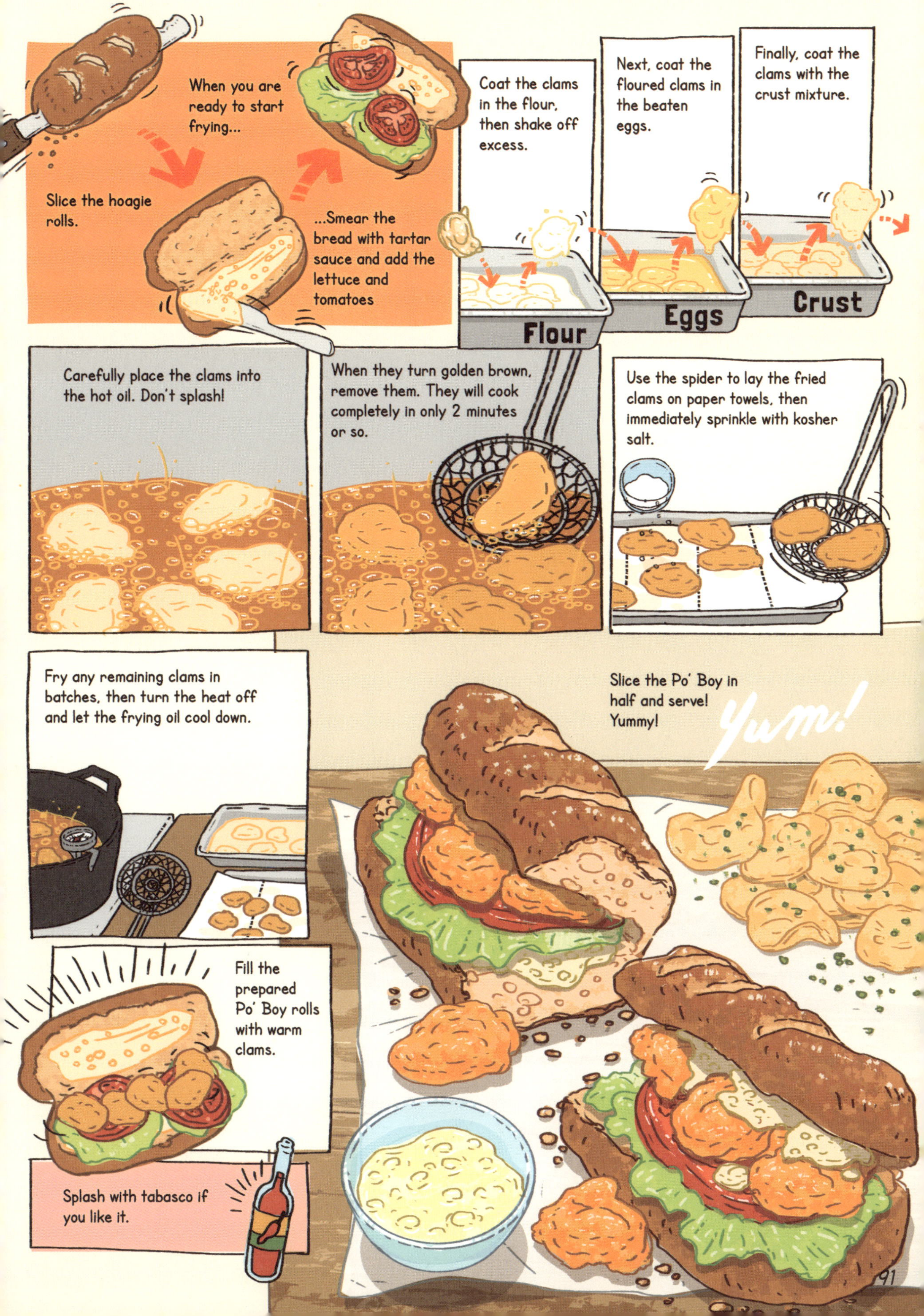
Slice the hoagie rolls.
When you are ready to start frying...
...Smear the bread with tartar sauce and add the lettuce and tomatoes
Coat the clams in the flour, then shake off excess.
Next, coat the floured clams in the beaten eggs.
Finally, coat the clams with the crust mixture.
Flour
Eggs
Crust
Carefully place the clams into the hot oil. Don't splash!
When they turn golden brown, remove them. They will cook completely in only 2 minutes or so.
Use the spider to lay the fried clams on paper towels, then immediately sprinkle with kosher salt.
Fry any remaining clams in batches, then turn the heat off and let the frying oil cool down.
Fill the prepared Po' Boy rolls with warm clams.
Splash with tabasco if you like it.
Slice the Po' Boy in half and serve! Yummy!
Yum!

Technique 10

BRAISING

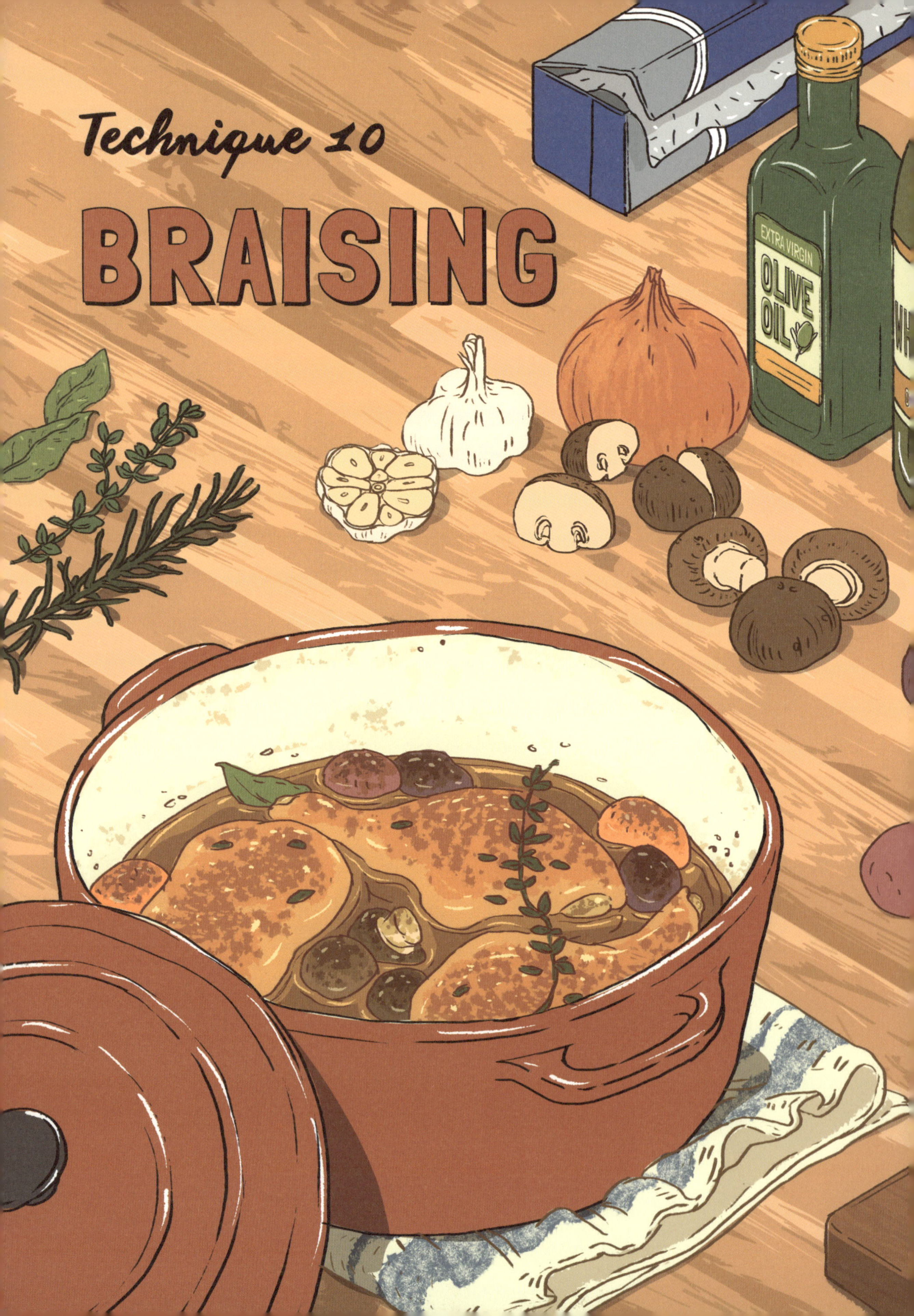
EXTRA VIRGIN
OLIVE OIL

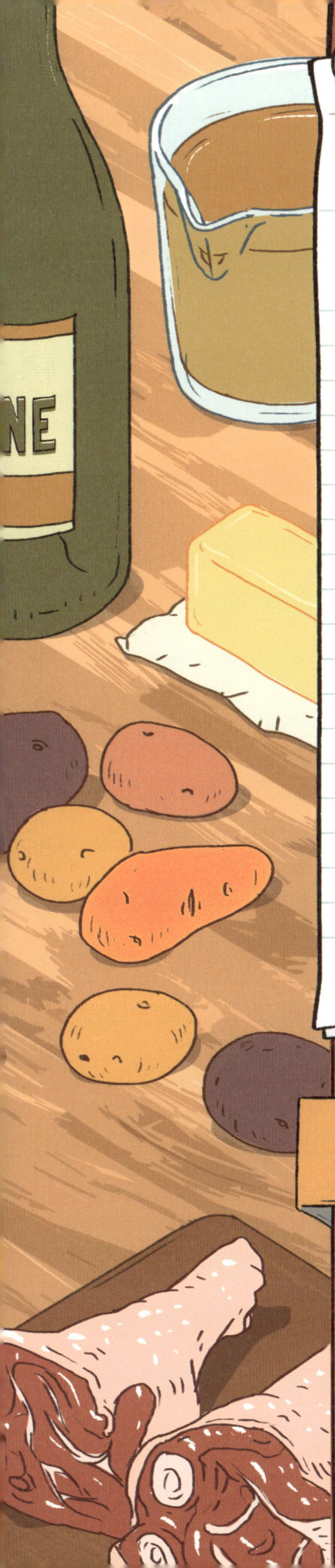

Chef's Note

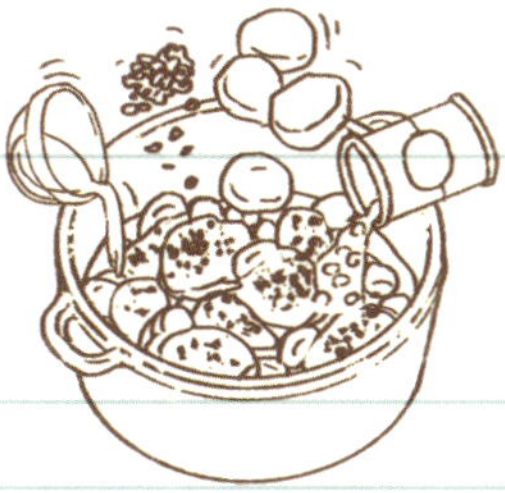

Braising has been around for longer than the Crockpot, and the truth is you can get better results in your oven than you can on your kitchen counter.

Braising is the best way to use those tougher, cheaper cuts of meat. The good news is that when these cuts are treated with love they are packed with flavor. The best way to turn these cheap cuts into flavorful, tender morsels is to cook them in a covered pot, in liquid, at a low temperature, for a long time. It's very easy, all you have to do is plan ahead!

You shouldn't make plans to leave the house when your braise is in the oven though, so make sure you set aside the time you need. Don't try to speed it up by cranking the oven above 325°F, because then you'll just be boiling it in the oven.

SKILL BADGES

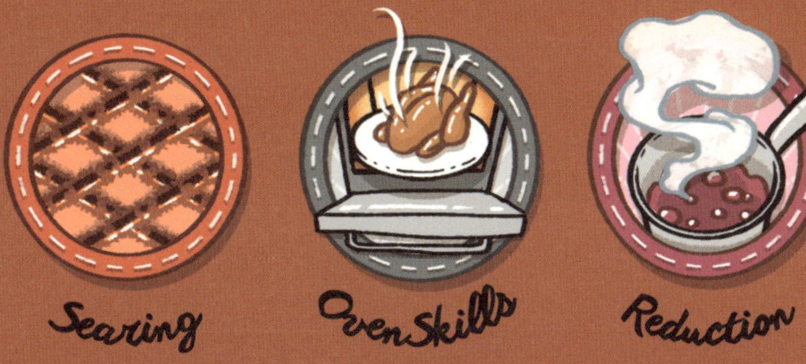
Searing
Oven Skills
Reduction

BRAISING TECHNIQUE

All a great braise needs is **time**, so make sure that you set aside enough time to let the meat cook and **relax** in the oven. Tough cuts of meat are full of connective tissue between the muscle fibers, and that is what makes them tough. When this tissue is exposed to relatively low heat for a long time, the tissue breaks down into gelatin, so the meat becomes very **tender**, and you end up with a rich sauce to serve with it too! The ideal temperature range for this process is 200°F to 325°F. Any higher than that and your food will boil, but any lower, and you will have to worry about food safety.

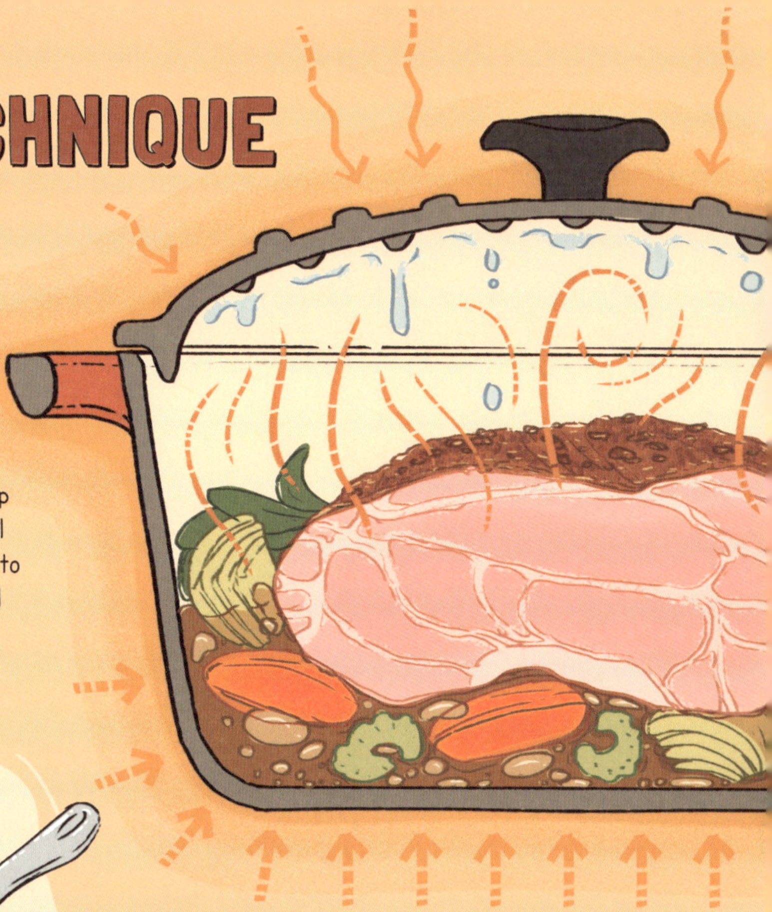

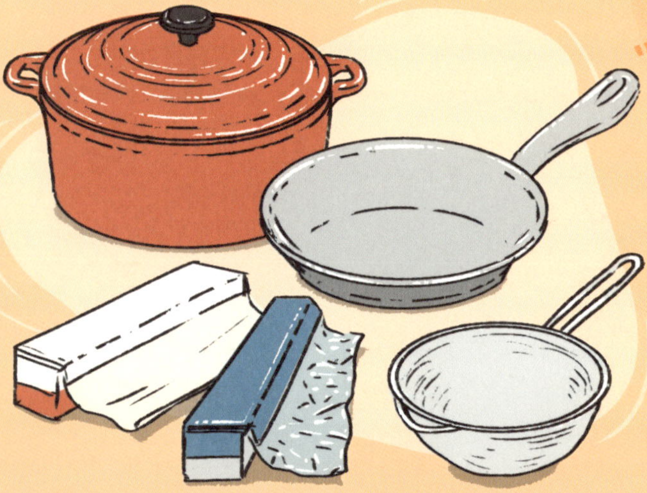

Equipment Necessary

- **Braising pan** The best choice for this is a dutch oven (if you don't have the lid you can use aluminum foil). If you don't have one you can use a casserole dish that has high sides. You just need something tall enough to accomidate the liquid and the braising item.
- **Large sauté pan**
- **Strainer**
- **Parchment paper**
- **Aluminum foil**

Let's Get Cooking!

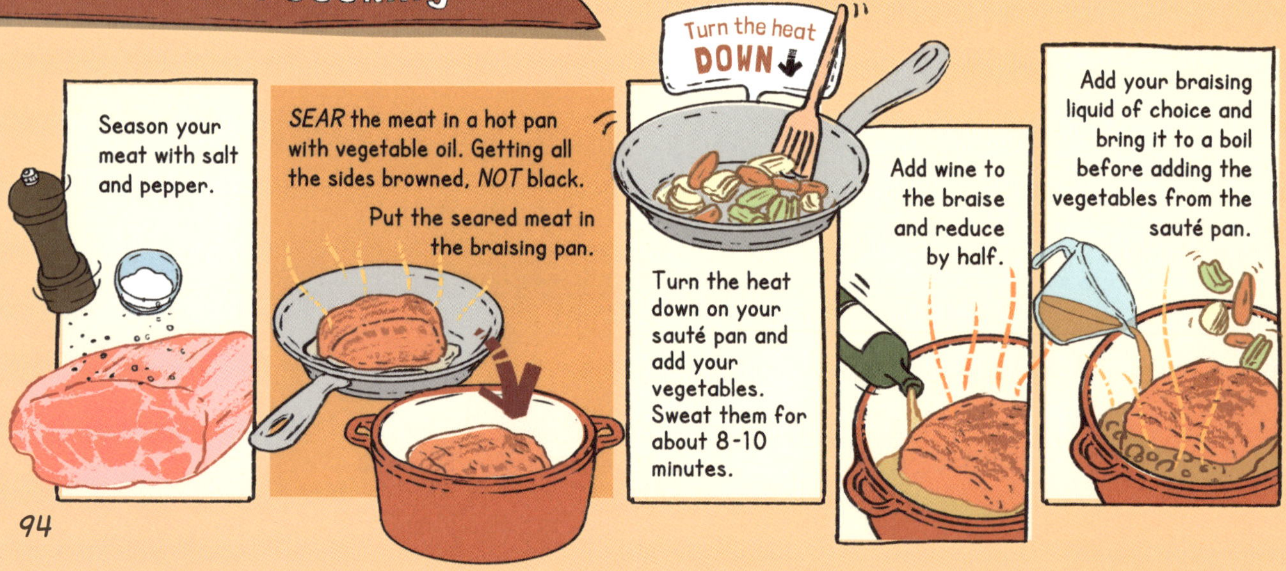
Season your meat with salt and pepper.
SEAR the meat in a hot pan with vegetable oil. Getting all the sides browned, NOT black.
Put the seared meat in the braising pan.
Turn the heat DOWN
Turn the heat down on your sauté pan and add your vegetables. Sweat them for about 8-10 minutes.
Add wine to the braise and reduce by half.
Add your braising liquid of choice and bring it to a boil before adding the vegetables from the sauté pan.

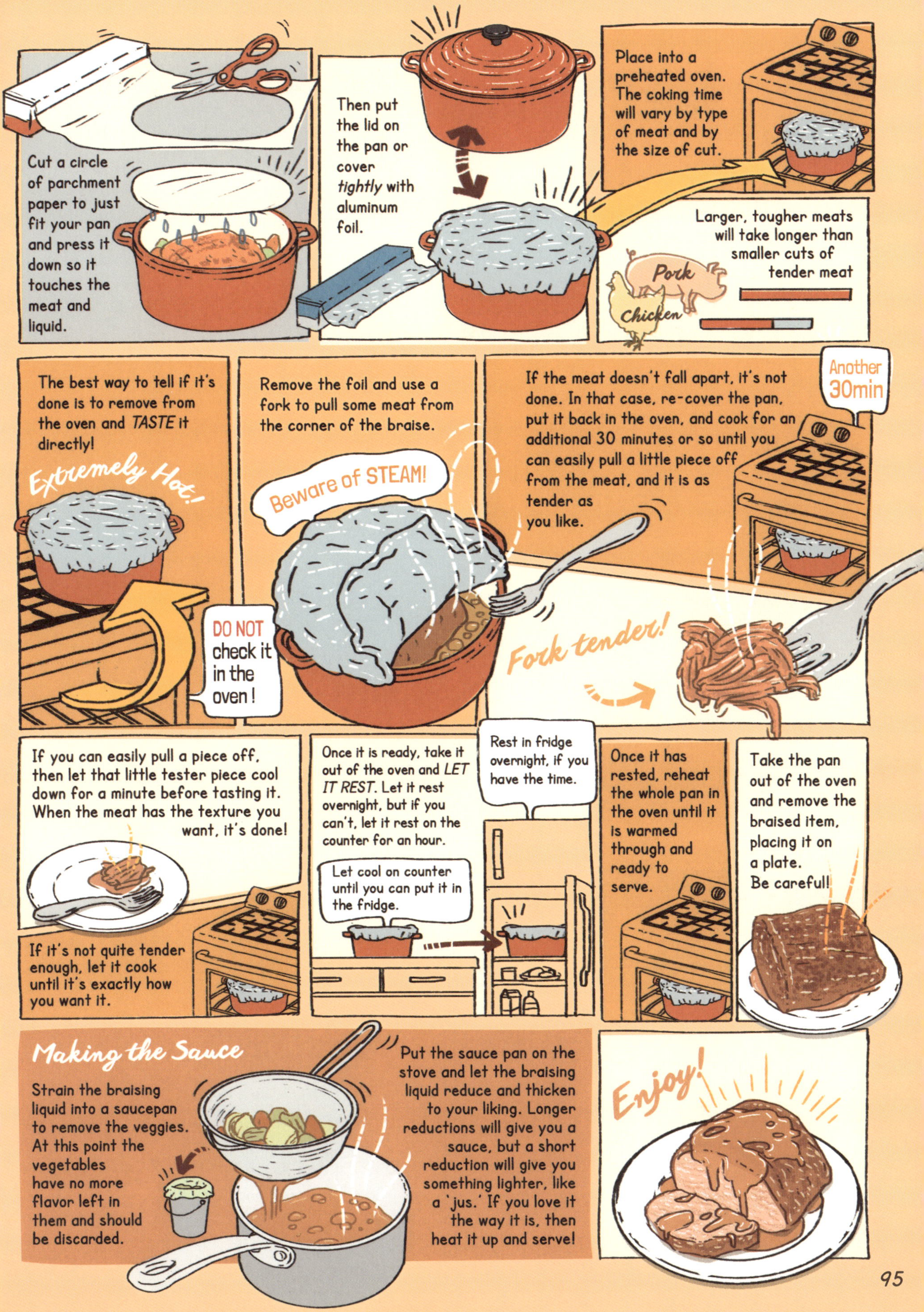

Cut a circle of parchment paper to just fit your pan and press it down so it touches the meat and liquid.
Then put the lid on the pan or cover *tightly* with aluminum foil.
Place into a preheated oven. The coking time will vary by type of meat and by the size of cut.
Larger, tougher meats will take longer than smaller cuts of tender meat
Pork
Chicken
The best way to tell if it's done is to remove from the oven and *TASTE* it directly!
Extremely Hot!
DO NOT check it in the oven!
Remove the foil and use a fork to pull some meat from the corner of the braise.
Beware of STEAM!
If the meat doesn't fall apart, it's not done. In that case, re-cover the pan, put it back in the oven, and cook for an additional 30 minutes or so until you can easily pull a little piece off from the meat, and it is as tender as you like.
Another 30min
Fork tender!
If you can easily pull a piece off, then let that little tester piece cool down for a minute before tasting it. When the meat has the texture you want, it's done!
If it's not quite tender enough, let it cook until it's exactly how you want it.
Once it is ready, take it out of the oven and *LET IT REST*. Let it rest overnight, but if you can't, let it rest on the counter for an hour.
Let cool on counter until you can put it in the fridge.
Rest in fridge overnight, if you have the time.
Once it has rested, reheat the whole pan in the oven until it is warmed through and ready to serve.
Take the pan out of the oven and remove the braised item, placing it on a plate. Be careful!
Making the Sauce
Strain the braising liquid into a saucepan to remove the veggies. At this point the vegetables have no more flavor left in them and should be discarded.
Put the sauce pan on the stove and let the braising liquid reduce and thicken to your liking. Longer reductions will give you a sauce, but a short reduction will give you something lighter, like a 'jus.' If you love it the way it is, then heat it up and serve!
Enjoy!

Recipe 18

Lamb Shanks with Cheesy Polenta

Lamb shanks are the perfect cut of meat to show off the **magic** of braising. They might seem tough at first, but by the time this dish is ready they are tender and flavorful. The **tender** lamb sits atop a cheesy polenta that soaks up all the delicious braising liquid. A perfect winter dish!

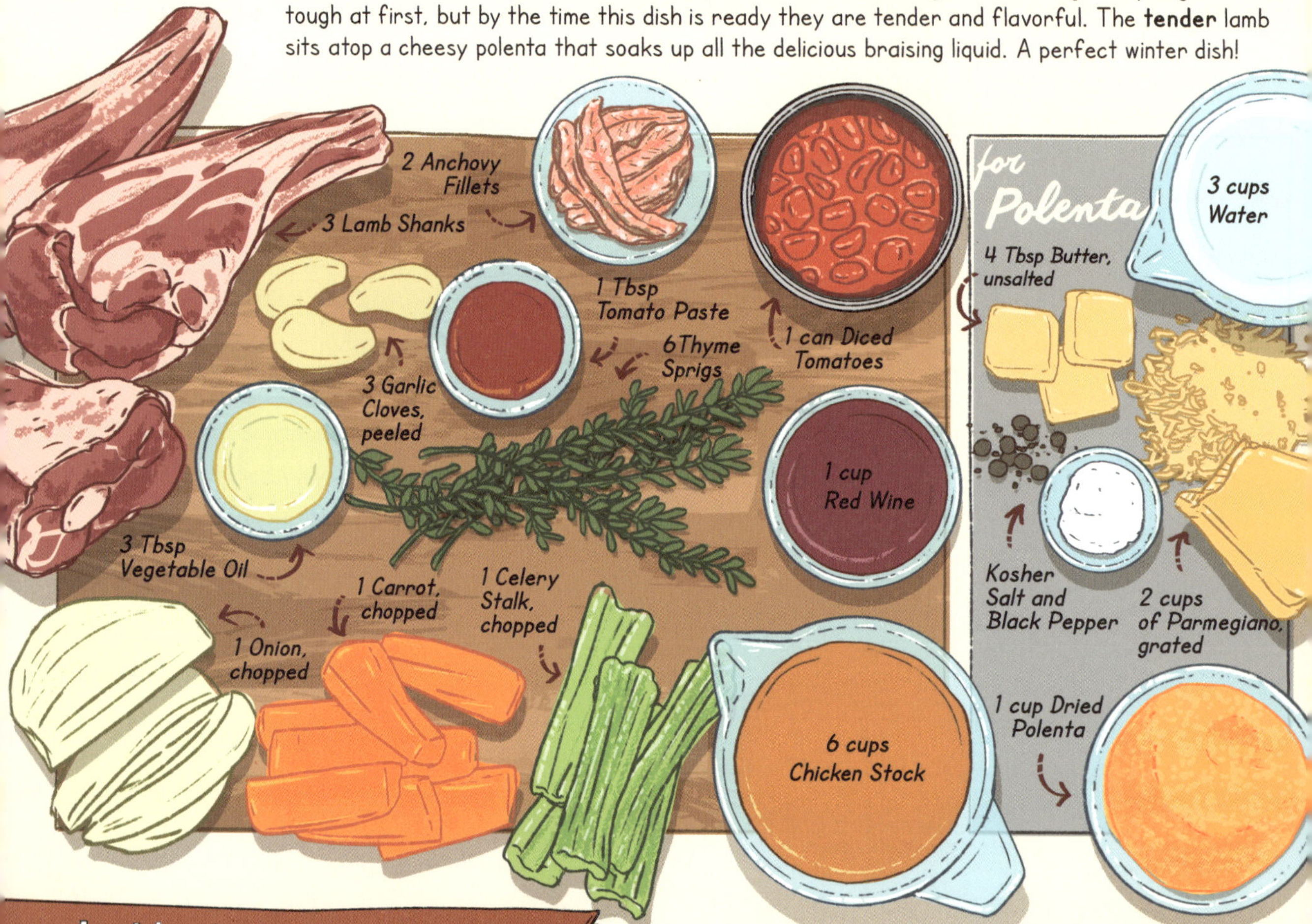
2 Anchovy Fillets
3 Lamb Shanks
1 Tbsp Tomato Paste
6 Thyme Sprigs
1 can Diced Tomatoes
3 Garlic Cloves, peeled
1 cup Red Wine
3 Tbsp Vegetable Oil
1 Carrot, chopped
1 Celery Stalk, chopped
1 Onion, chopped
6 cups Chicken Stock
for Polenta
3 cups Water
4 Tbsp Butter, unsalted
Kosher Salt and Black Pepper
2 cups of Parmegiano, grated
1 cup Dried Polenta

Let's Get Cooking!

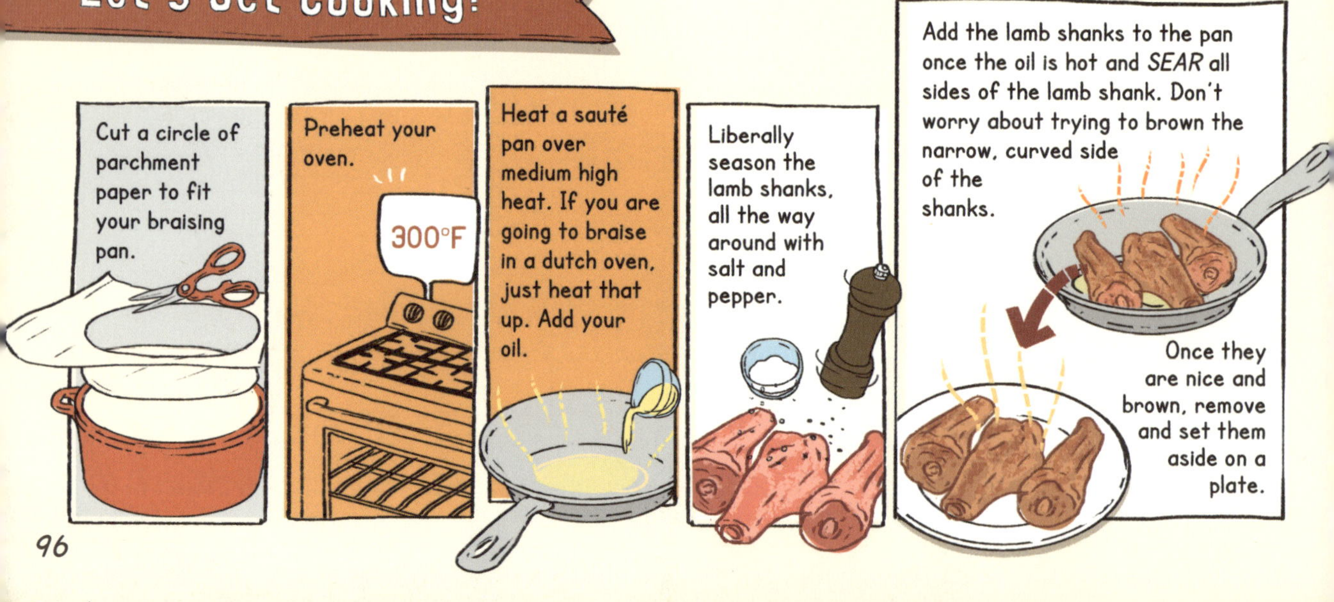
Cut a circle of parchment paper to fit your braising pan.
Preheat your oven.
300°F
Heat a sauté pan over medium high heat. If you are going to braise in a dutch oven, just heat that up. Add your oil.
Liberally season the lamb shanks, all the way around with salt and pepper.
Add the lamb shanks to the pan once the oil is hot and SEAR all sides of the lamb shank. Don't worry about trying to brown the narrow, curved side of the shanks.
Once they are nice and brown, remove and set them aside on a plate.

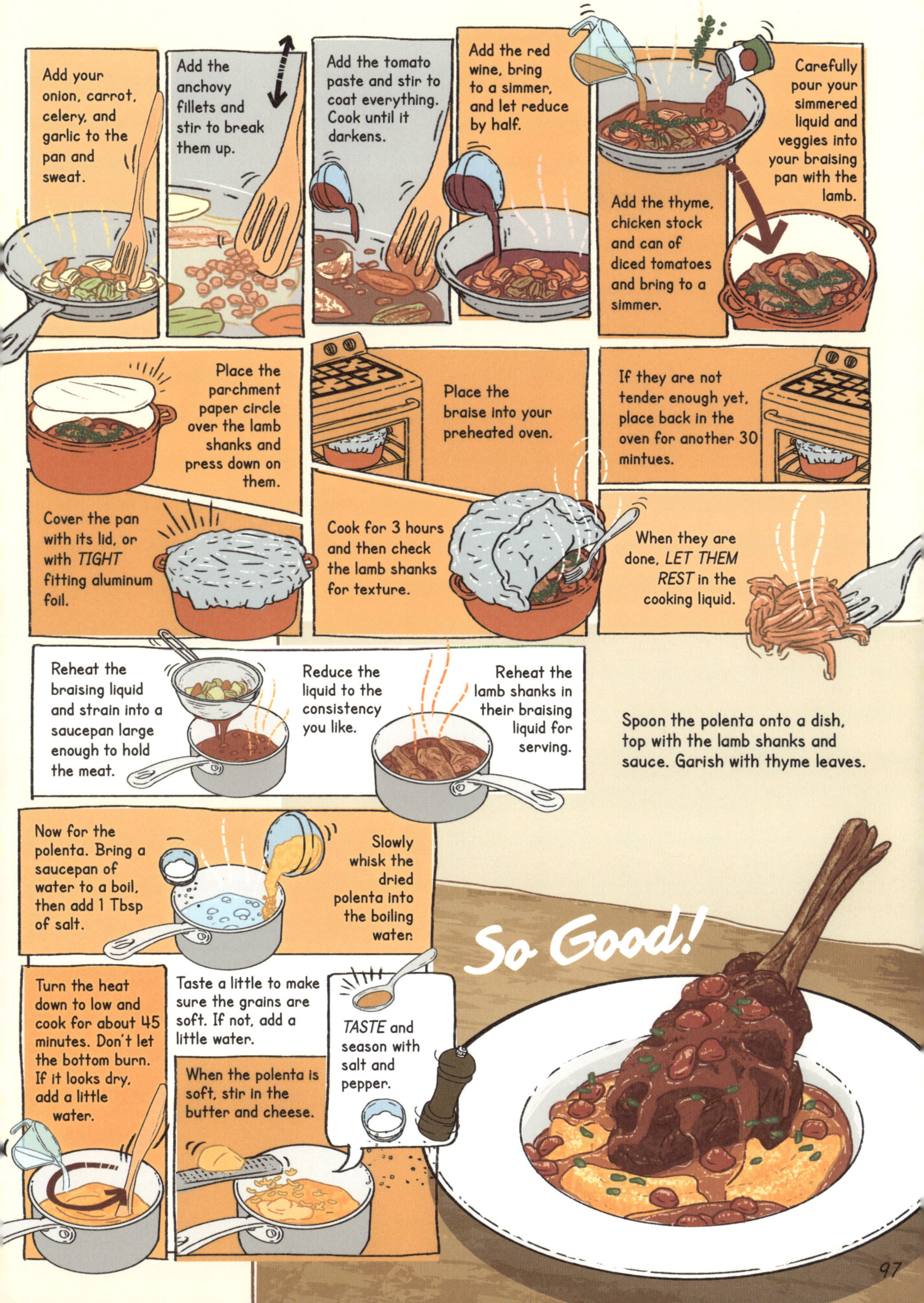

Add your onion, carrot, celery, and garlic to the pan and sweat.
Add the anchovy fillets and stir to break them up.
Add the tomato paste and stir to coat everything. Cook until it darkens.
Add the red wine, bring to a simmer, and let reduce by half.
Add the thyme, chicken stock and can of diced tomatoes and bring to a simmer.
Carefully pour your simmered liquid and veggies into your braising pan with the lamb.
Place the parchment paper circle over the lamb shanks and press down on them.
Cover the pan with its lid, or with TIGHT fitting aluminum foil.
Place the braise into your preheated oven.
Cook for 3 hours and then check the lamb shanks for texture.
If they are not tender enough yet, place back in the oven for another 30 mintues.
When they are done, LET THEM REST in the cooking liquid.
Reheat the braising liquid and strain into a saucepan large enough to hold the meat.
Reduce the liquid to the consistency you like.
Reheat the lamb shanks in their braising liquid for serving.
Spoon the polenta onto a dish, top with the lamb shanks and sauce. Garish with thyme leaves.
Now for the polenta. Bring a saucepan of water to a boil, then add 1 Tbsp of salt.
Slowly whisk the dried polenta into the boiling water.
Turn the heat down to low and cook for about 45 minutes. Don't let the bottom burn. If it looks dry, add a little water.
Taste a little to make sure the grains are soft. If not, add a little water.
When the polenta is soft, stir in the butter and cheese.
TASTE and season with salt and pepper.
So Good!

Recipe 19

Chicken with Garlic, Balsamic & Potatoes

This is a great one-pot dish that packs a lot of flavor. Chicken does not take very long to braise so it is incredibly **easy** to cook the whole meal in one pot and have everything turn out just right. The rich, **sweet balsamic** turns this into something special. Serve with crusty bread.

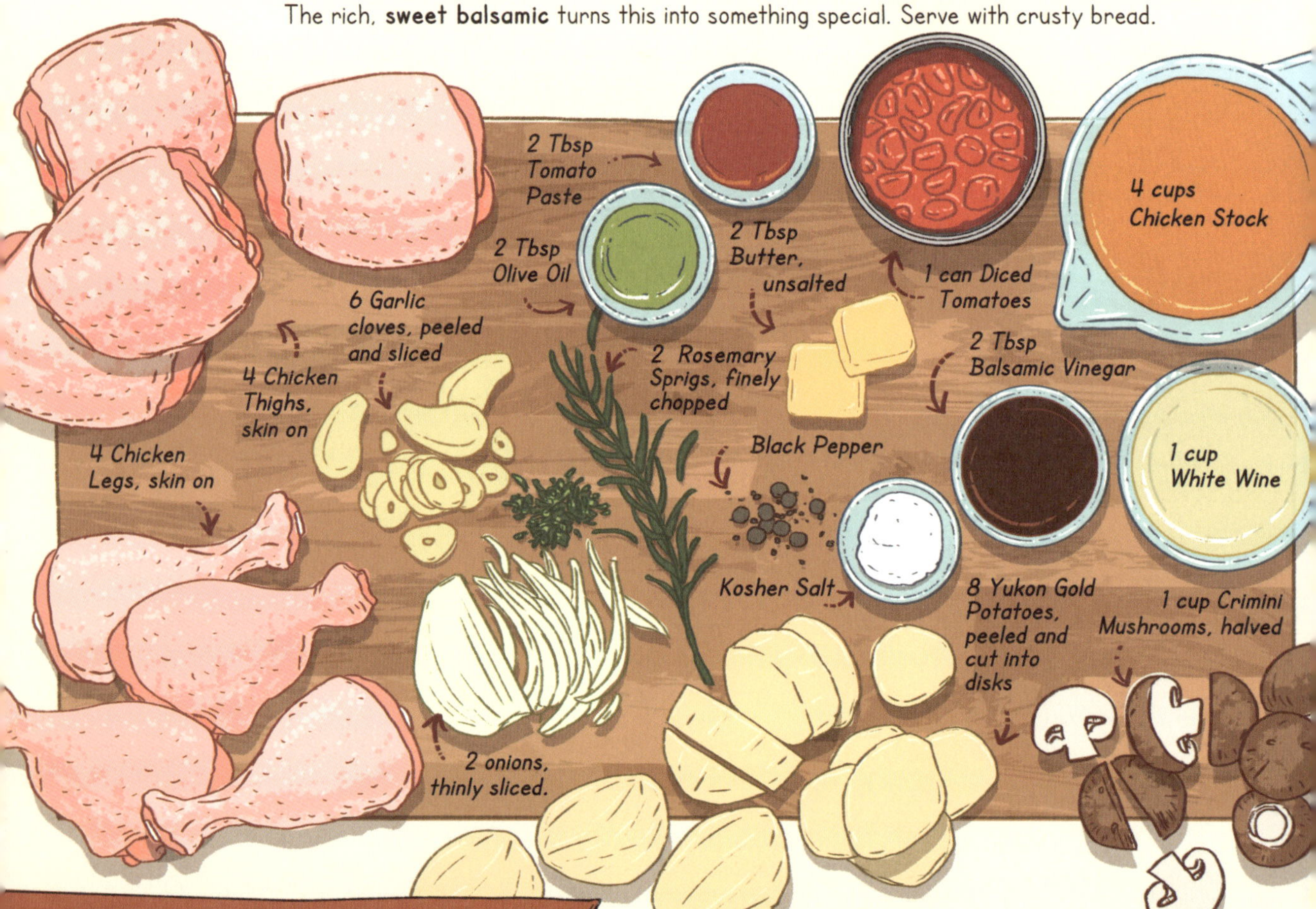

2 Tbsp Tomato Paste
2 Tbsp Olive Oil
2 Tbsp Butter, unsalted
1 can Diced Tomatoes
4 cups Chicken Stock
6 Garlic cloves, peeled and sliced
4 Chicken Thighs, skin on
2 Rosemary Sprigs, finely chopped
2 Tbsp Balsamic Vinegar
Black Pepper
1 cup White Wine
4 Chicken Legs, skin on
Kosher Salt
8 Yukon Gold Potatoes, peeled and cut into disks
1 cup Crimini Mushrooms, halved
2 onions, thinly sliced.

Let's Get Cooking!

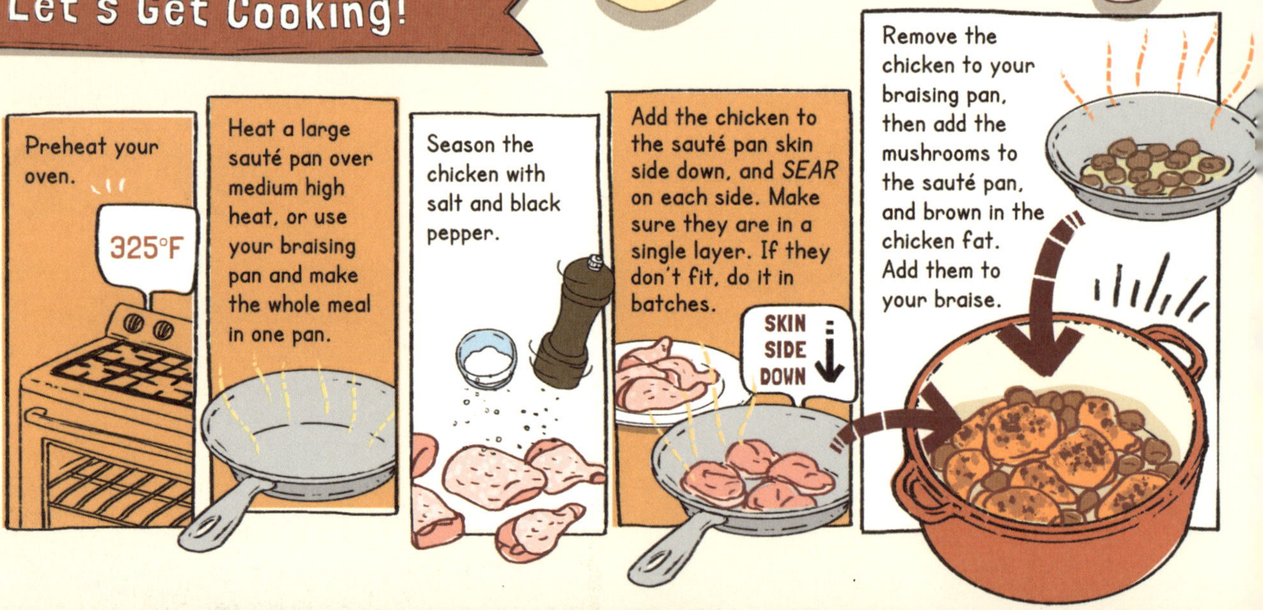

Preheat your oven.
325°F
Heat a large sauté pan over medium high heat, or use your braising pan and make the whole meal in one pan.
Season the chicken with salt and black pepper.
Add the chicken to the sauté pan skin side down, and SEAR on each side. Make sure they are in a single layer. If they don't fit, do it in batches.
SKIN SIDE DOWN
Remove the chicken to your braising pan, then add the mushrooms to the sauté pan, and brown in the chicken fat. Add them to your braise.

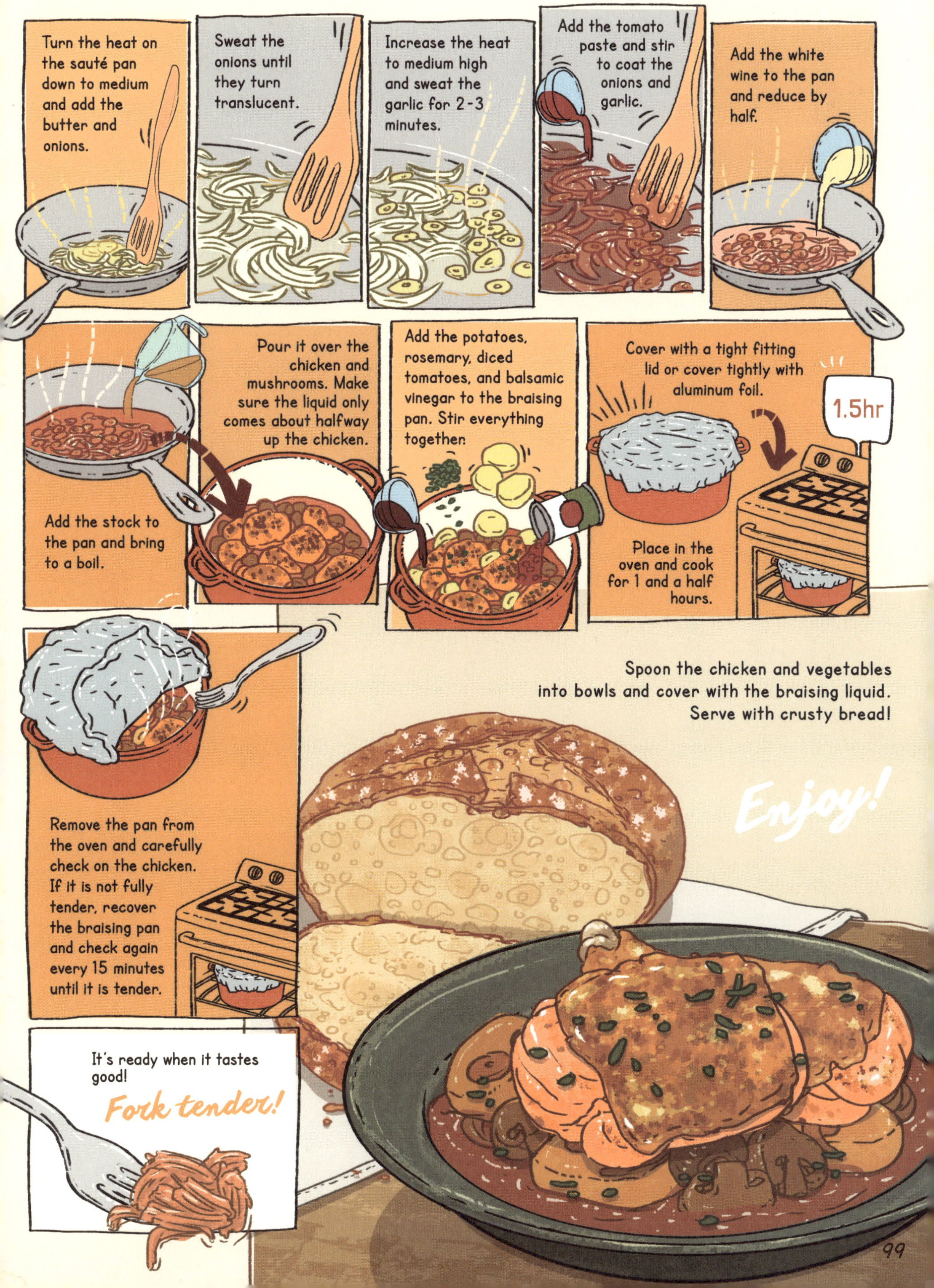
Turn the heat on the sauté pan down to medium and add the butter and onions.
Sweat the onions until they turn translucent.
Increase the heat to medium high and sweat the garlic for 2-3 minutes.
Add the tomato paste and stir to coat the onions and garlic.
Add the white wine to the pan and reduce by half.
Add the stock to the pan and bring to a boil.
Pour it over the chicken and mushrooms. Make sure the liquid only comes about halfway up the chicken.
Add the potatoes, rosemary, diced tomatoes, and balsamic vinegar to the braising pan. Stir everything together.
Cover with a tight fitting lid or cover tightly with aluminum foil.
1.5hr
Place in the oven and cook for 1 and a half hours.
Remove the pan from the oven and carefully check on the chicken. If it is not fully tender, recover the braising pan and check again every 15 minutes until it is tender.
It's ready when it tastes good!
Fork tender!
Spoon the chicken and vegetables into bowls and cover with the braising liquid. Serve with crusty bread!
Enjoy!

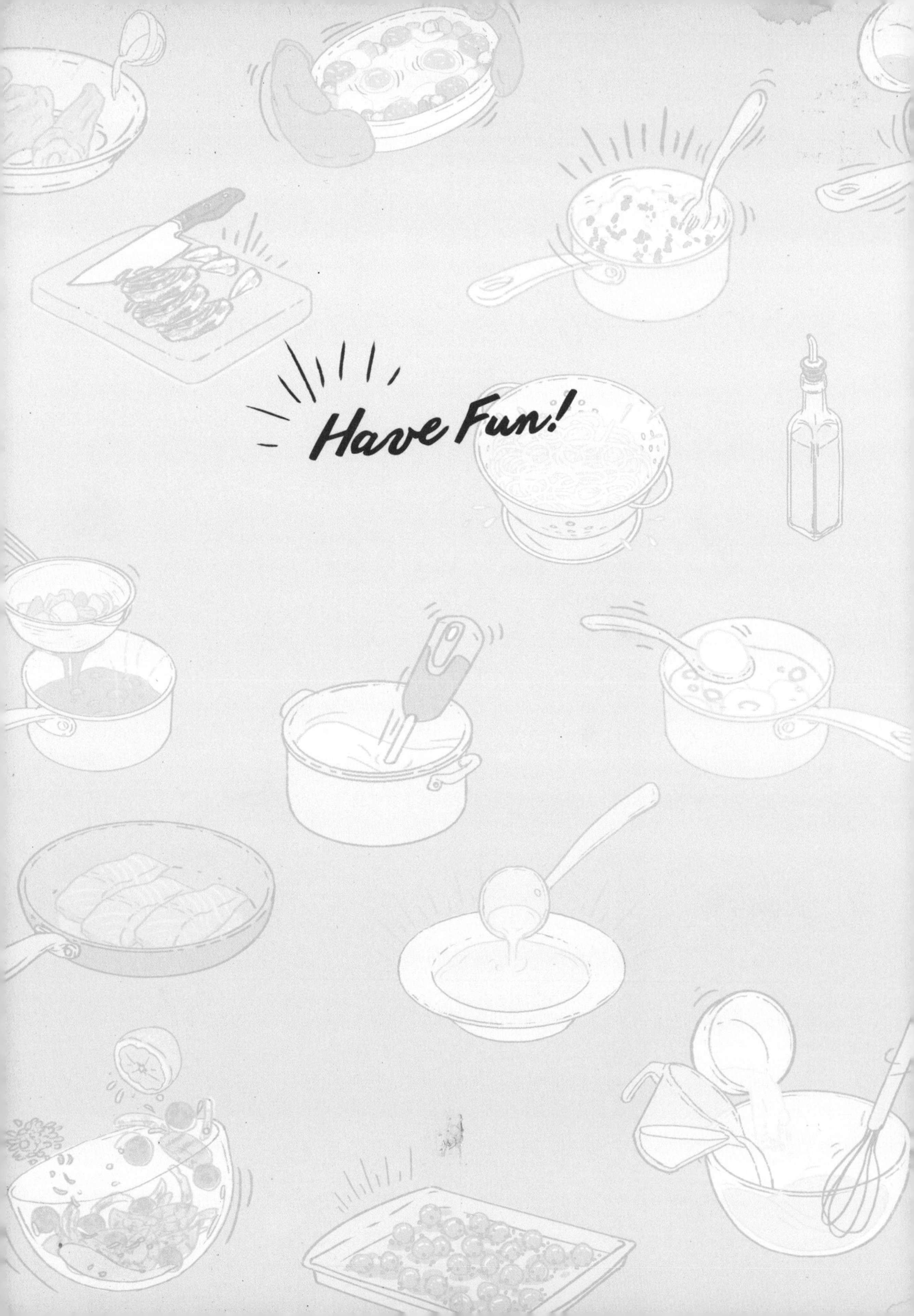
Have Fun!